"As pattern-seeking creatures, we look out to the objective world to make sense of our environment. In the age of datafication, the received wisdom is that the process has been reversed: corporations look into the subjective world of people's data patterns in order to surveil and anticipate. This much is true, but as this 'pattern-breaking' collection shows, much more happens besides. From the aesthetic to the temporal and from the cultural to the biopolitical, there is a fast-paced evolutionary struggle taking place for the perpetuation of the aeonic patterns of life against the growingly powerful machine-based intelligence of computation. *Big Data—A New Medium?* is the most important and encompassing analysis yet on the struggle for the 'soul' of human creativity, diversity and autonomy".

Robert Hassan, *University of Melbourne, Australia*

"This is a breath-taking and kaleidoscopic series of reflections on one of the most important phenomena of our age. It tells the compelling story of its subject's 'quest to anticipate and harness the individual and collective unconscious' and is by turns surprising, complex, thought provoking, dizzying and mind-blowing ... just like Big Data itself".

Steve Dixon, *President of LASALLE College of the Arts, Singapore*

"As the control of data surpasses the regulation of populations, new modes of government emerge: as well as stripping the earth of its resources we are also stripping our lives of the data they produce. At the same time, new forms of mutant expression are emerging that offer alternative modes of life because, as this volume makes strikingly evident, patterns are always more than they seem. Infinite processes sit buried within finite algorithms. Figuring out the relationship between data mining and its various forms of expression is an urgent task, one that the contributors to this volume take on with a critical intent that steers them away from platitudes and toward inventive insights for our age of control".

Iain MacKenzie, *University of Kent, UK*

"This multidisciplinary volume is perfectly timed to help us consider our increasing immersion in data and its insidious integration with our current experience. Lushetich and the writers she collects in this volume help us rethink our relationship with data in a new way, focusing on its potential as a medium by which to reconsider the phenomena of our 21st century culture and how it affects our fundamental sense of being in the world".

Kevin LaGrandeur, *New York Institute of Technology, USA*

"This mind-opening book cultivates an aesthetic appreciation for, even empathy with, the creative capacities of informational patterning. Certainly these authors critique the crude deployment of big data for profit and power. But more strikingly, they value seemingly nonhuman forms of perception and thought that liberate the human to surf within populations of patterned being".

Laura Marks, *Simon Fraser University, Vancouver, Canada*

"This timely and lively collection offers a broadening of the understanding of big data, drawing on the arts, humanities and social sciences to put big data in a bigger picture".

Matthew Fuller, *Goldsmiths, University of London, UK*

BIG DATA—A NEW MEDIUM?

Drawing on a range of methods from across science and technology studies, digital humanities and digital arts, this book presents a comprehensive view of the big data phenomenon.

Big data architectures are increasingly transforming political questions into technical management by determining classificatory systems in the social, educational, and healthcare realms. Data, and their multiple arborisations, have become new epistemic landscapes. They have also become new existential terrains. The fundamental question is: can big data be seen as a new medium in the way photography or film were when they first appeared? No new medium is ever truly new. It is always remediation of older media. What is new is the medium's re-articulation of the difference between here and there, before and after, yours and mine, knowable and unknowable, possible and impossible.

This transdisciplinary volume, incorporating cultural and media theory, art, philosophy, history, and political philosophy is a key resource for readers interested in digital humanities, cultural, and media studies.

Natasha Lushetich is Professor of Contemporary Art & Theory at the University of Dundee. Her research is interdisciplinary and focuses on intermedia, biopolitics and performativity, the status of sensory experience in cultural knowledge, hegemony, and complexity.

ROUTLEDGE STUDIES IN SCIENCE, TECHNOLOGY AND SOCIETY

37 Future Courses of Human Societies
Critical Reflections from the Natural and Social Sciences
Edited by Kléber Ghimire

38 Science, Africa and Europe
Processing Information and Creating Knowledge
Edited by Patrick Harries, Martin Lengwiler and Nigel Penn

39 The Sociology of "Structural Disaster"
Beyond Fukushima
Miwao Matsumoto

40 The Cultural Authority of Science
Comparing across Europe, Asia, Africa and the Americas
Edited by Martin W. Bauer, Petra Pansegrau and Rajesh Shukla

41 Blockchain and Web 3.0
Social, Economic, and Technological Challenges
Edited by Massimo Ragnedda and Giuseppe Destefanis

42 Understanding Digital Events
Bergson, Whitehead, and the Experience of the Digital
Edited by David Kreps

43 Big Data—A New Medium?
Edited by Natasha Lushetich

44 The Policies and Politics of Interdisciplinary Research
Nanomedicine in France and in the United States
Séverine Louvel

For the full list of books in the series: www.routledge.com/Routledge-Studies-in-Science-Technology-and-Society/book-series/SE0054

BIG DATA—A NEW MEDIUM?

Edited by Natasha Lushetich

LONDON AND NEW YORK

First published 2021
by Routledge
2 Park Square, Milton Park, Abingdon, Oxon OX14 4RN

and by Routledge
52 Vanderbilt Avenue, New York, NY 10017

Routledge is an imprint of the Taylor & Francis Group, an informa business

© 2021 selection and editorial matter, Natasha Lushetich; individual chapters,
the contributors

The right of Natasha Lushetich to be identified as the author of the
editorial material, and of the authors for their individual chapters, has been
asserted in accordance with sections 77 and 78 of the Copyright, Designs
and Patents Act 1988.

All rights reserved. No part of this book may be reprinted or reproduced or utilised
in any form or by any electronic, mechanical, or other means, now known or
hereafter invented, including photocopying and recording, or in any information
storage or retrieval system, without permission in writing from the publishers.

Trademark notice: Product or corporate names may be trademarks or registered trademarks,
and are used only for identification and explanation without intent to infringe.

British Library Cataloguing-in-Publication Data
A catalogue record for this book is available from the British Library

Library of Congress Cataloging-in-Publication Data
A catalog record has been requested for this book

ISBN: 978-0-367-33383-6 (hbk)
ISBN: 978-0-367-33384-3 (pbk)
ISBN: 978-0-429-31955-6 (ebk)

Typeset in Bembo
by Newgen Publishing UK

CONTENTS

List of figures	*ix*
List of contributors	*xi*
Acknowledgements	*xv*

Prologue: Why ask the question?   1
Natasha Lushetich

PART I
Patterning knowledge and time   **15**

1   Big data and/versus people knowledge: On the ambiguities
of humanistic research   17
Ingrid M. Hoofd

2   Simulated replicants forever? Big data, engendered determinism,
and the end of prophecy   32
Franco 'Bifo' Berardi

3   "Visual hallucination of probable events": On environments
of images, data, and machine learning   46
Abelardo Gil-Fournier and Jussi Parikka

viii Contents

PART II
Patterning use and extraction 61

  4 Biometric datafication in governmental and personal spheres 63
     Btihaj Ajana

  5 Digital biopolitics and the problem of fatigue in platform capitalism 80
     Tim Christaens

  6 Appreciating machine-generated artwork through deep
     learning mechanisms 94
     Lonce Wyse

PART III
Patterning cultural heritage and memory 113

  7 Data to the Nth degree: Zooming in on *The Smart Set* 115
     Craig J. Saper

  8 Intellectual autonomy after artificial intelligence: The future
     of memory institutions and historical research 130
     Nicola Horsley

  9 *BeHere*: Prosthetic memory in the age of digital frottage 145
     Natasha Lushetich and Masaki Fujihata

PART IV
Patterning people 161

10 Surfaces and depths: An aesthetics of big data 163
     Dominic Smith

11 POV-data-doubles, the dividual, and the drive to visibility 177
     Mitra Azar

12 Reading big data as the heterogeneous subject 191
     Simon Biggs

13 Epilogue: Telepathic exaptation in late cognitive capitalism:
     A speculative approach to the effects of digitality 206
     Warren Neidich

Index   *221*

FIGURES

3.1   Abelardo Gil-Fournier, *An Earthology of Moving Landforms*, 2018.
      Samples of data sets of planetary surface behaviours   51
3.2   Abelardo Gil-Fournier, *An Earthology of Moving Landforms*, 2018.
      A series of predictions of the movements of the fast meandering
      Ucayali River in Perú   54
4.1   Gym turnstiles with facial recognition cameras, 2019.
      Photo: Btihaj Ajana   63
4.2   Facebook responses, 2019. Photo: Btihaj Ajana   64
6.1   *Woman in Wood* 2017. Photo: Creative Commons   95
6.2   Model of neurons. Figure: Lonce Wyse   97
6.3   Layers and Cells. Figure: Lonce Wyse   98
6.4   An original image presented to the DeepDream network.
      Images: Creative Commons and Mordvintsev et al. 2015   99
6.5   Photo by Andreas Praefcke rendered in the styles of *The
      Shipwreck of the Minotaur* by JMW Turner, 1805; *The Starry
      Night* by Vincent van Gogh, 1889; and *Der Schrei* by
      Edvard Munch. Figure by Gatys, Ecker, and Bethge 2016   101
6.6   RNN with recurrent connections. Figure: Lonce Wyse   103
6.7   Predictive RNN. Figure by Radford, Jozefowicz, and
      Sutskever 2017   104
6.8   Compact distributed representation. Figure: Lonce Wyse   106
6.9   Vector representations. Figure: Creative Commons   107
6.10 Tom White, *Perception Engine*, 2018   109
7.1   BE Hefner, James Madison University, "Circulating American
      Magazines: Visualization Tools for U.S. Magazine History"
      big data project 2020   116

x List of figures

9.1 Masaki Fujihata, *BeHere*, Wan Chai, Hong Kong, 2018.
Photo: Shuichi Fukuzawa 148
9.2 Masaki Fujihata, *BeHere* photogrammetry, screen capture, 2018 152
12.1 Simon Biggs, *Babel*, 2001. Photo: Simon Biggs 196
12.2 Simon Biggs, *Dark Matter*, 2017. Photo: Simon Biggs 198
12.3 Simon Biggs, *Heteropticon*, screen still, 2018 200
13.1 Warren Neidich, *Telepathy Drawing*, 2019. Photo: Warren Neidich 217

CONTRIBUTORS

Editor

Natasha Lushetich is Professor of Contemporary Art & Theory at the University of Dundee and AHRC Leadership Fellow (2020–2021). Her research is interdisciplinary and focuses on intermedia, biopolitics and performativity, the status of sensory experience in cultural knowledge, hegemony, disorder, and complexity. She is the author of two books: *Fluxus: The Practice of Non-Duality* (2014) and *Interdisciplinary Performance* (2016). She is also co-editor of 'On Game Structures', a special issue of *Performance Research* (2016), editor of *The Aesthetics of Necropolitics* (2018) and editor of 'Beyond Mind', a special issue of *Symbolism* (2019).

Contributors

Btihaj Ajana is Reader (Associate Professor) in the Department of Digital Humanities, King's College, London. Her academic work is interdisciplinary in nature, spanning areas of digital culture, media praxis, and biopolitics. She is the author of *Governing through Biometrics: The Biopolitics of Identity* (2013) and editor of *Self-tracking: Empirical and Philosophical Investigations* (2018) and *Metric Culture: Ontologies of Self-tracking Practices* (2018).

Mitra Azar is an eclecto-nomadic video-squatter and ARTthropologist. For the last ten years, he has been investigating crisis areas, building an archive of site-specific works through the lens of visual art, filmmaking and performance. He is currently a PhD candidate at Aarhus University and part of the Geneve2020 think tank (Institute of Research and Innovation, Pompidou Centre, Paris). His theoretical and practice-based work has been shown at the Museum of the Moving

xii List of contributors

Image New York; Spectacle Cinema NYC; the Havana Biennial; The Influencers; Fotomuseum Wintertur; The Venice Biennial; Transmediale Festival; Macba [Sonia] Podcast, and Berlinale Film Festival.

Franco 'Bifo' Berardi is a contemporary writer, media-theorist and media-activist. He founded the magazine A/traverso (1975–1981) and was one of the contributors to Radio Alice, the first free radio station in Italy (1976–1978). In the 1980s and 1990s he took part in the promotion of cyberculture. He has been a contributor to *Semiotexte* (New York), *Chimeres* (Paris), *Metropoli* (Rome) *Musica 80* (Milan), and *Archipielago* (Barcelona), among others. He has published books about social movements, art, and communication. Among his publications are *The Soul at Work* (2009) *Futurability* (2015) *Fenomenologia del fin* (2017), and *Breathing* (2018).

Simon Biggs is a media artist, writer, and curator. His work has been presented at Tate Modern, Tate Liverpool, National Film Theatre, ICA, FACT, Ikon, Pompidou, Academy de Kunste, Maxxi, Macau Arts Museum, Walker Art Center, San Francisco Cameraworks, Total Seoul, Art Gallery of New South Wales, and Adelaide and Edinburgh Festivals. Publications include *Remediating the Social* (ed., 2012), *Autopoeisis* (with James Leach, 2004), *Great Wall of China* (1999), *Halo* (1998), *Magnet* (1997) and *Book of Shadows* (1996). He is Professor of Art at the University of South Australia.

Tim Christaens is a PhD candidate at RIPPLE in the Institute of Philosophy of the KU Leuven. His research focuses mainly on contemporary economic issues, such as financialisation, socio-economic exclusion, and digital labour, viewed from the lens of Italian and French critical theory (Foucault, Deleuze, Agamben, post-operaismo, etc.). He is a founding member of the Low Countries chapter of the Italian Thought Network and of Rethinking Economics Leuven. His research has been published in journals such as *Theory, Culture & Society*, *The European Journal of Social Theory*, *Cultural Critique*, and *Critical Sociology*.

Masaki Fujihata is a pioneer of new media art. His CG work was celebrated in the 1980s, before his interests shifted to creating 3D sculptures from data using 3D printing, as in *Geometric Love* and the stereo-lithography *Forbidden Fruits*. In the mid-1990s Fujihata produced canonical pieces of what would later be called 'interactive art', *Beyond Pages* and *Global Interior Project*. He has, since then, created many landmark pieces such as the 2003 *Field-work@Alsace*, and the 2012 *Voices of Aliveness*. Fujihata's *Global Interior Project #2* won the 1996 Golden NIKA Award while *Voices of Aliveness* won an Ars Electronica Award of Distinction in 2013. Fujihata has held professorships at Keio University; Tokyo University; Ritsumeikan University, Paris VIII; Art University, Linz; Hong Kong Baptist University and University of California, Los Angeles.

Abelardo Gil-Fournier is an artist and researcher currently working on the project on Operational Images and Visual Culture (2019–2023) at FAMU at the Academy of Performing Arts, Prague. His work, which addresses the material interweaving between the contemporary image and the living surfaces of the planet, has been shown and discussed at venues such as Transmediale Berlin, Matadero Center of Art, Galeria Millenium (Lisbon), MUSAC, Fundación Cerezales Antonino y Cinia, Medialab Prado, IKKM, Baluarte, Laboral Center of Art as well as in the cultural centres of Spain in Mexico, Nicaragua, and El Salvador.

Ingrid M. Hoofd is Assistant Professor in the Department of Media and Culture at Utrecht University, the Netherlands. Her research interests are issues of representation, feminist and critical theories, philosophy of technology, game studies, and information ethics. She is the author of *Higher Education and Technological Acceleration: The Disintegration of University Teaching and Research* (2016), and *Ambiguities of Activism: Alter-Globalism and the Imperatives of Speed* (2012). Her research outlines the accelerated tensions and relationships between various new technologies (e-learning platforms, big data, and social media) and activist-academic moral imperatives from a critical–cultural and deconstructionist perspective.

Nicola Horsley has researched and published on the dominance of scientific and technical knowledge as bases for policy and practice, digital minoritisation and the future of knowledge in the big data era and beyond, and challenges in feminist research methods. Her qualitative research critiques the marginalisation of the social in discourses including citizenship, datafication, education, and family policy. Her writing has most recently focused on current questions of data, truth and knowledge complexity by applying a cultural lens to the challenges big data poses for society.

Warren Neidich is a conceptual artist and theorist based in Berlin and Los Angeles. He is the founding director of Saas-Fee Summer Institute of Art and the English editor of Archive Books, Berlin. He founded the website Artbrain.org which includes the *Journal of Neuroaesthetics* in 1997. Recently published books include *Glossary of Cognitive Capitalism* (2019) and *Neuromacht* (2017). He has been guest tutor at Goldsmiths College, London 2004–2007 and the Weissensee Kunsthochschule, Berlin 2016–2018, as well as lecturing at such institutions as Harvard University, Columbia University, Princeton University, Brown University, University of Oxford, and University of Cambridge.

Jussi Parikka is Professor at University of Southampton and Visiting Professor at FAMU at the Academy of Performing Arts, Prague where he leads the project on Operational Images and Visual Culture (2019–2023). His work has addressed questions of virality and computer accidents – *Digital Contagions: A Media Archaeology of Computer Viruses* (2016) and ecology and media in books such as *Insect Media* (2010) and *A Geology of Media* (2015). His forthcoming publications include the co-authored *The Lab Book* (with Darren Wershler and Lori Emerson) and the co-edited *Photography Off the Scale* (with Tomas Dvorak).

xiv List of contributors

Craig J. Saper, Professor in Language, Literacy & Culture Doctoral Program, UMBC, published *Artificial Mythologies* (1997), *Networked Art* (2001), *The Amazing Adventures of Bob Brown* (2016), and *Intimate Bureaucracies* (2012). He co-edited volumes: *Electracy* (2015), *Imaging Place* (2009), *Drifts* (2007), and *Mapping Culture Multimodally* (2007); edited and introduced six volumes in new critical facsimile editions: *The Readies, Words, Gems, 1450–1950* (2014), *Houdini* (2017), and *Readies for Bob Brown's Machine* (2020). He also published chapters and articles on digital humanities, co-curated *TypeBound* (on typewriter and sculptural poetry), built readies.org and co-founded folkvine.org. He co-publishes Hyper-Electric Press's digital-book-equivalent series, and is on the editorial boards of *Rhizomes*.net, *HyperRhiz*.io, *Textshop Experiments*, and *Inscription: The Journal of Material Text*.

Dominic Smith is Senior Lecturer in Philosophy at the University of Dundee, where he researches philosophy of technology. He is interested in bringing the continental tradition in philosophy (e.g. phenomenology, critical theory, poststructuralism, new forms of realism, and materialism) to bear on philosophy of technology and media. His latest book is *Exceptional Technologies: A Continental Philosophy of Technology* (2018). His next project involves thinking about how philosophy of technology can be broadened to speak to issues in philosophy of education, design, and creativity, with a focus on the work of Walter Benjamin.

Lonce Wyse is an Associate Professor with the Department of Communications and New Media at the National University of Singapore, and holds a PhD in Cognitive and Neural Systems (1994). He serves on the editorial boards of the *Computer Music Journal, Organized Sound*, and *The International Journal of Performance Arts and Digital Media*. He teaches courses on software studies, creative coding, media art, and interactive audio. His recent research area spans sound perception, real-time musical communication and notation, and networked music making. His current focus is on developing neural networks as interactive sound and music synthesis models.

ACKNOWLEDGEMENTS

First and foremost, I would like to thank the contributors to this volume for being wonderful fellow travellers on this journey, which began as a symposium at LaSalle College of the Arts, Singapore, in May 2018. I am grateful for the many interesting conversations that have animated this venture both during and since the symposium, in verbal and written form. My heartfelt thanks also go to Wolfgang Münch for his thoughtfulness and support, and to Lev Manovich, Randall Packer, and Gray Wetzler for thinking with the volume.

I acknowledge that Abelardo Gil-Fournier and Jussi Parikka's chapter "'Visual Hallucination of Probable Events': On Environments of Images, Data, and Machine Learning" builds on an earlier version of this text published as "'Visuelle Halluzination von möglichen Ereignissen' oder: Über Umweltbilder und Maschinelles Lernen" in *Archiv für Mediengeschichte* 18. Significant sections of this chapter are direct quotations of the German text. I would also like to thank Shuichi Fukazawa for the permission to use a photograph of Masaki Fujihata's project *BeHere*. Last but certainly not least, I am indebted to my editor at Routledge, Simon Bates, and editorial assistant ShengBin Tan, for all their help and care.

PROLOGUE

Why ask the question?

Natasha Lushetich

In a well-known rumination on biological and machinic ecologies, Wiener writes:

> [o]ur tissues change as we live: the food we eat and the air we breathe become flesh and bone of our body and the momentary elements of our flesh and bone pass out of our body every day with our excreta. We are but whirlpools in a river of ever-flowing water. We are not stuff that abides, but patterns that perpetuate themselves.
>
> *(Wiener 1950, p. 96)*

Seventy years later, patterns – or, more precisely, pattern recognition – have a bad name.

Machine learning, understood as a mode of perception, rather than cognition (Bratton 2015; LeCun 2018) has extended visual pattern recognition to the processing of the widest variety of data. In machinic, as in human perception, pattern recognition is an ordering principle. It establishes relationships between elements in a repetitive sequence (Nolan 2009). In machine learning, the learning algorithm extracts patterns from the training data by establishing a connection between the input and the output. It then 'writes' a statistical description of that correlation and applies it to new data. The learning algorithm is considered as successfully trained when it can recognise patterns and detect anomalies with an acceptable margin of error, although what that margin should be remains a hot topic of debate in many fields (Bolukbasi et al. 2016; Eubanks 2018; Noble 2018; Frank 2019).

There are two understandable fears associated with the binary separation of patterns from anomalies. The first is the replication – in an automated and thus even more problematic form – of a millennia-old dualism, which separates identity from alterity, stasis from change, 'good' from 'bad', 'worthy' from 'unworthy' further perpetuating classism, racism, sexism, and speciesism. The second is the elimination of the future, or the imposition of *le futur* over *l'avenir*. In French, there are two words for the future. *Le futur* is "programmed to come" (Derrida 2002, np.). We could say that, once born, every living being is 'programmed' to die. *L'avenir*, on the other hand – which, literally translated, means 'to come' (*à venir*) – surpasses human understanding, 'natural' as well as 'artificial' programmability. As Derrida notes, *l'avenir* is "nothing of which it might be possible to say: 'this is' (with any complement of being) in the way that Hegel was able to say 'this is an oak in which we discern the development of an acorn'" (Derrida 1988, p. 152). Rather, *l'avenir* is "the evaporation (*échéance*) of any variety of acorns"; it is "unforeseeable, free of ulterior expectations, and in no way subject to teleological maturation" (152). Complexity theorists would say that the unpredictability of much (although not all) of life comes from the fact that stable systems occasionally produce random behaviour while chaotic systems produce ordered behaviour (Volk 1995; Capra 1997). All networks – biological, geological, informational, or social – are, likewise, by definition, non-linear; they are modulated by negative and positive feedback. Negative feedback negates disturbances and creates stability; positive feedback amplifies disturbances and creates turbulence, allowing for the bottom-up emergence of new relationships as well as distorted feedback loops (Papetin 1980; Waldorp 1992; Bell 1999).

It will not come as a surprise that the reduction of *l'avenir* to *le futur*, or prediction based on poor information, over-simplified interpretation, or simply 'blind' prejudice, has disastrous effects. Infamous examples range from Google's algorithms auto-tagging pictures of black people 'gorillas' (Mulshine 2015), and the US penal system algorithms predicting recidivism in criminals by 'reading' their levels of education against their family's incarceration history (O'Neill 2016), to drones mistakenly opening fire on innocent civilians because they mistook their umbrellas for guns (Chamayou 2015). Unfortunately, these problematic ramifications of what we could call 'dogmatic' pattern recognition do stand in an oak–acorn relationship with the word's etymology. The Middle English *patron*, which means "serving as a model" is derived from the Latin *patronus*: protector and father (OED 2019, np.). It refers to authority, the order imposed by that authority, and its attendant zones of epistemic exclusion or cultivated ignorance: that which the authority refuses to know (Sedgwick 2008).

But patterning is not just a unidirectional or unilateral process. It is a process of formation and dissipation of structures – as well as their nesting substructures – and not just a process of calibration, although, in machine learning, calibration is key. If an algorithm's learning is too limited it will fail to recognise objects with any margin of difference from the training data – a process also called overfitting or appaternicity; if it is too broad, the algorithm will create too many connections and fail to distinguish 'signal' from 'noise', subject matter from background – a process called underfitting or patternicity (Shermer 2008; Bratton 2015). What this margin of variability shows, however, is that patterning is a 'phase' or 'transition'

Prologue: Why ask the question? **3**

space as every pattern changes when placed in even a marginally different context, whether visual, auditory, or textual (Toussaint 1978, 2013). This further means that patterning cannot be thought of as a monolithic process. Patterning encompasses multiple processes at different levels of structuration where microscopic changes, lines of resistance, thwarting forces, and errors interfere and intertwine. This collection takes patterning as its organising principle to think the social, biological, epistemic, mnemonic, environmental and aesthetic changes that the phenomenon referred to as big data – big 'givens' – has brought about. The book consists of four Parts: Patterning Knowledge and Time; Patterning Use and Extraction; Patterning Cultural Heritage and Memory; and Patterning People.

It has by now become customary to talk about big data in terms of size: 40 Zettabytes (40 x trillion Gigabytes) of data that, at the time of writing, even supercomputers with a processing power of 200 petaflops cannot process (Sun and Huo 2019). More importantly, the term denotes a multifaceted socio-technical process of generating temporally enduring 'givens' through online activities, mobile phone use, commercial transactions, sensors, sequencers, and crowdsourcing. This process, also known as datification (Mayer-Schönberger and Cukier 2013) includes textual, numeric, visual, and audio-visual data distributed across machine-to-machine communication, cyber-physical systems, sensor circuits, social media, and Internet of Things. The euphemistic agricultural term 'data harvesting' refers to three forms of data extraction: directed extraction, which relies on human-controlled systems such as CCTV; automated extraction, which includes data-capturing systems such as clickstream data, transponders, barcodes, and, more generally, all digital devices that communicate the history of their own utilisation; and voluntary extraction, via social media or crowdsourcing (Kitchin 2017). Data harvesting is accompanied by an entire array of operations such as data cleaning, ordering, formatting, linking, storing, curating, visualising, interpreting, sharing, and recycling.

What big data is – as process and product – is, by necessity, constantly revised, often in acronyms borrowed from business, such as the seven Vs: volume, variety, velocity, variability, visualisation, value and veracity; or the three Hs: high dimension, high complexity and high uncertainty (Sun, Strang, and Li 2018; Sun and Huo 2019). Many of these terms remain debatable, however. Contrary to what may be expected, 'veracity' does not refer to a form of advanced empiricism but is a euphemism for data cleaning, itself a euphemism for removing 'confusing' data. A case in point is Booz Allen Hamilton's (IT consultancy company) analysis of five-star hotel demographics where consumption patterns of large groups of Middle Eastern teenagers were eliminated from the data set as 'noise' because the combination of 'young', 'coloured' and 'rich' seemed incongruous to the analysts, the assumption being that 'rich' may go with 'young' but does not go with 'coloured' (Kopytoff 2014; Steyerl 2018). Value, too, is debatable. The fact that big data stands for a continuously changing constellation of human and machinic behaviour, where every action, however trite, is captured and quantified, means that over 80 per cent of data remains unstructured (Gandomi and Haider 2015; Kong 2019).

It also means that due to the velocity of data production, data analyses are not synchronised (Jukić et al. 2015) and that the compatibility of data sets remains questionable (Jiang et al. 2015). Despite these persisting question marks, there are disciplines that have benefitted from exhaustive data collection and analytics more than others. In the sciences, big data analytics have pioneered a blended inductive–deductive approach, which combines the formerly separate empiricism (where data are thought to speak for themselves) with the deductive, theory-based approach (Kitchin 2014). In health, water, waste, and traffic management real-time data analysis and scenario modelling have enabled detection of early warnings of flu outbreaks, more efficient waste management, and safer traffic regulation (Abella, Ortiz de Urbina-Criado, and De-Pablos-Heredero 2017; Rathore et al. 2017; Sun and Scanlon 2019).

In the arts and (digital) humanities, however, the use of big data remains a contentious issue not only because data architectures are increasingly determining classificatory systems in the educational, social, and medical realms, but because they reduce political and ethical questions to technical management (Rouvroy in Rouvroy and Berns 2013; Rouvroy and Stiegler 2016; Panagia in Panagia and Çağlar 2017). Panagia's apt term *#datapolitik* is an umbrella term for a set of operations that regulate circulation through space and time, at micro and macro levels, bringing together machinic perception, the cybernetic feedback loop, practices of tracking and capture, and beliefs of a threat or potential catastrophe (Panagia in Panagia and Çağlar 2017, np.). By treating citizens as a moving target, indistinct from any other automated object, such as a missile, *#datapolitik* reduces the political horizon to conformity enforcement and difference control. Zuboff is equally adamant in her astute critique of instrumentarianism, which she correctly distinguishes from digital totalitarianism, a term favoured by theorists such as Hendricks and Vestergaard (Hendricks and Vestergaard 2019). The problem with a (historical) term like totalitarianism is that it fails to reflect the contemporary condition. Relentless data extraction, of which humans are mostly unaware, has little to do with the totalitarian ambition to master the entire semantic field in order to control "everyone in every aspect of their life" (Arendt 1951, p. 456). Rather, data extraction is a mode of production as well as a mode of exchange. Situating contemporary data extraction practices within the broader context of surveillance capitalism, Zuboff argues that, in instrumentarianism, "users are no longer ends-in-themselves" but "a means to profits in new *behavioral futures markets*" in which they are neither buyers nor sellers nor products", but "the *human natural* source" (Zuboff 2019, p. 13; emphasis original). Clearly, data and their multiple arborisations have become economic and political strategies as well as existential territories. Our homes are existential territories in the sense that our bedrooms afford sleeping, our bathrooms bathing, our kitchens cooking. So do our numerous apps: Google maps, Skype, Todoist Karma, Smarty Pig or Nike Plus. Like the built environment, they *conjugate* our existence, cue habits, and modify our neural synapses (Malabou 2008) creating both unprecedented opportunities for memory inscription, and overwhelming us with a deluge of (often) unintelligible data.

Prologue: Why ask the question? **5**

In the arts, design, and architecture, the intelligible, unstructured data patterning has a long history. At the beginning of the last century, Constructivism emerged as a bottom-up method of enquiry in poetry, painting, literature, theatre, and film. Relying on the juxtaposition of incongruous parts to create a new perceptual landscape in which 'meaning' was derived not from neatly organised semantic parts but from the associative repercussions of incongruous elements, films like Vertov's 1929 experimental documentary *Man with a Movie Camera*, used an array of cinematic techniques – slow and fast motion, double exposure, freeze frames, tilted angles, tracking shots, jump cuts, backward projection, and stop motion animation – to show a complex coalescence of crowds, streets, factories, sport stadiums, amusement parks, concert halls, beaches, and bars, all intercut with sequences of joy, sorrow, marriage, divorce, death, and birth. Vertov and his numerous *kinoks* – cinema eyes – recorded life-facts as they were. The explicit purpose of such cinematic 'data collection' was to penetrate beneath the surface of external reality and "reveal processes inaccessible to the naked eye", made visible through the "recording of movements composed of the most complex combinations" (Vertov quoted in Petrić 1993 [1987], p. 4). Similarly, in the post-Second World War United States, the MIT designer Kepes pioneered the deluvial use of visual data in his explorations of "patterns of order" emerging from incongruous "landscapes of sense", recorded by radars and computers (Kepes 1956, p. 24). This non-apparent order transformed "data from measured quantities" into qualities or "forms that exhibited properties of harmony, rhythm, and proportion" (22–24). Bringing together Gestalt psychology's focus on "the phenomenal nature of perceiving 'gestalten' of a pattern's structure" (Golec 2002, p. 8), and the "syntactical dimension of perception" (4), Kepes' landmark 1944 book *Language of Vision* signalled the possibility of order emerging spontaneously from disorder two decades before the chaos theory (Gleick 1987). Kepes firmly believed that data collected by automated devices such as radars, X-rays, and computers enabled designers to access "levels of the unformed world" (Golec 2002, p. 5). In a similar rejection of representation, Kepes' contemporaries, the design couple Eames, used an excess of audio-visual data as a methodology. The role of design was, for the Eames, to *amplify* information, enable idiosyncratic individual reception of informational patterns, and forge new aesthetic connections (Eames 1974, pp. 14–15). In similar fashion, architect and polymath Fuller argued that, in education, ten-hour lectures, reminiscent of Satie's 1893 24-hour piano solo *Vexations*, with hundreds of slides, relentless repetition, and iteration, stimulated an "awareness of the processes" that led to "new degrees of comprehension" (Fuller 1975, np.). Fuller claimed that what "to the careless listener or reader" might "seem tiresome" was "to the *successful explorer* [...] the essential mustering of *operational strategies* from which alone new thrusts of comprehension" could arise (np.; emphasis original). For all these artists and designers, whose influence on future generations cannot be overestimated – think of Cage, Maciunas, or the Fluxus group, among others – the avalanche of unstructured or semi-structured data stood for the liberation from the narrow confines of subjectivity and the perceptual paths prescribed by tradition. The production of data gathered with an array of recording technologies, the use of novel spatial and temporal positions, points of view, and velocities, were a mode of exploration that embraced indeterminacy, ambiguity, and repetition *as* difference, purposefully conflating process with product.

In this (narrow) sense, we could answer the question 'is big data a new medium?' effortlessly in the affirmative, and corroborate the statement with reference to contemporary artists such as Miebach who converts layers of geological and meteorological data as well as data related to the gravitational influence of the sun and the moon, to create quizzical material objects (Miebach nd.). But the question whether big data is a new medium is both more comprehensive, and more ontological than epistemological. Derived from the Latin for "middle, midst, intermediate course", a medium is always lodged between two "degrees, qualities, or classes"; it is a "channel of mass communication"; a "physical material" used for "reproducing data, images, or sound"; a "substance through which a force acts on objects at a distance or through which impressions are conveyed to the senses"; as well as "a person or thing which acts as an intermediary" (OED 2019, np.). A medium essentially stands for two things: relationality, and the channelling or modification of difference. Relationality is similar to gravity. It is a perpetually acting force that does not privilege stable entities over their processes of creation or dissipation, a force which in constituting relationships between entities, *constitutes* and *reconstitutes* the entities within these relationships (Lushetich 2014). The channelling or modification of difference can, for its part, take many forms: transposition, cross-pollination, adaptation, interpenetration, or assimilation. What the combination of these two forces or processes shows is that the ontology of media cannot be seen as separate from the ontology of human beings and the environment.

Kittler reminds us that Aristotle, in his reference to air and water as two 'betweens', adapted the common Greek preposition – *metaxú* or between – into a "philosophical concept: *tò metaxú*, the medium" (Kittler 2009, p. 26). He further suggests that that which exists "'[i]n the middle' of absence and presence, farness and nearness, being and soul" is, by analogy, not "nothing" but a "mediatic relation" (26). Pondered by many theorists, this relation has perhaps been most accurately articulated by Vismann, for whom gadgets and devices, and not just human agents, engage in auto-praxis [*Eigenpraxis*] (Vismann 2013, p. 84). Vismann argues that since a thing is never independent of its conditions of production, space, time, and environmental forces, it would be wrong to attribute agency solely to human beings, as the agent–thing *iteratively steers* emergent processes in new, and, for humans, often unpredictable and imperceptible directions (84). Reaching into deep, tectonic past, and referring to paleontologist Leroi-Gourhan – for whom the species-nature of humans arose from their use of objects, not only as tools, but as tools to make tools – Stiegler argues that the essence of human beings is technical. The history of humanity, as cultural transmission and sedimentation is, by analogy, inseparable from the history of technology (Stiegler 1998). In an ecological register and extending McLuhan's theorisation of media as environment (rather than as an extension of human beings, which is what McLuhan is perhaps most known for),

Parikka proposes a geological view of media where the earth, light, air, space, and time are related to technological devices as well as to copper, uranium, oil, and nickel (Parikka 2015).

But what does it mean, in the context of the above biosocial, evolutionary, and ecological relations, to ask whether big data is a new medium? First, a medium that may appear new at any given time, is always a remediation of older media; for example, film is a remediation of photography and radio (Bolter and Grusin 2000). Second, every new medium (re)articulates the difference between here and there, before and after, individual and communal, perceptible and imperceptible, possible and impossible. A new medium is thus always an emplacement and a new set of relations, inseparable from the socio-economic conditions of its epoch (McLuhan 1962; Benjamin 1969; Guattari 1995). As Benjamin notes, with the "increasing extension of the press", "an increasing number of readers became writers", making the distinction between author and reader "lose its character" (Benjamin 1969, p. 232). In recent years, we have witnessed yet another modification of the writer–reader relationship and their modes of exchange. As Dean notes, in communicative capitalism, prosumers' messages "no longer have use value"; their chief value is their "capacity to circulate, to be forwarded, counted", in other words: exchange value (Dean 2013, p. 66). The new additive value is based on "fundamental communicative equivalence" where "[n]o opinion or judgment is worth more than any other (they each count as one comment on my blog or one update of Facebook or a single tweet. Facts, theories, judgments, opinions, fantasies, jokes, lies – they all circulate indiscriminately" (66). What matters is not what is said but that something is said, and that this 'something' circulates and stimulates further communication – comments, questions, and responses.

Writing in the wake of the above-mentioned 1950s artistic, scientific, and educational explorations, McLuhan presciently theorises media as constellations. Privileging process over staticity, relationships over stable entities, he focuses on their transformation. In *The Gutenberg Galaxy*, McLuhan writes: "the galaxy or constellation of events [...] is a mosaic of perpetually interacting forms that have undergone kaleidoscopic transformation" (McLuhan 1962, p. 7). Referring to all forms of automation, such as electric light, print, the telegraph, and the railway (McLuhan 1964, pp. 23–24) and not just media like photography, the radio, or film – which, in addition to their transmitting, recording, and transcoding functions also have a *poietic* function – media are, for McLuhan, in a perpetual process of communication with other media. They reverse themselves in what he calls a "reversal of pattern" and have a "break boundary" (49) caused by the "cross-fertilization" of new, incoming media (50). Most importantly, they bypass human consciousness. For McLuhan, as for Benjamin, media alter human sensory balance. They recode perception, changing (or de-patterning and re-patterning) the landscape and structure of unconscious thought and impulses. As Benjamin writes of the advent of film:

> Our taverns and our metropolitan streets, our offices and furnished rooms, our railroad stations and factories appeared to have us locked up hopelessly.

8 Natasha Lushetich

> Then came the film and burst this prison-world asunder by the dynamite of the tenth of a second, so that now, in the midst of its far-flung ruins and debris, we calmly and adventurously go traveling. With the close-up, space expands; with slow motion, movement is extended [...] The camera introduces us to unconscious optics as does psychoanalysis to unconscious impulses.
>
> *(Benjamin 1969, pp. 236–237)*

Referring to the above passage, Han suggests that big data can be understood "in analogy to a movie camera" (Han 2017, p. 64). As a "digital magnifying glass", data mining, processing, and interpreting enlarges human actions; it discloses "another scene shot through with unconscious elements [...] behind the framework of consciousness" (65). Such "microphysics" makes "actomes" – micro-actions that elude detection by the waking mind – visible by bringing to light collective patterns of behaviour that render the "collective unconscious accessible" (65). Han calls this "microphysical or micropsychical web of relations", after Benjamin's optical unconscious, "the digital unconscious" (65). The problem, however, is that Han's discussion of big data is entirely anthropocentric. If big data can be thought of as a new medium, it is, of course, important to ask questions such as 'how does it conjugate human existence?' But it is also important to ask how big data (re)articulates time, space, the material and immaterial world, the knowable and the unknowable; how it navigates, or alters, hierarchies of importance. Particularly useful in this respect is McLuhan's later, tetradic approach to media. Building on amplification as extension, obsolescence as a content–form relationship (where one medium becomes the content of another), retrieval (where a medium retrieves what has been obfuscated earlier) and reversal (when a medium reaches its limit and reverses into a form that will drive itself into obsolescence), McLuhan's later media analysis centres on four questions: "what does it enhance?"; "what does it obsolesce?"; "what does is retrieve?" and "what does it turn into when pushed to the limits of its potential?" (McLuhan 1977, p. 175).

The chapters gathered in this transdisciplinary volume – authored by a diverse group of scholars: media, cultural, and literary theorists, artists, philosophers, political philosophers, historians, communication and computer scientists – approach big data by addressing, in broad terms, the tendencies that big data, as a potential new medium, enhances, obsolesces, retrieves, and pushes to the limits of potentiality. Taking a critical yet non-prejudicial view of this complex phenomenon, the volume does not set out to prove that automated prejudice is worse than non-automated prejudice or that ubiquitous surveillance is worse than surveillance limited to the disciplinary institutions studied by Foucault – the school, the prison, and the hospital (Foucault 1991). It obviously is. Rather, this volume asks questions about big data as a *constellation* and a multifaceted process of *transformation* that, like all medial operations, occurs largely beyond the realm of human consciousness.

Part I, Patterning Knowledge and Time, opens with Hoofd's "Big Data and/ versus People Knowledge: On the Ambiguities of Humanistic Research". In this chapter, Hoofd suggests that big data renders its object of analysis both more knowable and more unknowable, which, she argues, amplifies the *aporia* at the heart of the humanistic enterprise: the simultaneous desire to probe and to liberate alterity. In "Simulated Replicants Forever? Big Data, Engendered Determinism and the End of Prophecy", Berardi contemplates the constitution of what he terms the 'cognitive automaton'. Mapping different forms of linguistic inscription of the future in the present, such as injunction, code, paradoxical injunction, and prophecy, he anchors the operation of the cognitive automaton to natural as well as programming languages. In "'Visual Hallucination of Probable Events': On Environments of Images, Data, and Machine Learning", Gil-Fournier and Parikka use nowcasting and Next Frame Prediction to analyse the interfacing of images and data. Highlighting the umbilical relationship between the production of possible futures, scenario modelling, and the temporal feedback loop characteristic of such data sets, Gil-Fournier and Parikka elaborate upon the relationship between visual and spatial prediction techniques and the management of environments.

In Part II, Patterning Use and Extraction, in "Biometric Datafication in Governmental and Personal Spheres", Ajana suggests that the convergence of biometrics and big data is a mode of governance. Focusing on two different examples – refugee management technologies and consumer products of self-tracking and health monitoring – she analyses the biometric datification of the body from two perspectives: the top-down and the bottom-up. In "Digital Biopolitics and the Problem of Fatigue in Platform Capitalism", Christaens compares the old industrial problem of physical exhaustion highlighted by Marx to Berardi's theorisation of nervous exhaustion, characteristic of the twenty-first century. Christaens analyses strategies employed by the algorithmically operated gig economy, suggesting that platforms need to be re-designed as open and alterable (rather than as black boxes) based on Le Corbusier's 'open architectural object' priory Sainte-Marie de La Tourette. In the following chapter, "Appreciating Machine-generated Artwork through Deep Learning Mechanisms", Wyse focuses on the use of neural networks. Arguing that the hitherto existent discussions of machine art, which evaluate the artefact by comparing it to human artworks, yet disregard important considerations used in human art evaluation (the art-historical background or the artist's process and methodologies), Wyse provides a close reading of several neural network mechanisms in order to deepen the understanding of non-human 'backgrounds' and processes.

Part III, Patterning Cultural Heritage and Memory, opens with Saper's "Data to the Nth Degree: Zooming in On *The Smart Set*". Using a graph from "Circulating American Magazines: Visualization Tools for U.S. Magazine History" as content, and the Eames' 1968 film *The Powers of Ten* as a methodology, he discusses *The Smart Set*, a literary magazine founded in 1900. Zooming in and out in the manner of a cinematic shot (and the Eames' film), Saper engages a spectrum of perspectives, distant, and close readings, suggesting that this way of reading data might allow literary and cultural scholars to better grasp issues and problems that large data sets expose. In "Intellectual Autonomy after Artificial Intelligence: The Future of Memory Institutions and Historical Research", Horsley focuses on the fact that in recent years, memory institutions (archives, libraries, and repositories) have witnessed a re-making of the historical record as a data mine. Her investigation of the decision-making processes characteristic of machine classification, datification, and the increasing presence of machinic methodologies in a knowledge commons, poses questions about researchers' future capacity to discover diverse historical resources and the effect of the data-mine approach on the intellectual autonomy. In "*BeHere*: Prosthetic Memory in the Age of Digital Frottage", Lushetich and Fujihata discuss Fujihata's augmented reality project *BeHere* (2018–). Focusing on the latent or semi-visible image emerging from what they call 'digital frottage' (a digital variant of the Surrealist technique), remediated co-presence (of passed-away city inhabitants, actors and viewer/interactants), and the affective anarchive (an archive that is not an archive), they interrogate the ways in which vast quantities of found, data-processed images of a bygone era, co-create and amplify prosthetic memory.

In Part IV, Patterning People, in "Surfaces and Depths: An Aesthetics of Big Data", Smith considers contemporary data-analytical methods through the trope of the oceanic image. Referring to Floridi, Dean, and Deleuze, he argues that one way to enrich how we sense our way around big data in daily life is to understand the images that mediate our experience of it, not as superficial clichés but as instructive media in their own right. In the following chapter, "POV-Data-Doubles, The Dividual, and the Drive to Visibility", Azar addresses the twofold meaning of Deleuze's 'dividual': as the dispersal of the subject into bits of information, and as the intrinsic quality of affects that constitute the fabric of subjectivity. Exploring the tension between these two perspectives in the digital regime of visibility, he compares the cinematic POV (the subjective point of view in which the camera shows what the actor sees) to the POV-data-double – a data stand-in for the digital user and repository of their digital traces. In the final chapter in this Part, Biggs, in "Reading Big Data as the Heterogeneous Subject", analyses the relationship between Perec's notion of the infra-ordinary (Perec 1974), big data, and the related 'black-box' social ontology in order to shed light on the concept of iridescence as a big-data-mediated, multiplicitous, and discontinuous construct. Finally, in the epilogue entitled "Telepathic Exaptation in Late Cognitive Capitalism: A Speculative Approach to the Effects of Digitality", Neidich speculates on potential repercussions of some of the existing and emerging tendencies discussed in the preceding chapters. Mobilising Darwinian, Baldwinian, and Lamarkian evolutionary arguments, he suggests that strategies similar to those responsible for the production of dedicated neural modules for reading and writing 5,000 years ago, might, in the future, become strategies of resistance to the controlling propensity of data-driven capitalism's neural economy.

References

Abella A, Ortiz de Urbina-Criado M, and De-Pablos-Heredero C 2017, "A Model for the Analysis of Data-driven Innovation and Value Generation in Smart Cities", *Ecosystems Cities*, vol. 64, pp. 47–53.

Arendt H 1951, *The Origins of Totalitarianism*. New York: Harcourt.

Bell S 1999, *Landscape: Pattern, Perception and Process*. New York: Routledge.

Benjamin W 1969, "The Work of Art in the Age of Mechanical Reproduction", in Arendt H (ed.), *Illuminations*, trans. Zohn H. New York: Schocken, pp. 217–251.

Bolter JD and Grusin R 2000, *Remediation: Understanding New Media*. Cambridge, MA: MIT Press.

Bolukbasi T et al. 2016, "Man is to Computer Programmer as Woman is to Homemaker? Debiasing Word Embeddings", *arXiv.org*, 21 July. Available from: arxiv.org/abs/1607.06520 [accessed 7 August 2019].

Bratton BH 2015, *The Stack: On Software and Sovereignty*. Cambridge, MA: MIT Press.

Capra F 1997, *The Web of Life: A New Synthesis of Mind and Matter*. London: Flamingo.

Chamayou G 2015, *A Theory of the Drone*, trans. Lloyd J. New York: The New Press.

Dean J 2013, "Communicative Capitalism: This Is What Democracy Looks Like", in Medak T and Milat P (eds.), *Idea of Radical Media*. Zagreb: Multimedijalni Institut, pp. 60–71.

Derrida J 1988, *Mémoire pour Paul de Man*. Paris: Galilée.

Derrida. 2002, documentary film. New York: Zeitgeist Films.

Eames C 1974, "Language of Vision: Nuts and Bolts", Bulletin, The American Academy of Arts and Sciences, 28 October, pp. 13–45.

Eubanks V 2018, *Automating Inequality: How High-Tech Tools Profile, Police, and Punish the Poor*. New York: St. Martin's Press.

Foucault M 1991, *Discipline and Punish: The Birth of the Prison*, trans. Sheridan A. London: Penguin.

Frank SA 2019, "How to Understand Behavioral Patterns in Big Data: The Case of Human Collective Memory", *Behavioral Science*, vol. 9, no. 40. Available from: doi:10.3390/bs9040040 [accessed 6 August 2019].

Fuller B 1975, *Synergetics: Explorations in the Geometry of Thinking*. New York: Macmillan.

Gandomi A and Haider M 2015, "Beyond the Hype: Big Data Concepts, Methods, and Analytics", *International Journal of Information Management*, vol. 35, pp. 137–144.

Gleick J 1987, *Chaos: Making a New Science*. London: Vintage.

Golec M 2002, "A Natural History of a Disembodied Eye: The Structure of Gyorgy Kepes's *Language of Vision*", *Design Issues*, vol. 18, no. 2, pp. 3–16.

Guattari F 1995, *Chaosmosis*, trans. Bains P and Pefanis J. Bloomington and Indianapolis, IN: Indiana University Press.

Han BC 2017, *Psychopolitics: Neoliberalism and New Technologies of Power*, trans. Butler E. London and New York: Verso.

Hendricks VF and Vestergaard M 2019, *Reality Lost: Markets of Attention, Misinformation and Manipulation*, trans. Høyrup S. Cham: Springer Open.

Jiang H et al. 2015, "Scaling up MaPREduce-based Big Data Processing on Multi-GPU Systems", *Cluster Computing*, vol. 18, no. 1, pp. 369–383.

Jukić, N et al. 2015, "Augmenting Data Warehouses with Big Data", *Information Systems Management*, vol. 32, no. 3, pp. 200–209.

Kepes G 1944, *Language of Vision*. Chicago, IL: Paul Theobald.

Kepes G 1956, *The New Landscape of Art and Science*. Chicago, IL: Paul Theobald.

Kitchin B 2014, *The Data Revolution: Big Data, Open Data, Data Infrastructures & Their Consequences*. London: Sage.

Kitchin B 2017, "Big Data", in Richardson D et al. (eds.), *The International Encyclopedia of Geography*. London: John Wiley & Sons Ltd. Available from: doi:10.1002/9781118786352.wbieg0145 [accessed 7 August 2019].

Kittler F 2009, "Towards an Ontology of Media", *Theory, Culture & Society*, vol. 26, nos. 2–3, pp. 23–31.

Kong H-J 2019, "Managing Unstructured Data in Healthcare System", *Healthcare Informatics Research*, January, vol. 25, no. 1, pp. 1–2.

Kopytoff V 2014, "Big Data's Dirty Problem", *Fortune*, 30 June. Available from: http://fortune.com/201/06/30/big-data-dirty-problem/ [accessed 8 August 2019].

LeCun Y 2018, "Learning World Models: The Next Step towards AI", Keynote lecture, International Joint Conference on Artificial Intelligence (IJCAI), July, Stockholm, Sweden.

Lushetich N 2014, *Fluxus: The Practice of Non-Duality*. Amsterdam and New York: Rodopi.

Malabou C 2008, *What Should We Do With Our Brain?*, trans. R and S. New York: Fordham University Press.

Mayer-Schönberger V and Cukier K 2013, *Big Data: A Revolution that Will Change How We Live, Work and Think*. London: John Murray.

McLuhan HM 1962, *The Guttenberg Galaxy: The Making of Typographic Man*. Toronto: University of Toronto Press.

McLuhan HM 1964, *Understanding Media: The Extensions of Man*. New York: Mentor.

McLuhan HM 1977, "Laws of the Media", *Et Cetera*, vol. 34, no. 2, pp. 173–179.

Miebach N nd., Artworks. Available from: https://nathaliemiebach.com/tide.html [accessed 7 August 2019].

Mulshine M 2015, "A Major Flow in Google's Algorithm", *Business Insider*, 1 July. Available from: www.businessinsider.com/google-tags-black-people-as-gorillas-2015-7?r=US&IR=T [accessed 13 August 2019].

Noble S 2018, *Algorithms of Oppression: How Search Engines Reinforce Racism*. New York: NYU Press.

Nolan G 2009, "What are Patterns?", Available from: http://philosophy-of-pattern.com [accessed 6 August 2019].

O'Neil C 2016, *Weapons of Math Destruction*. New York: Broadway Books.

Oxford English Dictionary (OED). 2019, Definition. Available from: www.oed.com/ [accessed 3 August 2019].

Panagia D and Çağlar K 2017, "#datapolitik: An Interview with Davide Panagia", *Contrivers' Review*. Available from: www.contrivers.org/articles/40/Davide-Panagia-Caglar-Koseoglu-Datapolik-Interview-Political-Theory/ [accessed 3 April 2018].

Papetin F 1980, "On Order and Complexity I. General Considerations", *Journal of Theoretical Biology*, vol. 87, pp. 421–456.

Parikka J 2015, *A Geology of Media*. Minneapolis, MN: University of Minnesota Press.

Perec G 1974, *Species of Spaces and Other Pieces*, trans. Sturrock J. Harmondsworth: Penguin.

Petrić V 1993 [1987], *Constructivism in Film: The Man with the Movie Camera A Cinematic Analysis*. Cambridge, MA: Cambridge University Press.

Rathore MM et al. 2017, "Advanced Computing Model for Geosocial Media Using Big Data Analytics", *Multimedia Tools and Applications*, vol. 76, pp. 24767–24787.

Rouvroy A and Berns T 2013, "Algorithmic Governmentality and Prospects of Emancipation", trans. Libbrecht E, *Réseaux 1*, no. 177, pp. 163–196.

Rouvroy A and Stiegler B 2016, "The Digital Regime of Truth: From the Algorithmic Governmentality to a New Rule of Law", trans. Nony A and Dillet B, *La Deleuziana* [Online] *Journal of Philosophy. Life and Number*, no. 3, pp. 6–27. Available from: www.ladeleuziana.org/wp-content/uploads/2016/12/Rouvroy-Stiegler_eng.pdf [accessed 7 August 2019].

Sedgwick E 2008, *Epistemology of the Closet*. Berkeley, Los Angeles, CA and London: University of California Press.

Shermer M 2008, "Patternicity: Finding Meaningful Patterns in Meaningless Noise", *Scientific American*, vol. 299, no. 5, pp. 48–49.

Steyerl H 2018, "A Sea of Data: Pattern Recognition and Corporate Animism", in Aprich C et al. (eds.), *Pattern Discrimination*. Minneapolis, MN and London: University of Minnesota Press and Meson Press.

Stiegler B 1998, *Technics and Time 1: The Fault of Epimetheus*, trans. Beardsworth R and Collins G. Stanford, CA: Stanford University Press.

Sun AY and Scanlon BR 2019, "How Can Big Data and Machine Learning Benefit Environment and Water Management: A Survey of Methods, Applications and Future Directions", *Environmental Research Letters*, vol. 14, no. 7. Available from: https://iopscience.iop.org/article/10.1088/1748–9326/ab1b7d [accessed 8 August 2019].

Sun Z and Huo Y 2019, "The Spectrum of Big Data Analytics", *Journal of Computer Information Systems*. Available from: doi:10.1080/08874417.2019.1571456 [accessed 2 August 2019].

Sun Z, Strang K and Li R 2018, "Big Data with Ten Big Characteristics", *Proceedings of 2018 The 2nd International Conference on Big Data Research (ICBDR 2018), October 27–29*. Weihai, China: ACM, pp. 56–61.

Toussaint GT 1978, "The Use of Context in Pattern Recognition", *Pattern Recognition*, vol. 10, pp. 189–204.

Toussaint GT 2013, *The Geometry of Musical Rhythm*. Boca Raton, FL: Chapman and Hall/CRC Press.

Vismann C 2013, "Cultural Techniques and Sovereignty", trans. Iurascu I, *Theory, Culture & Society*, vol. 30, no. 6, pp. 83–93.

Volk T 1995, *Metapatterns – Across Space, Time and Mind*. New York: Columbia University Press.

Waldorp MM 1992, *The Emerging Science at the Edge of Order and Chaos*. London: Viking.

Wiener N 1950, *The Human Use of Human Beings: Cybernetics and Society*. Boston, MA: Houghton Mifflin.

Zuboff S 2019, "Surveillance Capitalism and the Challenge of Collective Action", *New Labor Forum*, vol. 28, no. 1, pp. 10–29.

PART I

Patterning knowledge and time

1

BIG DATA AND/VERSUS PEOPLE KNOWLEDGE

On the ambiguities of humanistic research

Ingrid M. Hoofd

Introduction: big data, the neo-liberal evil?

Many universities across the globe have undergone radical changes with the advent of the so-called big data techniques. From new ways of generating global university rankings, to new computer-driven research methods in Social Sciences and Humanities, these techniques have led to novel, and, at times, more efficient ways of conducting teaching and research and managing large academic institutions. Big data techniques are a central aspect of what some scholars have termed the drive towards "informatization" under "cognitive capitalism" – terms that mark the increasing importance of cognitive work and the manipulation of symbols in order to spur economic growth (Hardt and Negri 2000, p. 280; Moulier-Boutang 2011, p. 47). Yet many scholars lament the advent of big data in universities, a phenomenon they see as constitutive of the near-pervasive "audit culture" (Shore and Wright 2000, p. 57; Strathern 2000, p. 2; Shore 2008, p. 278; Morrish 2017, p. 142). In these well-argued narratives, oppressive evaluation and audit practices are generally attributed to post-1980s neo-liberalisation that saw the demise of the welfare state and the devaluation of educational institutions in favour of a more market-driven approach (Shore 2008, p. 280; Watts 2017, p. 112).

While I certainly sympathise with these critiques of neo-liberalisation and its imbrication in the demise of healthier university practices, I would nevertheless like to invite you to consider the possibility that the problem of big data audit culture in academia – the continued assessment and surveillance of staff and students through digital-platform- and social-media-generated analytics – is actually more complex and cannot be situated in an 'evil' capitalist force residing outside the university walls alone. Resisting both the problematic covert nostalgia of the 'demise' of a 'nobler' past university, and the overly optimistic interpretations of the supposedly emancipatory potential of big data techniques, I suggest that the

18 Ingrid M. Hoofd

encroachment of data surveillance on the university, is, in fact, a continuation of a longer history of the university's entanglements with 'modern' technologies that date to the European Enlightenment. I develop this argument by zooming in on debates around the advent of big data in Humanities that have given rise to a new field: Digital Humanities. Proponents of big data in Humanities have so far argued that the automated gathering and visualisation of data affords new insights into social and human relations, as well as into the larger Republic of Letters (Burdick et al. 2012, p. 4; McGann 2014, p. 4). However, opponents bemoan the increasing encroachment of neo-liberal techniques of automation on the Humanities, arguing that they signal the demise of rich research and teaching practices such as "close reading" (Grusin 2014, p. 85); some scholars have complicated the opposition between "close" and "distant" reading by claiming that big data techniques generate sophisticated novel interpretations of classical texts (Hammond, Brooke, and Hirst 2016, p. 50).

In order to move beyond the too-convenient (even if partially justified) 'neo-liberalisation' narrative, I further complicate this adversarial 'for-or-against' stance by teasing out the ambiguities of big data's implementation in staff and student surveillance, curriculum changes, new research and teaching methods, and student surveys in the Humanities Faculty at Utrecht University. Founded in 1636, Utrecht University is one of the larger Dutch research universities, with approximately 6,000 staff and 30,000 students. Currently, the Faculty uses a plethora of big-data-analytics-generating platforms: Elsevier's research performance platform Pure, the online teaching and learning environment *BlackBoard*, course evaluation tool *Caracal*, *Peergrade* peer evaluation tool, the network analysis and visualisation software Gephi, and CLARIAH, a distributed infrastructure for archival work in Humanities. This chapter will illustrate that the turn to big data in Humanities signals a more profound conundrum in the concept of the university dating to its idealistic beginnings than a mere spat-around Digital Humanities. This deeper conundrum pivots on the paradoxical claim that big data renders its object of analysis simultaneously more *unknowable* (or superficial) and more *knowable* (or deep), a paradox inseparable from the *aporia* inherent in the humanist endeavour to understand yet liberate alterity, to totalise yet render un-finishable the project of totalising knowledge. Following this line of argument, I suggest that the very quest for knowledge – especially knowledge about people/s, which ties the university project to the history of colonialism – is becoming a near-pervasive 'exposing-itself' of academia. The Humanities' debates around big data illustrate that the problem of the university today consists of a cybernetic *acceleration of the university's idealistic yet oppressive mission*. Moreover, as much as academia never has been an isolated 'ivory tower', with no connection to 'the market', this 'exposing-itself' is similar to the effect the widespread use of social media has in all spheres of life. However, academia's self-exposure also utilises new, supposedly 'postcolonial' ethnographic methods that romanticise 'direct contact' with peoples and 'nature' beyond neo-liberal perversities that obviously damage 'natural' and human habitats and communities. My radical conclusion is that the most cherished ideals of Utrecht University – emancipation, innovation, and knowledge accumulation and exchange – are therefore precisely what produces unjust and unsustainable practices, both 'within' and 'without' Higher Education institutions in Dutch (and global) society.

Historical traces of big data: Utrecht University's missions and visions

As a large teaching and research university, Utrecht University has, in the past decade, embraced big data technologies in many realms. Every year, its students participate in the National Student Survey (Nationale Studenten Enquête or NSE), which ranks degree programmes ranging from 1 (very poor) to 10 (excellent) across the country by digitally analysing tens of thousands of online questionnaires. The 'grades' that degree programmes 'earn' are independent of the global university or department rankings. Students evaluate teaching through anonymous online forms eight times per year. The Department of Media and Culture's curriculum has recently wholeheartedly embraced 'data' as part of its teaching content, too; feedback to students is increasingly located in 'rubrics' where skillsets are evaluated by way of ticks or numbers, rather than narrative comments. Such 'datafied' assessment and feedback tools usually consist of 5 to 20 rubrics – for example, 'method', 'readability', and 'analysis'. They are marked with a plus or a minus, or numbers from 1 to 5 so that a pass or fail can be transparently calculated. Meanwhile, staff in Medical and Social Sciences are taught the intricacies of Python, a computer programming language developed for large database management. Humanities have jumped on the Digital Humanities bandwagon by instituting their own Centre for Digital Humanities, which "aspires to accelerate [sic] and support the development of these digital methods, in order to gain new insights in all of the humanities" (Centre for Digital Humanities 2019). In its 2016–2020 Strategic Plan, Utrecht University stated that it will "future-proof its educational model by implementing innovative pedagogical models that revolve around technical and educational support in the use of IT such as blended (online and classroom) learning" (Utrecht University Strategic Plan 2016, p. 6). It will also prioritise multidisciplinary research (especially between Science, Technology, Engineering, and Mathematics (STEM), Social Sciences and Humanities) by investing in research infrastructures (Utrecht University Strategic Plan 2016, p. 7), a large part of which will go to the Research IT programme that comprises "a high-quality network, capacity for the storage of research data and facilities for high-performance computing" (23).

In its Strategic Plan, Utrecht University justifies all these developments and investments by appealing to its primary responsibility to society:

> Developments in the field of digitalisation are changing the landscape of teaching and research. Society expects academics to find solutions to major global issues such as climate change, an ageing population and migration.

20 Ingrid M. Hoofd

> Society is also placing increasingly higher demands on our transparency and financial accountability.
>
> *(Utrecht University Strategic Plan 2016, p. 8)*

These are not mere neo-liberal catchphrases; the demand for transparency and accountability resonates with the University's mission, which revolves around "innovation, new insights and societal impact" (6), and with its motto, "Sol Iustitiae Illustra Nos" (May the Sun of Righteousness Enlighten Us), engraved in the University's emblem at the time of its inception in 1636. Plain here are Utrecht University's connections with the Dutch Reformed Church; the motto is taken from Malachi 4:2 of the Latin Bible. The Dutch Reformed Church (Nederlandse Hervormde Kerk) constituted the largest protestant denomination since the 1571 Reformation in the Netherlands until its disbandment in 2004 and has historically close ties with the Dutch government and its economic policies. Interestingly, a variation on the Utrecht University motto returns in the US Rutgers University's emblem which reads "Sol Iustitiae Et Occidentem Illustra" ("May the Sun of Righteousness Also Shine Upon the West"). Founded by Dutch Reformed colonists in 1766, Rutgers, like Utrecht, initially admitted only male students, and subsequently only the cultured elites.

Innovation, transparency, and social responsibility imperatives seem to be at the idealistic heart of the university. Far from being propaganda or facile PR strategy, they continue the University's moral trajectory towards techniques like big data and fields like Digital Humanities. This is not to say that neo-liberalisation plays no role, but that the neo-liberal management, teaching, and research techniques are appealing because they are steeped in certain deep-seated Christian, 'enlightened', and humanist moral imperatives. As with the university's initially positive, optimistic mission, and its simultaneous embroilment in deeply problematic practices (colonialism, patriarchy, and class elitism), it is these very imperatives and their aporetic tensions – for example, the transparentisation, through ethnographic research, of the precise number of 'natives' in a newly colonised territory (Jenkins 2003; Manickam 2015) – that lead to an aggravation of these long-lasting tensions through the accelerated communication and computation tools. The aporetic logic of these 'moral imperatives' and their accelerated aggravation – staff and student disorientation, stress, and distress – is operative in a host of problematic oppositions (such as "close" and "distant" reading) that typify the turn to big data in the university. In the face of these imperatives' accelerated implementation, their grounding aporetic logic fractures in a potentially indefinite number of signifiers, which, in our current cybernetic condition, are imbricated in the fundamentally binary logic of computing, leading to a variety of exhausted polarisations. While computer programming seems to offer a method for controlling vast data sets, the exponentially growing size of big data undermines procedural knowledge, which leads to an increase of uncertainty. Paradoxically then, it is these polarisations that keep the debate alive; they are not only unresolvable but fuel the infrastructural machines that have, from the historical beginnings of the university, through the 'Republic of Letters', been intimately intertwined with scientific research, collaboration, and publishing. An obvious example, of course, is this chapter itself, which productively challenges the opposition between the university's 'moral core' and its 'evil' neo-liberal 'environment', which the following section details in order to draw out the ambiguities and alternative futures of humanistic research in the era of big data.

Complicating oppositions in the Digital Humanities

In "Building Theories or Theories of Building?" Warwick recounts the "methodology storms" that have marred the birth and establishment of Digital Humanities, pointing out the difference between positions that emphasise "making" or "doing" and those that favour "theorising" or "critique" (Warwick 2016, p. 540). By helpfully tracing these "storms" to their historical precedents in English Studies and History, she argues that any young field tends to be marred by such oppositional in-fights, which are, or at least can be, "healthy" for the field's development (541). She shows that there are elements of "thinking" in "making" and vice versa – for instance, English composition is envisioned as contributing to Critical Media literacy, while Critical Making teaches coding to make transparent to students the power of computing. However, she also observes that much of these historical and contemporary "storms" take place within their pertaining communication technologies; fervent arguments in old printed pamphlets in English versus impassioned Twitter debates in Digital Humanities. Moreover, Warwick relates these "storms" to uncertainty about how to measure what counts as *proper scientific knowledge* in those fields, given the lack of appropriate parameters and objective values, which, in turn, leads to uncertainties about whose research is evaluated and who gets hired (546).

Given the above-mentioned aporetic entanglement of academic aspirations and new technologies, the uncertainty inherent in traditional Humanities, and now, again, in Digital Humanities, goes much deeper than teething problems. It concerns no less than the fundamental epistemological questions about the nature of knowledge and its (technical) procurement and ratification. In proposing this, I heed Frabetti's suggestion in "Have the Humanities Always Been Digital?" that such foundational epistemological concerns in Sciences and Humanities emphasise the need to "understand how exactly new technologies change the very nature and content of academic knowledge" (Frabetti 2012, p. 168). She does this by looking at how software engineering, in its attempt to control the "constitutive fallibility of software-based technology", *undoes* itself through the "unexpected consequences" of the very technologies it relies on (167). This, Frabetti claims, is not only true for optimising and adaptive algorithms, but for computer software in general. Software is always open to the world; it comes into existence through use. In other words, Frabetti suggests that cybernetic machines and their software programming always already deconstruct themselves, generating elements that are in excess of their instrumentalist attempt at control (the word 'cybernetics', after all, comes from the Greek κυβερνήτης: to govern or steer). This, in turn,

22 Ingrid M. Hoofd

means that "software is *always* both conceptualised according to ... a metaphysical framework *and* capable of escaping it" so that if we "uncover the conceptual presuppositions", we can better understand what counts as academic knowledge, especially in Humanities, so that we may, in turn, politicise concerns around cybernetic machines better (167; emphasis original). I would add that, in the spirit of deconstruction, uncovering such presuppositions necessarily also entails picking apart the problematic oppositions surrounding these machines. While Warwick's argument does a good job of uncovering the historical backdrop of one of these oppositions, we need a more fine-grained understanding of how and why this exhausted opposition between theory and practice appears in fields that are pressed to contribute to the general social good. One may think here, for instance, of socialist scholarship that devalues theory in favour of a revolutionary practice following Marx's famous 11th Thesis on Feuerbach, which reads: "Philosophers have hitherto only interpreted the world in various ways; the point is to change it" (Marx 2000 [1938], p. 170). However, computers complicate this opposition, since computing straddles thought and action with its logic of commanding and organising. In order to work through this problematic opposition and illustrate its intimate connection to ancient imperatives and the current cybernetic techniques in Science and Philosophy, I turn to the work of the 'deconstructive' scholars Derrida and Lyotard. I do so also to show that the ambiguities of big data in Humanities run much deeper than neo-liberal surveillance or ranking, a problem that requires effective politicisation.

Important to stress, at this point, as Frabetti also does, is that when looking for 'the digital' in our cybernetic machines we are left with vague answers at best. Is 'the digital' hardware or software? Or, where does the hardware end and the software begin? Indeed, software may be "unobservable" and marks the point of "deep opacity" in any system that signals its deconstructive aspect (Frabetti 2012, p. 165). The etymology of the word leads us to the proto-Indo-European *deyǵ-, which means "to show, point out, pronounce solemnly" and which informed the Latin *digitus*, a human finger or toe (Online Etymology Dictionary 2019). Related to the digital in the sense of "pointing out", one can discern a host of concepts like digits, points, numbers, counting, calculating, and even calculus, accountability, algebra, and algorithm. Likewise, utilising digital as finger (as part of the human hand), one can segue into grasp, understand, control, manipulate, touch, stroke, caress, tact, and tangent. In his remarkable *On Touching – Jean-Luc Nancy*, Derrida traces the elaborate conceptual "history of touch" vis-à-vis its much more written-about counterpart, vision (Derrida 2005, p. 6). More specifically, he traces the continuities and discontinuities around touch, and their entanglements with (ideas of) vision that have led to contemporary techniques and technologies of knowing. He begins this tracing with the enigmatic question "When our eyes touch, is it day or is it night?" (2), which can be read as a question about our related-ness to cybernetic technology – where touch and vision seem to 'short-circuit' in a self-regulating closed data-gathering system – and as a question concerning knowledge (better or worse knowledge through cybernetic machines?) as well as a question about the larger social-political context (hopeful or dark times ushered in by the new technologies?) In order to shed light on this question – and Derrida is well aware of the paradoxes surrounding his attempt to shed light on these matters in ever darker times – he goes back to Aristotle's puzzlements in *On the Soul* about the assumption that our senses operate in unison, as well as that our senses and the object sensed are in unison in order for valid knowledge to be generated in the human and social mind (Derrida 2005, pp. 2, 4). Aristotle is quick to notice several problems with these "necessary" assumptions, for instance, the problem of where touch begins or ends (comparable to the above-mentioned problem of hardware/software); how the relationship between the other senses is constituted, even if they seem disjointed in space and time (touch is "direct" while vision is "over a distance"); why touch does not have a privileged object (like hearing = sound, or taste = flavour) (5). Quoting Nancy, Derrida stresses that "there is no 'the' sense of touch" (111, 138–139, 217).

Touch has a *fraught* relationship with vision. Moreover, these unanswered questions or foundational assumptions constitute the "forgotten" in Western science and philosophy (6–7; see also Stiegler 1998, pp. 250–252). Touch is the shadow of vision, haunting metaphysics, leading the history of Western metaphysics through the development of vision technologies of vision-up, what Derrida calls all kinds of "tangents". Indeed, the structure of Derrida's book is one of accumulation of such tangents, illustrating the indebtedness of his reasoning to Western metaphysics, which allows him to question the supposed epistemic or revolutionary break that is cybernetic theory in favour of demarcating a certain 'trend in Western Science and Philosophy that remains radically undetermined or "open" (Derrida 2005, p. 217) for other modes of being and becoming. This openness therefore remains the *central yet opaque* feature of cybernetic technologies, even if, as Frabetti rightly notes, or perhaps rather *because*, such technologies seek to abolish openness or uncertainty in favour of control or optimisation models. This attempt at continuous or total control is, of course, discernible in the history of thought about modern communications that followed in the footsteps of Shannon and Weaver's mathematical engineering model for "combat[ting] noise" in computational communications, which erroneously led to the instrumentalist sender-channel-receiver model in *human* communications theories (Shannon 1948, p. 398). It has also led to the (mis)conception in neuroscience that thinking is a form of computation, and 'thought threads' bits of information. In *The Computer and the Brain* for instance, Von Neumann (in)famously compares the human brain and its neuronal network to an input and output system akin to the workings of a digital computer. This (mis) conception arose in tandem with the externalisation and objectification of thought threads, which, as Chun insightfully points out in "Software: a Supersensible Sensible Thing", can be sold on the market as actual (digital) objects (Chun 2011, p. 5). The marketisation of academic knowledge – whether 'sold' through teaching or research – is therefore not linked to its recent neo-liberalisation, but to a constitutive opacity or indeed *intangibility* that resides at the heart of the Western metaphysical endeavour, manifested in technological innovation. This intangibility is, as

Derrida also argues, twofold: it refers to that which cannot be wholly touched or grasped – the constitutive opacity of metaphysics – however, it also refers to that which *may* not be touched as it requires a certain "tact"; a "respect" for metaphysics' inner workings that should not be tampered with (Derrida 2005, p. 66) in so far as these workings generate actual knowledge; the "aporias of touch" flowing into "tact", leading to an "impossible knowledge", or at the very least to "a thinking of impossible knowledge" (68).

I propose that the aforementioned 'forgotten' aspect of Western Science and Philosophy is precisely the opaque or the moment of excess constitutive of big data technologies and their instrumentalist implementation, which lead to unexpected consequences, even if these consequences manifest as surprising 'tangents' that are, indeed, impossible to grasp or anticipate. Mellamphy and Mellamphy make a similar claim in "An Algorithmic Agartha" where they suggest that today's global landscape consists of a convergence of politico-military, market-economic, and techno-scientific forms of governance, which attempt to, but *do not*, form one perfectly unified global mechanism of governing societies. In fact, the situation is one of "synarchic regulation", in which the continuous overproduction and harnessing of information and incessant stacking of complex algorithmic layers generates "friction", "operational obscurity", and "uncertainty" (Mellamphy and Mellamphy 2015, pp. 164–165). "Equilibrium never occurs"; as such synarchic governance will continue to "elude public scrutiny and societal deliberation" (173). Likewise, Han in *Psychopolitics* argues that big data, in its very quest to anticipate and harness the individual and collective unconscious and thereby enlist each human as the self-same object and programme in the future, in fact remains "wholly *blind to the event*"; after all, "the *singular*, the *event* – will shape history, in other words, the *future* of mankind. Thus, Big Data is *blind to the future* too" (Han 2017, p. 76, emphases in original). I would add to Han's and Mellamphy and Mellamphy's insights that the exacerbation of internal tensions also allows for the 'unforeseen' beyond such governing by excess. To bring the discussion back to the university: if Western Science and Philosophy seeks to unify the senses and amalgamate the world into a universal whole – and we need to remind ourselves that the term 'university' comes from the Latin *universitas* which means "totality" or total community (Online Etymology Dictionary 2019) – then this desire for epistemological unity that we as academics constantly pay tribute to, is doomed to failure from the very start. However, it is then, paradoxically, also this failure that might give rise to a radically different future.

Now, challenging the idea of thought as computation or bits of information as well as communication as a perfect transmission of meaning through some sort of channel, in "Something Like: 'Communication … without Communication'" Lyotard sets out to understand the implications of cybernetic techniques, like big data, on Humanities. Focusing on aesthetic experience, he notes that Kant and Adorno, respectively, suggest that good taste should be "universally communicable", and that art should *not* be addressed "through categories of communication" (Lyotard 2012, p. 567). Indeed, Lyotard observed the emergence of a "communicationalist ideology" in the realm of aesthetic experience at the heart of modern Western reason, while Adorno was very suspicious of the ways in which this ideology addresses and oppresses (567). For Kant, this universal communicability of beauty requires a *"sensus communis"* or a "community of feeling"; Lyotard wonders "what happens to aesthetic feeling when calculated situations" such as those created by computers or other cybernetic machines "are put forward as aesthetic?" (Lyotard 2012, p. 568). To answer this question, he argues that aesthetic feeling requires "a state of passability", by which he means not only ability to pass as aesthetic according to prevalent conventions, but particularly the possibility of experiencing a "donation" or something given to us from outside and beyond ourselves that "precisely ... we cannot calculate"; a possibility that 'the Other' can "seize us ... [which gives us] matter for reflection". What is required is a certain "presentation, the fact that something is *there now*" (569; emphasis original). However, communication technologies *re*-present, forgetting the "there now" that binds a community. In an attempt to determine what they communicate, communication technologies actually destroy "space and time as forms of donation of what happens", leading to a feeling of the sublime (in the Kantian sense of an overwhelming experience of limitlessness), rather than the beautiful (the merely pleasant experience of form); that is, to an anxious apprehension of the technological spectacle as a "failing of space and time" that marks the "retreat of donation" in postmodern times, the hallmark of which is the feeling that "nothing happens, that we are not destined" (570). New technologies attack space and time, and, thus, also, the body and its potential to be in a state of "passability" (572). The result is the false notion that such a state is one of mere *passivity* which needs to be countered with *(inter)activity* for anything to happen; however, in interactivity one "react[s], repeat[s], at best conform[s] ... to a game that is already given or installed" (573).

And it is this state that has a devastating effect on the staff and student body in the university beyond the perverse commodification and ranking of teaching and research, namely a generalised sense of panic, fragmentation, disorientation, and existential confusion. These sensations are, in turn, symptomatic of the university's entanglement with techniques and desires − both digital and philosophical − of control, governance, and understanding. Regarding this, Lyotard admonishes teachers: "we imagine that minds are made anxious by not intervening in the production of the product, whereas the real problem today is that contemplation is perceived as devalorised passivity", leading to an "ontological melancholy" (574). "*Not* to be contemplative [has become] a sort of implicit commandment for responsible academics and citizens", which indeed leads to overwrought appeals to be active through new technologies and in classrooms at Utrecht University (574; emphasis mine). We can, of course, see the imperative to be (inter)active using new technologies and social media platforms to establish one's existence in the world despite surveillance, however, also, in more obscure ways in certain 'tangents' in contemporary research theories and practices in Humanities. It is to the example of such an ambiguous practice that I turn in the next section, bringing my argument,

26 Ingrid M. Hoofd

that technologies profoundly impact epistemologies, to its cybernetic – or not? – full circle.

Backing away from neo-liberalism? Anti-colonial ethnography and digital techniques

As already mentioned, the Enlightenment and humanist imperatives animating Utrecht University have led to investments in a number of technological infrastructures such as large data storage servers and digital networks. One example of an already operating elaborate server-space plus online platform is its I-Lab project, which allows for "interdisciplinary data analysis … to identify factors which would not be evident from a monodisciplinary approach" (Utrecht University 2016, p. 21). It has also tried to push innovative research through interdisciplinary collaboration between different fields. Two examples of such productive interdisciplinary research spanning the Natural Sciences, Arts, and Humanities, are the focus group around "new materialism" (New Materialism 2015) and the Terra Critica research network (Terra Critica 2012). Both research endeavours fruitfully combine insights from Physics and Biology with those of Humanities from a range of perspectives: postcolonial, anti-capitalist theories, and activist practices. As an in-depth discussion of these networks' research is beyond the scope of this chapter, I will focus on one arguably exemplary paper they produced: "Becoming Sensor in Sentient Worlds: A More-than-natural History of a Black Oak Savannah" by Canadian anthropologist Myers (Myers 2018). While very specific, this example will provide an insight into the ways in which the turn to digital technologies affects what counts as valid knowledge, or valid scientific practice, as well as the extent to which such promising research is marked by the technological acceleration of the university's aporetic mission.

Myers prefaces her chapter in the volume with her own introduction (even though she is not the volume's editor) titled "This is an Introduction, or, *What is happening?*" (Myers 2018; emphasis original). The title conveys certain desperation in relation to the world, which Myers counters by asking whether "an artful anthropology might be able to conjure up another world" (Myers 2018, p. 12). She explains that this requires a "conjuring practice" of "tuning in" in order to access the "muted registers of being and becoming" (12). Stressing that such a practice is different from other sensing practices – especially military ones and surveillance – she admits that such "worlding" might not be innocent, but "may be haunted by horrors, ghosts, harm" (13). Her subsequent chapter discusses the ways in which the land she is talking about is haunted by the violence of the colonial settlers, capitalism, even the present-day ecological caretakers that displaced the original population and their practices, which kept the savannah alive. However, this violence is opaquely reproduced in the conceptualisation and practices that Myers proposes, despite her goal to combat violence by unsettling "assumptions about the innocence of the ecological sciences" which, Myers claims and I wholeheartedly agree, is "founded in settler colonial logics" so as to "monetize lands and bodies" (Myers 2018, p. 75). What Myers then sets out to do is to rediscover other forms of "sentience" through new

> ways to reach towards the unknowable, the imperceptible, the ineffable, and the numinous. Not with the desire to capture some truth, or attempt to render the world legible to the constrains of our colonized imaginations, but rather to learn how to step into *not knowing* as an ethic and practice.
>
> *(75)*

She does this by "becoming sensor" in order to find out that the trees and plants in the park are not "mere vegetation ... that mute-passive undergrowth"; rather, the "plant and trees here are active participant-observers" (79). She sees this work as "an effort to invent protocols for an 'ungrid-able ecology' that includes 'documenting the beings and doings of these bodies and lands" (86). The three techniques for the scholar-activist to "become sensor" are "kinestetic imaging", "kinestetic listening", and "kinestetic smelling" (87–89). All three involve ready-at-hand technologies such as a camera or a digital audio recorder. The camera is used to record a time-lapse image leading to an aesthetic of 'wiped' ghostly photos; the digital recorder allows for the editing of recording – speeding up or slowing down – in order to uncover "otherwise unimaginable worlds" (88).

I agree that these sensor experiments certainly lead to interesting audio and visual imagery that would not be easily qualifiable as scientific representations, since they do not appeal to any kind of realist conventions or statistical data visualisations. But what such imagery primarily reveals, is that such 'deeper' uncoverings tell us more about *the aesthetic of the technological machinery* – its sequencing, spacing and temporalisation – than about the trees and the plants themselves. In its attempt to deepen our understanding, then, through these technologies, knowledge, in Myers' elegant experiment, becomes more 'superficial', as these technologies highlight and intensify the fundamental aporia at the heart of the Enlightenment knowledge enterprise to *produce* research outcomes. Rather than merely recording some kind of 'reality' out there, technologies are always *constitutive* of knowledge. This means that their specific ways of ordering are present in the kinds of knowledge and categories that are produced or invoked. While Myers claims to uncover something about the park or former savannah, she accidentally uncovers the *nature of our academic entanglement with technology*. With her paradoxical claim that such methods purport to set up an ethics of *not* knowing, she unwittingly performs an incisive desire to know, to bring 'the beyond', the intangible, *into her realm*, whether this concerns plant secrets or those of the savannah's former inhabitants. Here, too, the peoples native to North America become the idealised "Others" of a well-meaning anthropological project that, in its very attempt at breaking with the dark past of the discipline, unwittingly reproduces (a part of) its former colonialist logic. American Indians are romantically portrayed by Myers as perfect caretakers, while plants and trees are not only anthropomorphised but 'anthropolomorphised' as "participant-observers" (Myers 2018, p. 79). All this – together with the rather grandiose claim that Myers herself has learned "to tune her sensorium to the plants, to learn how to sense alongside them" (76) – has the unwitting effect of making the 'sensor-becoming' anthropologist look ethically superior while hubristically describing the methodology as a beautiful conjuring to purify the discipline's tainted scientific identity. Myers' chapter also unwittingly celebrates the ingenuity and flexibility of Western techno-science and anthropology, and the supremacy of sentience so essential to all academic work. Yet the point of my argument is not to chide Myers for doing so, but to point out that her dutifully performed, socially concerned academic responsibility leads to an accelerated reproduction, use and celebration of (new) technologies and their metaphysical underpinnings. One may well wonder with Lyotard whether the produced aesthetic constitutes art that manages to "seize us" in our "passability", or rather a type of sublime experience inseparable from these technologies' powers that we as academic "*sensus communis*", share. The *appeal* of Myers' research to fellow academics from the innovative Terra Critica network lies in this romantic attitude to technological innovation which silently solidifies our identity as socially responsible researchers. At the same time, her research narrative upholds the illusion that one can be tactful and caring with technologies that are overwhelmingly intrusive. Sadly, it is precisely these technologies and their ceaseless neo-liberal optimisation that underlie the fundamental violence against plants, trees, animals, and numerous former inhabitants of this planet. This constitutive violence at the heart of any contemporary university practice – indeed, its "darker" side (Derrida 2005, p. 2) – is what big data and Digital Humanities "storms" (Warwick 2016, p. 546) attest to.

Conclusion: from knowledge to the mystical?

The main argument of this chapter has been that the promises and perils of big data are absolutely intrinsic to the modern university's aporetic mission. Continuous technological acceleration of this aporia is what causes interesting shifts in pedagogies and research, staff and student management, however also an intensification of the university's 'dark side' – its colonial and elitist history. The chapter has demonstrated this through Utrecht University's imperatives and their entanglements with past practices where a postcolonial research 'tangent', at first sight far removed from big data's penetrative techniques, nonetheless affirms Humanities-centred perspective through modern technology in a paradoxical manner: in the form of an ethical response to contemporary technology's anthropocentrism. This means that, despite the fact that the 'neo-liberalisation evil' narratives are not groundless, as academic-activists we need to pose deeper questions about where our responsibilities in relation to big data techniques lie, to find a more *originary* responsibility that precedes academic institutions. The imbrication of academia with technologies is a constitutional yet dialectical relationship, in which technologies are much more than a mere *means* for teaching and research. Instead, they are paradoxically exposed – or they expose themselves – as *enablers* and *frustraters* of the humanistic academic ideal. Therefore, the ideal omniscience – and its contemporary incarnation, data-driven technologies – is itself just as ambiguous and finally ungraspable as the nature of academia as such.

A final paradox arises here. The central logic of the university today, due to the ambiguity, and the ambiguous relationship of automation and transparency, consists of a pervasive *stealth* or unknown quality. This is especially the case with the technologies of automation that facilitate current teaching and research, which, as Frabetti and Chun have pointed out, rely on obscuring their operations (Chun 2011, p. 9; Frabetti 2012, p. 165), which, in turn, results in the contemporary university increasing success at hiding its oppressive operations to create a false image of 'objectivity' and of 'being at the forefront' of knowledge, transparency, innovation, and truth. This 'stealth' is intimately connected to the military logic that slumbers in all cybernetic technology. The productivist principle that reigns at Utrecht University has a repressive working on contemplation and deeper responsibility. It relegates everything or anyone that does not comply with this productivist logic to the zone of incomprehensibility, as many of us in the Humanities Faculty who question the institution, can attest to. The *transparency–stealth nexus* gives rise to tensions and schizoid experiences among university staff and students; however, it also prompts a rethinking of the university mission beyond the IT and big-data bandwagon. What might be required, then, is for thought in Humanities to *render the world more opaque, mystical, and fatal*, instead of more transparent, calculated, and known, because, as Han claims, "digital psychopolitics" that big data creates by increasingly "interven[ing] in psychic processes" in order to instrumentalise thought, could become "*faster* than free will", marking the ultimate curtailment of freedom of being and thinking (Han 2017, p. 63). I hope in this chapter to have initiated the long-overdue gesture towards the mystical at the expense of the instrumental. But, finally, who is to know whether this will *work*? After all, Utrecht University, its Strategic Plan notwithstanding, cannot and *should not* in any way be 'future-proofed', also not by its academics, that is, me. Only the paradoxical duty to its own demise can open it to alternative insights and ways of being.

References

BlackBoard. Available from: www.blackboard.com/en-eu and https://uu.blackboard.com [accessed 18 November 2019].

Burdick A et al. 2012, *Digital Humanities*, Cambridge, MA: MIT Press.

Caracal. Available from: https://caracal.science.uu.nl [accessed 12 December 2019].

Centre for Digital Humanities. 2019, "Accelerating the Development of Digital Methods". Available from: www.uu.nl/en/research/digital-humanities [accessed 24 July 2019].

Chun W 2011, "Introduction: Software: A Supersensible Sensible Thing", in *Programmed Visions: Software and Memory*, Cambridge, MA: MIT Press, pp. 1–12.

Common Lab Research Infrastructure for the Arts and Humanities (CLARIAH). Available from: www.clariah.nl/en [accessed 17 December 2019].

Derrida J 2005, *On Touching – Jean-Luc Nancy*, trans. Irizarry C. Stanford, CA: Stanford University Press.

30 Ingrid M. Hoofd

Frabetti F 2012, "Have the Humanities Always Been Digital? For an Understanding of the 'Digital Humanities' in the Context of Originary Technicity", in Berry D (ed.), *Understanding Digital Humanities*. London: Palgrave, pp. 161–171.

Gephi. The Open Graph Viz Platform. Available from: https://gephi.org [accessed 28 November 2019].

Grusin R 2014, "The Dark Side of Digital Humanities: Dispatches from Two Recent MLA Conventions", *Differences: A Journal of Feminist Cultural Studies*, vol. 25, no. 1, pp. 79–92.

Hammond A, Brooke J, and Hirst G 2016, "Modeling Modernist Dialogism: Close Reading with Big Data", in Ross S and O'Sullivan J (eds.), *Reading Modernism with Machines. Digital Humanities and Modernist Literature*. London: Palgrave Macmillan, pp. 49–77.

Han B-C 2017, *Psychopolitics. Neoliberalism and New Technologies of Power*. London: Verso.

Hardt M and Negri A 2000, *Empire*. Cambridge, MA: Harvard University Press.

Jenkins L 2003, "Another 'People of India' Project: Colonial and National Anthropology", *The Journal of Asian Studies*, vol. 62, no. 4, pp. 1143–1170.

Lyotard J-F 2012 [1991], "Something Like: 'Communication … without Communication'", in Chang B and Butchart G (eds.), *Philosophy of Communication*. Cambridge, MA: MIT Press, pp. 567–574.

Manickam S 2015, "Of Sakai and the Census", in *Taming the Wild: Aborigines and Racial Knowledge in Colonial Malaya*. Singapore: National University of Singapore Press, pp. 98–126.

Marx K 2000 [1938], "Theses on Feuerbach", in *The German Ideology*. London: Electric Book Company, pp. 167–170.

McGann J 2014, *A New Republic of Letters: Memory and Scholarship in the Age of Digital Reproduction*. Cambridge, MA: Harvard University Press.

Mellamphy D and Mellamphy N 2015, "An Algorithmic Agartha: Post-App Approaches to Synarchic Regulation", *The Fibreculture Journal*, No. 25. Available from: http://twentyfive. fibreculturejournal.org/fcj-185-an-algorithmic-agartha-post-app-approaches-to-synarchic-regulation [accessed 28 November 2019].

Morrish L 2017, "Neoliberalism in the Academy: Have You Drunk the Kool-Aid?" in Mooney A and Sifaki E (eds.), *The Language of Money and Debt: A Multidisciplinary Approach*. London: Palgrave Macmillan, pp. 137–161.

Moulier-Boutang Y 2011, *Cognitive Capitalism*, trans. Emory E. Cambridge: Polity Press.

Myers N 2018, "This is an Introduction, or *What is happening?*" and "Becoming Sensor in Sentient Worlds: A More-than-natural History of a Black Oak Savannah", in Bakke G and Peterson M (eds.), *Between Matter and Method: Encounters in Anthropology and Art*. New York: Bloomsbury, pp. 12–13 and 73–96.

New Materialism. 2015, "How Matter Comes to Matter". Available from: https://newmaterialism.eu/ [accessed 26 July 2019].

Online Etymology Dictionary. 2019, "Digital". Available from: www.etymonline.com/ [accessed 24 September 2018].

Peergrade ApS. Available from: www.peergrade.io [accessed 12 December 2019].

Shannon C 1948, "A Mathematical Theory of Communication", *The Bell System Technical Journal*, Vol. 27, pp. 379–423. Available from: www.math.harvard.edu/~ctm/home/text/others/shannon/entropy/entropy.pdf [accessed 25 July 2019].

Shore C 2008, "Audit Culture and Illiberal Governance: Universities and the Politics of Accountability", *Anthropological Theory*, vol. 8, no. 3, pp. 278–298.

Shore C and Wright S 2000, "Coercive Accountability: The Rise of Audit Culture in Higher Education", in Strathern M (ed.), *Audit Cultures: Anthropological Studies in Accountability, Ethics, and the Academy*. London and New York: Routledge, pp. 57–89.

Stiegler B 1998, "The Disengagement of the *What*", in *Technics and Time 1: The Fault of Epimetheus*, trans. Beardsworth R and Collins G. Stanford, CA: Stanford University Press, pp. 239–278.

Strathern M 2000, "Introduction: New Accountabilities", in Strathern M (ed.) *Audit Cultures: Anthropological Studies in Accountability, Ethics and the Academy*. London: Routledge, pp. 1–18.

Terra Critica. 2012, "About Us". Available from: http://terracritica.net/about/ [accessed 26 July 2019].

Utrecht University Strategic Plan. 2016, "Strategic Plan 2016–2020". Available from: www.uu.nl/en/organisation/strategic-plan-2016–2020 [accessed 10 July 2019].

Warwick C 2016, "Building Theories or Theories of Building? A Tension at the Heart of Digital Humanities", in Schreibmann S, Siemens R, and Unsworth J (eds.), *A New Companion to Digital Humanities*. New York: John Wiley & Sons, pp. 538–552.

Watts R 2017, "Universities Under the Sign of the Market", *Public Universities, Managerialism and the Value of Higher Education*, London: Palgrave Macmillan, pp. 105–146.

2

SIMULATED REPLICANTS FOREVER?

Big data, engendered determinism, and the end of prophecy

Franco 'Bifo' Berardi

Fading Hegel

In the preface to *Symbolic Exchange and Death*, a book initially published in French in 1976, Baudrillard writes: "Les finalités ont disparues, c'est sont les modèles qui nous génèrent" [Finalities have disappeared, models are generating us] (Baudrillard 1976, p. 8). The modern cultural tradition conceived of the historical process as of the actualisation of projects, the projection of conscious will, and the pursuit of rational goals. In the present epoch, the modern age seems to have culminated in the aggressive Futurist assertion of the *Will zur Macht*, embodied in the new divinity, the Machine. According to the Futurist belief, technology was going to submit 'nature' and 'time' and, obviously, the 'woman' (this capricious animal suspended between the supposedly superior race of white males and the kingdom of Chaos). In the age of modernity, finalities were turned into projects. They were supported by state power in order to make possible the political actualisation of the Future. But, according to Baudrillard, something radically new happened in post-modernity: in the post-modern sphere we live under the domination of models. Finalities have lost their effectiveness. Will and consciousness no longer have the power to generate events. Morphogenesis is the result of the process of generation based on models, instead of on intentions. Info-generation (the generation of information through algorithmic and data-based procedures), and bio-generation (genetic generation) produce models that make up the bio-info Automaton. In the last moments of modern history, the ideological background of 1968 resembled the Hegelian yearning for dis-alienation, *totalizierung*, recomposition, and unification of the fragmented subjects of history. But the movement of 1968 was torn between two poles: on the one hand, we aspired to fulfil the modern promise, on the other, we expressed a nostalgia for the romanticised human freedom that modernisation was thought to have erased. The Hegelian *Aufhebung* (sublation)

Simulated replicants forever? **33**

here met the Situationist nostalgia for lost authenticity. In Hegel, the final historically dialectical moment is supposed to bring forth the identity of historical reality and the ideal nature of the human essence. Debord and many other Situationists expressed nostalgia for the authenticity lost through alienation, under the rule of capitalism as spectacle (Debord 1983). The year of 1968 was, therefore, conceived as the beginning of the process of a final and irrevocable reiteration of authenticity, the final realisation of what had, until then, been seen as human nature. However, the Hegelian framework failed in the decades following '68, while Baudrillard's framework has shown itself to be much more far-reaching, surpassing both Hegel and the ideological framework of '68. It is not *Aufhebung* but *simulation* that marks the end of history, or the shift beyond modernity: not dis-alienation but the full implementation of alienation, the replacement of the world with a copy of that world. In Baudrillard's vision, modernity dissolves because the project of dis-alienation meets the perfect alienation of the simulacrum. And the simulacrum is a copy without a prototype, an alienation that forbids the very imagination of authenticity. The technical perfection of the human being is not the realisation of some original essential authenticity, but the implementation of generative models. The ambiguous intentions of politics are replaced by the automatism of technological simulation. Finalities give way to generative models. It is at this point that the pan-logical, recombinant project of Leibniz gains the upper hand in the philosophical landscape of late modernity, replacing the pan-logistical – the spiritual and historical – project of Hegel. The bio-info destiny is inscribed in the logical concatenation of necessity, not in the historically conflictive dimension of possibility. In what follows, I trace the transformation of the social world into simulated representation, through the datification of social actors and the interfacing of data with logical devices, which turns social language into an automated self-fulfilling prophecy, and rules of governance into performative acts.

The comeback of Leibniz

Two panlogical projects loom large in the landscape of modern philosophy, the recombinant project of Leibniz, and the dialectical project of Hegel. In Hegel, the logos finds its embodiment in the dialectical drama of history: it is through bloody and tortuous events, which turn daily life of the people into history (*Geschichte*), that reason asserts itself. But the experience of the twentieth century did not affirm the dialectical expectation; the historical panlogism failed. Fragmentation has taken the place of totalisation, and chaos is spreading in the social and geopolitical sphere. A second panlogical project is emerging, based on the algid and glimmering process of computational recombination that is the legacy of Leibniz's philosophy. For Leibniz, rationality dwells in the abstract sphere without bodies. The Leibnizian computational theology is based on the idea of a generative God, who is the source of mathematical recombinations. In this space of recombinant determination, bodies can act effectively only if they are compatible with the format of the reigning mathematical theology. Otherwise, they are marginalised

34 Franco 'Bifo' Berardi

as irreducible residuals. Leibniz's computational panlogic does not deal with the physical and historical reality of bodies and environments, but with the virtual condition of computational monads that real bodies are obliged to conform to. In the post-dialectical century in which we are currently living, historical bodies (nations, society, political order) explode and dissipate the prospect of progress and *Aufhebung*. At the same time, in the virtual bunker, a sort of Leibnizian Computing Ur-Monad is generating the connective concatenation: a continuous flux of disembodied recombination. Leibniz's monad is the zero-dimensional generative potency of information. Leibniz actually spoke of "incorporeal automata" in his most famous book *Monadology*:

> [o]ne could give the name *entelechies* to all simple substances or created monads. For they all have in them a certain perfection (*echousi to enteles*); there is a certain self-sufficiency (*autarkeia*) that makes them sources of their own internal actions and, so to speak, incorporeal automata.
>
> *(Leibniz and Recher 1991, p. 87)*

In his short essay titled "Principles of Nature and Grace, Based on Reason", Leibniz writes that "each living mirror that represents the universe according to its own point of view, that is, each *monad*, each substantial center, must have its perceptions, and its appetites as well ordered as is compatible with all the rest" (Leibniz 1989, p. 211). Leibniz refers to a principle of algorithmic regulation proceeding from the all-generating computer whose name is God, and whose emanating power permeates the entire universe to inform each fragment according to a recombinant methodology. This generative panlogism, perfectly epitomised in the digital principle of recombination, is not affected by the suffering or the agonising of living bodies; it does not perceive the chaotic violence of exploitation, corruption, and war, but only recognises the flow of data that gives artificial life and syntactic exchangeability to the informational units that work, produce value, and interact in the space of the theological economy. God is the binary principle of generation from which perfectly compatible recombined units emanate. Leibniz's panlogical vision seems well poised to prefigure the combinatory digital concatenation of the contemporary world. In Hegel's panlogism, the dynamics of history are based on the methodology of disjunction and overcoming (*Aufhebung*). Truth is revealed at the end of the historical process as an effect of conflict and recomposition, in other words, of dialectical disjunction and conjunction. In Lebniz's postmodern comeback, however, the logic of disjunction and conjunction is replaced by the logic of computation, where reason is not the endpoint of the historical process, a *telos* pursued by the conscious action of human beings, but its beginning, the generative source of countless recombinations. Although Baudrillard does not refer to Hegel or Leibniz, the incisive density of the sentence I quoted above – "*les finalités ont disparues, c'est sont les modèles qui nous génèrent*" – refers to this change in the philosophical backdrop.

The paradoxical annihilation of prophecy

Baudrillard's imagination was essentially prophetic, however his prophecies often had a reverse element in them: "the year 2000 will not take place" (Baudrillard 1986, p. 18); "the Iraqi war will not take place" (Baudrillard 1995, p. 23). The philosophical core of his prophetic discourse is paradoxical: events have been cancelled because finalities have been replaced by the code. Reality has been cleansed, smoothed, and finally digitalised. In the year 2000, as the Yugoslavian wars had brought back the horrors of ethnic cleansing, and simultaneously the digital technology was promising a bright future of immateriality, Baudrillard wrote:

> [c]leansing is the prime activity of this *fin de siècle*, the laundering of dirty history, of dirty money, of corrupt consciousness, of the polluted planet, the cleansing of memory being indissolubly linked to the (hygienic) cleansing of the environment and the ethnic cleanings of populations.
>
> *(Baudrillard 2000, p. 33)*

The paradoxical prophecy, for Baudrillard, is: "[p]rediction, the memory of the future, diminishes in exact proportion to the memory of the past. When there is overall transparence, when everything can be seen, nothing can be foreseen anymore" (Baudrillard 2000, p. 37). In this text, *The Vital Illusion*, Baudrillard anticipated the future connection between data and the automaton, the entanglement of consciousness, will, and action in a chain of predictive concatenations. In a paradoxical turn, prophet Baudrillard prophetises that prophecy is doomed to disappear, because the memory of the future is disappearing. All of future will be absorbed by the prescriptive machine. The code generates the networked reality, while living bodies convulse outside the castle of language, in the chaotic Babylonia of mutual incomprehensibility. Digital language, inserted in artificial intelligence devices, inscribes the *datum* into the future. Prescription replaces prophecy while computation replaces historical choice. The event is erased. The territory is replaced by a map. It's important to remind ourselves here that the critical analysis of capitalism, in Baudrillard, is framed in the language of semiotics. This is why it is possible to speak of semiocapitalism, when referring to the present relation between economy and the production of signs. The very concept of capital, in Baudrillard's work, is redesigned according to a semiological vision, and finally defined as a Code that shapes social life as simulation. This is why Baudrillard's thought may be read as an introduction to the neo-liberal transformation of capitalism. The integration of technology, finance, and the economy, while disabling the effectiveness of political will, has turned the entire process of value production into the deployment of the coded rule. The code submits social life to the automatic implementation of a set of (techno)-logical implications.

The effect of this semiological interpretation of the capitalist rule, of replacing the "event" with the abstract determinism of the code, is the end of the social. "We

36 Franco 'Bifo' Berardi

no longer feel the pulse of events, we are left with the cardiogram" (Baudrillard 1994, p. 33). Not the historical pulse of social upheavals, of uncertain or ambiguous events, but the cardiogram of the code-generating simulacra. I use the word 'generation' to refer to the rise of a replicant phenomenon from information, capable of giving form to reality. Info-generation (the algorithm) and biogenetics (replication and manipulation of DNA) here replace the intentionality of human acts. Baudrillard's *Symbolic Exchange and Death* can be read within the horizon of the creation of the bio-info-Automaton: the proliferation of devices inserting artificial intelligence into the flux of social behaviour and cognitive activity has replaced the living brain with techno-linguistic automatons. The bio-info destiny generated by the code is inscribed in the living body of society. This inscription acts as a *prescription* forbidding access to an alternative configuration of the real, making the event impossible. The world is reduced to simulation and recombinant replication. Forever? That remains to be seen.

Data extraction and insertion of automatic devices

Let us take a look at the current process of the datification of social life, and at the prospects emerging from this process. In November 2019, a federal investigation into Google's Project Nightingale (a deal with a large hospital group to build a new cloud-storage system for patients' medical data, which effectively placed that extremely sensitive and valuable data in Google's hands), disclosed that a networked data system had been built containing the most intimate features of our existence. The impending optimisation and acceleration of the network (which the implementation of the 5G system is sure to unlock) will manifest in the increased ubiquity of sensor data. Wearable technology will monitor every biological function of the body from heartbeat to blood sugar levels. Healthcare providers will be able to combine constant real-time monitoring with other data known to impact health, such as air quality, abrupt changes in temperature, and other environmental stressors. This holistic and real-time approach to healthcare is poised to transform the medical system, at least for the small minority of the population that will be allowed access. This trend has provoked vociferous objections from those who fear the loss of privacy, however this resistance does not seem to be able to effectively stop – or regulate – the overall extraction of data. We are witnessing the transformation of the recombinant machine into a fully fledged system that captures our personal data and turns it into interactive automatisms aimed at prescribing our future choices and actions. In her outstanding book, *The Age of Surveillance Capitalism*, Zuboff outlines this new stage of capitalism, focusing on the history of Google and the role that Google has played (and is still playing) in the evolution of the economy and in the anthropological sphere as a whole. She describes the effect of the ongoing process of massive data extraction as the capture of present behaviour by the machine, which turns information about the present into devices for the control of the future. Her definition of "surveillance capitalism" is intended to distinguish technology from its social use:

> Surveillance capitalism is not a technology; it is a logic that imbues technology and commands it into action. Surveillance capitalism is a market form that is unimaginable outside the digital milieu, but it is not the same as the digital.
>
> *(Zuboff 2019, p. 25)*

As technology is *not* the evolution of natural causes into natural consequences, but a social application of knowledge that varies with social interests, under the rule of a socio-economic system based on the extraction of surplus value and on accumulation of time transformed into value, the potential of digital technology is shaped according to the need for increasing profit. Zuboff focuses her analysis on a special aspect of value extraction: the creation of an all-encompassing system of surveillance delineating a sort of new totalitarianism based on the superimposition of a grid of prescriptive devices which transform the knowledge of the present behaviour into a project of total certainty, and reduce the future to the re-enactment of the recorded present. Zuboff emphasises the relationship between techno-corporations (particularly Google) and the U.S. military system, highlighting the integration of Google with military projects like Recorded Future, "a company whose mission is to strip out from web pages and sort who, what, when, where, why: sort of who's involved, where are they going, what kind of events are they going to" (Record the Future 2019, np.) and Total Information Awareness, developed by the National Security Agency in 2002 as a response to the terrorist acts of 9/11. Zuboff suggests that the convergence of massive data extraction and insertion of intelligent devices into the continuum of social communication is the all-encompassing trend of the present phase of techno evolution of the anthropo-sphere. It is also, and mainly, the ultimate instantiation of the logico-mathematical trap of financial semio-capitalism. This convergence is paving the way for the creation of the cognitive automaton, based on the inscription of the future in the computational combination of data extracted from the present. I use the word 'datification' to refer to the transformation of social relations into a process of manipulation of data by an agency endowed with intelligent devices. The cognitive automaton, the final avatar of the modern process of rationalisation, is emerging from the background of Chaos, amidst the mental maelstrom unravelling in the real world, outside the sphere of automatic language. In the sphere of language, the future is shaped in such a way that Chaos is converted into *automated order*, while the conjunctive mode is replaced by the connective mode: conjunction linguistically inscribes the future in an ambiguous way, as one possibility among many. Connection, on the other hand, inscribes the future as a logical computational necessity. I call conjunction the mode of relation between embodied agents of conscious and sensitive signification, while connection is the exchange of signs that function, according to the Code, between syntactic machines.

In the conjunctive mode, irregular bodies exchange ambiguous signs; in the connective mode, agents of communication exchange signs that are syntactically formatted according to the code of interpretation. Due to the connective transformation of the linguistic exchange, computing machines are able to extract enormous amounts of data from the behaviour of those who connect. Furthermore, the computing machine has the ability to detect the relevance of data for different aims and purposes (commercial or otherwise) according to the principle 'search not sort'.

> We humans need to sort (organize, classify, formalize, order, structure) a list to make it usable so we can organise ideas and things by hierarchy or orders of causation. Computers are not in the business of finding meanings and can use any huge messy untreated and unprocessed random inventory just fine: they can search without sorting: hence they can predict without understanding.
>
> *(Carpo 2017, p. 67)*

Automatic prescription

There are many semiotic forms of inscription of the future in the present: code, injunction, paradoxical injunction, and prophecy are some of these forms. However, the cognitive automaton is based on a different mode: automatic prescription. Let me explain. When the government decrees a law that commands or forbids, it inscribes the future in the present act of language. But citizens can violate the law, which they sometimes do, at their own risk. The code is different. The code is a linguistic tool that generates real objects according to a homogeneous format. It generates enunciations and objects that can only be actualised if they follow the format and the logical implication of the code itself. Prophetic prediction concerns the relation between an act of language and the event that will or will not actualise the content of the predictive enunciation. Consider the so-called self-fulfilling prophecy: the act of language that creates pragmatic conditions in which the content of the prediction is ordained to become true. If one enters a crowded space shouting that a catastrophe is going to happen, it's quite likely that the prophecy will be fulfilled, as a consequence of the panic created by the panicked prophesy. If a well-known rating agency predicts that the financial value of a company will dramatically collapse tomorrow, the collapse will probably happen, as an effect of the financial behaviour caused by the prediction itself. The speech act theory distinguishes between referential sentences and performative acts of language: performative utterances, in the appropriate circumstances, are neither descriptive nor evaluative, but may be seen as actions, as they create the situation rather than describing or reporting on it (Austin 1962). A performative act, uttered by the right person, under the right circumstances, has as a result a change in reality of the persons who utter the performative sentence or those involved in the situation. For example, 'I pronounce you husband and wife', uttered by a priest, in a church, with legal power, will have the evoked effect on the couple referred to as husband and wife after the performative has been uttered. The transformation of the social world into a sort of simulated representation, enabled by the datification of social actors allows data to interface with logical devices. This turns social language into an automated self-fulfilling prophecy, and turns the rules of governance into performative acts. In recent decades, political action has repeatedly shown itself to be impotent in the face of the financial rule, labelled 'governance'. Just think of what happened in Greece in the summer of 2015: the majority of the Greek people (62 per cent to be precise) voted against the application of the financial power troika's memorandum (IMF, Central European Bank, and the European Commission), but the Greek premier Tsipras was nevertheless obliged to bend to the troika's rule, as there was no possibility to act *outside* of financial governance. Financial rule is a generative code that *pre*-scribes social language, the machine that turns financial prophecy into prescription. Is political impotence to be seen as a temporary inability? Or, have we entered a sphere that is impervious to political action, impervious to human freedom, inasmuch as the data extracted from the present is linked automatically with artificially intelligent semiotic machines?

The Statisticon

There are many ways in which the future may be inscribed in language: promise, prediction, injunction, and prophecy are forms of conjunctive inscription of the future, while code, data and technical determination are forms of connective inscription. The conjunctive inscription is not deterministic: promises can be kept or broken, prophecy can be true or false, and the injunction of the authorities can be ignored by citizens if they choose to do so. The game of conjunction is open-ended; you never know whether the rules will be obeyed or not. The connective inscription, by contrast, is of a distinctly deterministic nature, because only if one obeys the rule of the game, is one part of the game. If you don't comply you are out. If your enunciation does not follow the rules, the machine will not work and your message will be lost. The cognitive machine can, at present, extract enormous amounts of data from the world, and insert this data into the generation of the world's future configurations. The shift here is one from the dimension of history, where events occur in the uncertain sphere of possibility, to the dimension of the Statisticon, where probability is transformed into necessity and where event uncertainty is turned into the certainty of compliant model reproduction. The expression 'statisticon', coined by the neuro-artist Neidich (Neidich 2017, np.) refers to the abstract concatenation in which data extraction is interfaced with the insertion of prescriptive devices. Thanks to data extraction, behaviours that take place in the real world (enunciations, exchanges, displacements, and so on) can be used as linguistic tools; thanks to metadata – data about data – it is possible to act in the real world so that the map of the present turns into a prescriptive tool for mapping the future. The map, that once upon a time was the representation of the territory, has turned into an interactive simulation of the territory. Suffice it to think of Google maps. The more we enter into the detail of the territory, the less the territory is distinguishable from the map. The relation between the map and the territory is in a permanent state of change as long as we can acquire data about the territory, almost perfectly reproduced by the map, and as long as the insertion of indexical devices leads to the incorporation of the map by the territory. Geo-referentiality is the best example of this: the global positioning system is not only a referential map, but also an index-ical tool for the representation of the position of the GPS user. The Statisticon is referential (it represents reality in the form of data) but it transforms the real world. If our freedom of interpretation is a function of the (un)predictability of the future, the accumulation of huge amounts of data about the present allows the extrapolation of a prescribed future. In the connective relation, where the code shapes the exchange and interpretation of signs, the process of signification is stripped of bodily singularisation, and reduced to re-cognition and re-framing. A machine may be able to re-cognise me due to a coded memory (my fingerprint or eyescan), but the interpretation is reduced to re-cognition of what has been previously recorded. The inscription of the future is based on de-contextualised re-cognition and on the automation of interaction. The Statisticon is a techno-informational automatism that captures data from the living flow of social activity in order to adapt the articulations of the global machine to the expectations of the social organism itself, and in order to adapt the expectations of the social organism to the articulations of the global machine. The shift from political government to techno-info governance is based on this reduction of social life to the Statisticon apparatus, due to the proliferation of automatisms in social language. I call 'automatism' the penetration of a logical device into the flesh of a linguistic agent. The infiltration of automatisms in the field of social action (in the economy, in language, in affective life) shapes the global cognitive automaton. In the process of (self)construction of the automaton, the prescriptive inscription replaces prophecy and law: it absorbs the code, and cancels the unpredictability of the future, which refers to the (relative) autonomy of the future from the present. The system (the statistical machine) is evolving together with the environment (social life), but the condition of this co-evolution is the pre-inscribed structural homology that is a pre-condition for making social inter-action possible in the sphere of automated governance. In order to enter the sphere of effective communication, the agent of enunciation is forced to use the format of the machine, and to speak the language that the machine understands. Once the agent of enunciation has accepted the format that makes interaction possible, the interaction can evolve, and the machine can evolve and adapt to the living organism in so far as the living organism has evolved adapting to the machine. The Statisticon implies two complementary actions: one is the recording of massive flows of data; the second is the adaptation of the machine to the living environment and the adaptation of the conscious living organism to the machine. Big amounts of data give the machine the ability to adapt. Simultaneously, the filter bubble induces living conscious organisms to comply with the expected responses to the machine. Pariser calls "filter bubble" the technique of customisation that enables Google and other search engines to anticipate our requests, and also the ability to shape and control our desires (Pariser 2012). Filter bubble is an example of the Statisticon: a reducer of future events to probability and predictability. Pre-emption is complementary to the statistical capture: pre-emptying the future means preventing future behaviour and emptying it of singularity, so formatting the political and economic acts of wide populations.

Connective simulation

According to Korzybski, language is a map, a means by which we collapse the incredible complexity of the world into a much simpler form (Korzybski 1958). The word for a thing is not the thing itself. Language allows humans to understand things in the world, even if that understanding is a simple representation of those things. Similarly, metadata is a map, "a means by which the complexity of an object is represented in a simpler form" (Pomerantz 2015, pp. 10–11). In a general sense, we may define language as a tool for the simulation of worlds. It is thanks to the emanation of linguistic signs, of symbols that acquire meaning in the process of exchange and communication, that worlds emerge in the space of communication. Reality is just a point of intersection of countless linguistic projections. But in the digital sphere, the performative function of language is enforced by technical simulations. In the last decades of the late-modern century, Baudrillard spoke of simulation in order to explain the performative function of the techno-communication in the post-industrial world. The universe as we know it (the cosmos, the ordered world) is a projection of mental frames. The question now is the following: How is the current linguistic mutation from conjunction to connection changing the simulation of our universe? The secretion of the universe in which we live (the UmWelt) is a semiotic affair: what we call the universe is, indeed, a matter of shared meaning. In the sphere of conjunction, meaning is produced through a process of signification that is the effect of vibrational interpretation in a particular context of ambiguous enunciations. In the sphere of connection, by contrast, the interpretation of meaning is based on the recognition of patterns, and the subject of enunciation is requested to follow syntactic chains of exactitude in order to make recognition unambiguously possible. There is no space for conflictive interpretations in the sphere of connection, so there is no space for ambiguity, irony, or poetic polysemics. Conjunction implies a semantic criterion of interpretation, while connection implies a purely syntactic criterion of interpretation. This means that the connective agent must recognise a sequence of signs and must fulfil the operation required by the general syntax (operational system). Connectivity and collectivity do not go together. The source of collectivity is conjunctive language. When sensible conscious organisms enter into a relation of reciprocal transformation, they conjoin; from their conjunction, an ambiguous conflictive, animated world emerges. Connectivity is, instead, based on the insertion of logical implications in the bio-info interfaces of techno-language. In a book devoted to the heuristics of digital language, Carpo writes:

> Cellular automata are rules or algorithms for very simple operations that computers can easily repeat an extraordinary number of times. Ostensibly, this is the opposite of the human logic: as human operations are slow and human time is limited, we generally prefer to go the other way, and human science takes a lot of time to develop, hone and refine a few very general laws that, when put to task, can easily lead to calculated results. Computers

prefer to repeat the same dumb operation almost ad infinitum until something happens. By letting computers do just that, this new kind of science can already predict complex natural phenomena such as the growth of crystals, the formation of snowflakes, or turbulences in fluid flow, that modern science has traditionally seen as indeterminate.

(Carpo 2017, p. 47)

Likewise, the social world, too, was a space of indeterminacy, at the time when the process of signification meant conjunction. But as the process of signification is now mostly the result of connective code, the social becomes a sphere of determination – a totalitarian sphere.

Engendered determinism

The interfacing of big data and artificial intelligence enables the insertion of automatisms into social language, so that an appalling (or reassuring?) perspective emerges: the future is no longer a range of possibilities, but a logically necessary sequence of states of the world. Power is based on a relation between forces. When a relation between forces is fixed, it can be described as a form. This form can translate into a tangle, and tends to shape the selection of contents. Once established, the power relation between forces forbids the expression of possibilities whose paradigm (format) is different from Gestalt. Gestalt turns into a tangle. As a Gestalt the established organisation of content obscures other possible content configurations. Power consists of a Gestalt that generates data through the force of limitation. It is the effect of semiotic delimitation of the space of collective action. At each historical bifurcation, the range of possibilities is limited by power and opened by the emerging subjectivities. If the emerging subjectivity has potency (internal consistence and projecting energy) it can bring the invisible possibility into the space of visibility, and it can actualise that possibility. Morphogenesis is the generation of a new form contained as a possibility: we can insert automated selections into the actualisation of a possibility. Automation is the replacement of human acts with machines, and also the submission of the cognitive activity to logical and technological chains.

This is exactly the origin of power: insertion of automated selections into the social vibration. Automation is programmed by the human mind according visions, ideologies, projects or pre-conceptions: programming automation is the fundamental act of power.

As power takes the form of techno-linguistic automatisms shaping future behaviour, it can be defined as a form of engendered determinism. If you don't pay your rent you'll be automatically evicted from your apartment. If you don't pay university fees you'll be automatically expelled from the university. The execution of the act of eviction from your apartment, or the expulsion from university, is not an act of a human agent that might be moved by compassion and change her mind. The above consequences exist in the technical machine as if they were logico-mathematical necessities. They are, of course, not logico-mathematical necessities, but the techno-semiotic machine of big data records behaviour and translates it into consequences: real events are activators of mathematical functions inscribed in the machine as logical necessities provoking a sort of pre-emption of life, and of will. Pre-emption can determine the future of the organism by the insertion of bio-technical mutations or techno-social mutations in a deterministic way. But beware: determinism is not to be seen as a philosophical methodology that describes the evolution in terms of causal implications: it is also a political strategy that aims to introduce causal chains in the world, and particularly into social language and in the biosphere itself. The effect produced on reality by a chain of automatisms has to be considered a *determinist trap*, a trap in which the possible is captured and reduced to a mere probability, and the probable is enforced as a necessity. The future is no longer a possibility, but the implementation of a logical necessity inscribed in the present. Is this subjection of the future to the logical structure of the present an irreversible mutation in human evolution? Is the reduction of the possible to the logical necessity doomed to last forever?

The apocalyptic comeback of the event

Baudrillard said: "finalities have disappeared, models are generating us", and therefore predicted the inscription of the prescribed model in the present in such a way as to erase the event, and replace it with a replicant simulation. However, we know that this prediction of Baudrillard's proved wrong; at a certain point Baudrillard himself acknowledged that the event had come back, although dramatically, apocalyptically indeed. In an essay titled *The Spirit of Terrorism*, written in the wake of the most spectacular terrorist act of all times, Baudrillard speaks of the ambiguous relief that everybody felt (although unspeakably) when the towers of the World Trade Center (the symbol of digital replication in his 1981 book *America*), were destroyed by the Islamist terrorist attack, on 11 September 2001:

> [t]he fact that we have dreamt of this event, that everyone without exception has dreamt of it – because no one can avoid dreaming of the destruction of any power that is hegemonic to this degree – is unacceptable to the Western moral conscience.
>
> *(Baudrillard 2003, p. 5)*

The event was back, at that point: the unpredictable, the unspeakable, the logically impossible was back. And this was the beginning of a series of frightening events: the spreading of suicidal terrorism in the European cities, the financial collapse of 2008 that Baudrillard could not witness (he died just a few months before) and the explosion of suprematist madness: Brexit, the victory of Trump, the Hindu nationalism of Modi, and the comeback of Nazism on a planetary scale. As reason has been absorbed by the all-encompassing logic of computation, the brainless body is exploding on the naked dishevelled scene of the real. History was finally back, and was horrible. "There is an end to your talk about the virtual. This is something real. Similarly, it was possible to see a resurrection of history beyond its proclaimed end" (Baudrillard 2003, p. 28). Since then, the dynamic of the new century has been suspended between two opposite polarities: chaos and automaton. What is chaos? Deleuze and Guattari speak of chaos in the last chapter of *What is Philosophy?* as a condition of the mind, when semiotic stimulations grow too fast for conscious elaboration (Deleuze and Guattari 1994). Chaos is not a real thing, something existing out there, but a relation between the rhythm of the brain and the rhythm of the Infosphere. As we are unable to deal with chaos, to find a rhythm harmonic with the surrounding noise, the light of reason is darkening: swift extinction of the light that pretended to enlighten the world in the past modern times. Dark Enlightenment, the ideological expression of the American alt. right, captures the movement from light to darkness that seems to characterise the new century. Everywhere democracy is overwhelmed, everywhere human rights are violated, everywhere the international institutions are disregarded, everywhere aggressiveness is winning over rational arguments. In addition, in a separate dimension, connection after connection, the automaton is taking shape and huge amounts of data are linked with devices of artificial intelligence. The bio-info technologies are converging towards the establishment of the cognitive Automaton. So the Automaton emerges in the social context of a spreading psychosis: demented obsessional need of aggressive identity. Identitarian dementia and the global cognitive Automaton are the actors of the imminent scene: the organic intelligence innervates the chaos of the social organism, once it has been uncoupled from consciousness. The transhumanist project, which takes shape in the space of American late-futurism, is based on the idea that technology will make possible the perfect simulation of intelligent life. However, this is going to be true only if intelligence is separated from consciousness. I call intelligence the ability to choose and to make decisions between decidable alternatives, and I call consciousness the ability to choose and to make decisions between undecidable alternatives. Intelligence implies computation, combination, and recombination of discreet elements, while consciousness acts in the dimension of the continuum of experience, and judgment is based on choices that have no foundations, no finite examination. The separation of intelligence from consciousness is the core of the contemporary project of datification of social reality, the reduction of the future to the intersection of big data and artificial intelligence. In the field of economic competition and in the field of war, intelligence is useful, while consciousness may be damaging. The less limited by consciousness and ambiguousness, the more intelligence can pursue its goals of domination. In the space of artificial intelligence the Automaton is asserting its power, but in the space of nature and life, chaos and dementia are destroying the legacy of humanism, and the very possibility of human life on the planet. The transhumanist project is flawed because Chaos takes the upper hand on the Automaton, and because consciousness is never annihilated, even if it re-emerges in the form of mental chaos.

References

Austin JL 1962, *How to do Things with Words*. London: Oxford University Press.

Baudrillard J 1976, *Symbolic Exchange and Death*. London: Sage Publications Ltd.

Baudrillard J 1986, "The Year 2000 Will Not Take Place", in Grosz EA et al. (eds.), *Future*Fall: Excursions into Post-Modernity*. Sydney: Power Institute and Sydney University.

Baudrillard J 1994, *The Illusion of the End*, trans. Turner C. Stanford, CA: Stanford University Press.

Baudrillard J 1995, *The Gulf War Did Not Take Place*, trans. Patton P. Bloomington, IN: Indiana University Press.

Baudrillard J 2000, *The Vital Illusion*, ed. Witwer J. New York: Columbia University Press.

Baudrillard J 2003, *The Spirit of Terrorism and Other Essays*, trans. Turner C. London: Verso.

Carpo M 2017, *The Second Digital Turn: Design Beyond Intelligence*. Cambridge MA: MIT Press.

Debord G 1983, *Society of the Spectacle*. Detroit, MI: Black and Red.

Deleuze G and Guattari F 1994, *What is Philosophy?* trans. Tomlinson H and Burchill G. London: Verso.

Korzybski A 1958, *Science and Sanity*, 4th edn. Baltimore, MD: The Institute of General Semantics.

Leibniz GW 1989, "Principles of Nature and Grace, Based on Reason", in *Philosophical Essays*, ed. and trans. Ariew R and Garber D. Indianapolis, IN: Hackett.

Leibniz GW and Recher J 1991, *G. W. Leibniz's Monadology: An Edition for Students*. Pittsburgh, PA: University of Pittsburgh Press.

Neidich W 2017, *Statisticon* [The Statisticon Neon]. Available from: www.warrenneidich.com/the-statisticon-neon-2017/ [accessed 23 October 2019].

Pariser E 2012, *The Filter Bubble: What the Internet is Hiding from You*. London: Penguin.

Pomerantz J 2015, *Metadata*. Cambridge, MA: MIT Press.

Record the Future. 2019, [online]. Available from: www.recordedfuture.com/ [accessed 23 October 2019].

Zuboff S 2019, *The Age of Surveillance Capitalism*. London: Profile Books.

3

"VISUAL HALLUCINATION OF PROBABLE EVENTS"

On environments of images, data, and machine learning

Abelardo Gil-Fournier and Jussi Parikka

Introduction

Contemporary images come in many forms. Importantly, they also come in many times. Screens, interfaces, monitors, sensors, and other devices that form part of data infrastructures create visualisations in so-called real-time. While data visualisation may not be that new a technical form of data-as-image organisation, it takes a particularly intensive temporal turn with networked data – discussed, for example, in the context of financial speculation where trading information is linked to visualisation software (Cubitt 2017). At the same time, these imaging devices are part and parcel of an infrastructure that does not merely 'observe' microtemporal moments in a passive manner. Rather, microtemporal moments are here an integral part of data mobilised to sustain a relation with a particular form of governance: data and projective temporalities governance. As we will show in this chapter,[1] in terms of geographical, geological, and, broadly speaking, environmental monitoring, the now-moment expands into near-future scenarios that offer a speculative set of possibilities for modelling future changes. We focus on imaging as a form of *nowcasting*, exposing the importance of understanding change changing. Images and sensors are subsumed under data-driven modelling techniques, which apply pattern recognition to the future. While this is, in itself, not a radical revelation – after all, future pattern recognition is one of the key features of climate modelling – it is an important category of knowledge that, according to Chun, challenges what is usually thought of as a form of knowledge particular to the Humanities (Chun 2015). For Chun, data and data modelling can be seen as forms of building modelled hypotheses:

> We need to address uncertainty as enabling rather than disabling, for it is by engaging this changing relationship between what is true and verifiable,

"Visual hallucination of probable events" **47**

theoretical and empirical, that we can form new associations between knowing and doing—new theories of cognition and new habits of correlation—that treat the nonexact coincidence between scientific predictions and observed reality as the promise, rather than the end, of science and of politics.

(Chun 2015, p. 678)

With regard to the politics of speed and the mobilisation of temporality/ies as a form of governance, Virilio's work stands as a central reference. In addition to his broader dromological project, of particular interest for our project are the ways in which 'environment control' functions in and through the photographic image. In Virilio's narrative, the interconnection between light (exposure), time, and space, is closely related to the disappearance of the external world's spatio-temporal coordinates (Virilio 2000, p. 55). We move from the 'real-space' to the 'real-time' interface and to the analysis of how the modelling and management of visual data detaches the time of the seasons, the *longue durée* of the planetary qualitative time from the light of the sun, and attaches it to the internal mechanisms of calculation pertaining to electric and electronic light. For Virilio, the photographic describes the exposure of the world: it is an intake of time, and of light. The time of the photographic development (Niepce), the cinematographic resolution of movement (Lumière), or the "videographic high definition of a 'real-time' representation of appearances" (Virilio 2000, p. 61) all form part of Virilio's chronology of time and light in a media-saturated culture. Operating on the world as active optics – which refers to the circulation of vision through screens and electronic streams of images that, for Virilio, differ from the passive optics of lenses and mirrors – these intakes constitute the temporal frame. They frame (and manage) environments with the aid of "operational images" (Farocki 2004, p. 17), which invariably influence our perception of geographic spaces, too.

However, what is only implied in this cartography of active optics is the mobilisation of time as prediction and forecasting, or, what Chun has called 'hypo-real tools' (Chun 2015). Operations and production of time/s have moved from meteorological forecasting to computer models, and from computer models to a plethora of machine-learning techniques applied to computer vision and image generation. These techniques are another site of transformation of what we used to call photography, and this transformation is closely related to big data that now routinely forms part of the image infrastructure. Zylinska terms this realm of operations (which detaches the image further from the historical legacy of anthropocentrism), "non-human photography", referring to other forms of representation and other temporalities (Zylinska 2017). Here, time and image techniques recode what is perceived as operatively real, questioning the technically induced forms of hallucination – or machine learning – that increasingly shape the production of information.

Digital culture's mass-compiling of images as data, that are, often, not visual in the traditional sense of the word, also means that images persist as markers of time in more than one sense. They refer to the photographic indexicality of past time (or that which the image records, the documentary status of the image as used in various administrative contexts) as well as to what can be predicted through data analysis and modelling based on pattern recognition, or even pattern hypotheses. In such contexts, machine-learning techniques are a central aspect of image making, re-making, and its multiple uses in contemporary culture: from video predictions of the complexity of multiple moving objects known as traffic (such as cars and pedestrians) to the satellite images monitoring agricultural crop growth. Such techniques have become a central example of Earth's geological and geographical changes, understood through algorithmic time, that is, through a microtemporal space of operations in which the rapidly changing vehicle traffic is treated in the same way as the much slower processes or crop growth. In all these cases, the ability to perceive space as composed of *temporally critical* patterns and micro-changes, and incorporate these patterns and micro-changes into decision-making processes, is key in an autonomous vehicle's environmental perception (Sprenger 2019, pp. 484–497) and a large-scale system's geographical data analyses. Computational microtemporality is essentially futuristic; algorithmic processes used to mobilise data sets in machine learning take the form of predictions and projections in a variety of institutional contexts. Virilio's politics of speed and time should be updated to include the microtemporal level of operations in complex environments of calculated abstractions as well as simulated systems' projections that operate in real-life settings, such as cities and forests. As future-producing techniques and hypo-real modelling tools, images run ahead of themselves. They run ahead of their time.

The present chapter is part of a larger project concerned with the visual culture of environmental imaging, upon which we elaborate with the aid of theoretical and artistic research methods. Here, we will address the relationship between environmental imaging and big data via an imaging technique relevant to time-critical images: Next Frame Prediction (NFP). Briefly, NFP names a set of techniques aimed to predict the following frame in a video frame sequence, used, for instance, in the development of self-driving cars or robotic movements. We address this media technique as related to the use of predictive imaging in contemporary environmental research, such as agriculture and climate. While questions about the "geopolitics of planetary modification" (Yusoff 2013) are central to how we think about the ontologies of materiality and the earth, our main interest here lies with the ways in which these materialities are produced at the level of images. In other words, we are interested in how images and environments interweave in a microtemporal grid underpinning calculations practised on the planet's surface. Real-time data processing of the Earth, not as a single-view entity, but an intensely mapped set of relations that unfold in data visualisations, is a way of continuing earlier, more symbolic, forms of imaging such as the Blue Marble – the famous photograph taken by Apollo 17 in 1972. If this view of the globe reduced the Earth to a seemingly unified object, current real-time visualisations have changed that view through complex models and simulations (Bratton 2013, pp. 200–203; Likavčan 2019). Despite the fact that microtemporal real-time imaging techniques[2]

"Visual hallucination of probable events" **49**

may not affect deep time in strict geological terms, they are an important way of understanding the visual culture of computational images that does not merely record and represent, but predicts and projects.

In the pages that follow, we focus on computational microtime, visualised and predicted Earth time/s, by focusing on that which they hinge: images. The various chrono-techniques (Ernst 2016) that have entered the vocabulary of Media Studies are particularly suited to provide a cartography of analytical procedures behind producing time, such as the mechanisms for the electro-technical synchronisation of signals or the operationalisation of the human perception thresholds that feature as critical sites in the televisual elaborations of time. However, the question here is not (only) about (the nature of) the temporal processes embedded in media techno-logical operations. It is about the *times responsible for the production of time*. Although this may sound like a merely tautological statement, we ask: what times of calcula-tion produce imagined futures, statistically viable cases, and predicted worlds? What microtemporal times are behind the sense of futurity conditioned in calculational, software-based, data set-determined systems? Finally, how can an analysis of such techniques be used to understand the use of data in the temporal governance of spatial territories?

Planetary images

As an after-effect of the twentieth-century rocketry, from the photographic cameras installed in V-2 to satellites, Earth is constantly visible. Often described in the lan-guage of optical visuality – as, for example, in Virilio's terminology of overexposure (1991) – Earth's constant visibility is also related to the calculation of visibility, a central theme in recent media theoretical discussions (Kaplan 2018; Parks 2018). As Gabrys points out: "[t]he architectures and algorithmic processes for relating sense data are a critical part of how sensor systems operate. They articulate how sense data will come together into arrangements indicative of environmental and planetary processes" (Gabrys 2016, p. 42).

Planetary visibility is calculated and composed in mathematical ways that have already introduced a form of imaging that shifts the focus from representations, or even images as such, to their constitutive infrastructures such as remote sensing or data-storage and processing. In this regard, Graham argues that the satellite-produced orbital image must be understood both through its infrastructures (some of which are on the ground level) and its production of Earth's surface *through* and *as* an image:

> Instead of invoking satellites as an absolute form of imperial vision, it is necessary, rather, to see satellite imaging as a highly biased form of visualizing or even simulating the earth's surface rather than some objective or apolitical transmission of its "truth".
>
> *(Graham 2016, p. 31)*

The calculational basis of the earth's simulated surface is subject to microtemporal operations that define it less as visual images than as statistical distributions even if they come out as temporal image series. Indeed, as Krapp argues in relation to the planetary networks of knowledge concerning polar regions, the image of the planet as a holistic entity of knowledge is underpinned by the issue of scale – both spatial and temporal – that includes the particular microtemporality of the calculations that constantly compose and recompose the planet in its projected sense (Krapp 2016). Satellite images become the backbone of the temporality of the planetary view. From an assumption of an eye in the sky, the more accurate way to understand the potential of images is to think of them as part of "diachronic omniscience", to use Parks' formulation:

> Archives of satellite image data [...] create the potential for diachronic omniscience – vision through time – because they enable views of the past (and future with computer modelling) to be generated in the present that have never been known to exist at all, much less have been seen. Our understanding of the temporality of the satellite image should be derived through the process of its selection, display, and circulation rather than formed at the instant of its acquisition.
>
> *(Parks 2005, p. 91)*[3]

Such images are revealed primarily as data sets; agricultural growth, deforestation, ice retreat and other surface level transformations become integrated through mundane techniques that already speak to this transformation of both images and satellite data. Still images transform into moving images that track changes:

> For a long time Earth observation was about the identification of specific features on an individual "still" image, starting with defense and security purposes, and then slowly spreading to other industries as well. While the stills part is true even today, with the introduction of ongoing monitoring programmes such as Landsat and Sentinel a new methodology appeared—the long-term observation of changes, developments, or simply monitoring vegetation growth. Having weekly (or better) coverage available over land worldwide makes it a uniquely powerful dataset.
>
> *(Milcinski 2018, np.)*

Historical data sets are instrumentalised as predictive patterns that can be updated in real time. The question of earth (surface) time condenses in the moment of calculation that is open to real-time input from various data sources considered relevant, such as the archives of the Landsat and Sentinel satellite programmes. Geological and geographical times are not merely presented, but forwarded towards various speculative futures.

One key technique that we are interested in, in this context, is 'video frame prediction', which attaches these images to the legacy of moving images while also

"Visual hallucination of probable events" 51

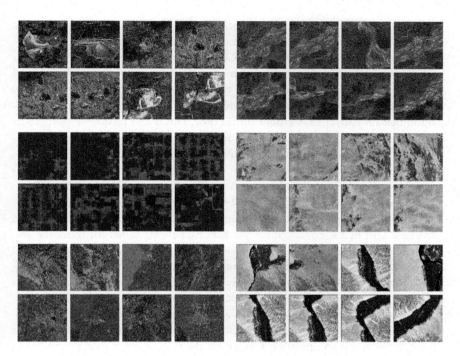

FIGURE 3.1 Abelardo Gil-Fournier, *An Earthology of Moving Landforms*, 2018 [workshop documentation]. A collection of samples of data sets of planetary surface behaviours. Clockwise, starting top left, they show: brown-coal mines, meanders of the Ganges River, dunes in the Sahara Desert, the agricultural lands by the Nile riverside, cities in China, and deforestation in the Amazon.

Source: © Abelardo Gil-Fournier

signalling their relevance in contemporary data cultures. In other words, questions of sequences of change become revised from visual content to (scientific and other) visualisation that maps change. Moving images – to stretch the connotations of these terms – are then present, at least to an extent, in GIF time-lapse images used to demonstrate annual change, often in public communication (for example, the disappearance of the Amazon rainforests, or the spread of urbanisation patterns). The revisualisation of archived images of environmental changes as time-lapse video sets the stage for the video prediction techniques that, as will be shown in the following section, are both part of the regime of digital images (codecs and compression) and of the large-scale planetary imaging.

Video prediction

Next Frame Prediction, or broadly speaking video prediction, names a strand of machine learning aimed at the algorithmic continuation of a given video. Explored

52 Abelardo Gil-Fournier and Jussi Parikka

so far in computer science environments, its main objective is to generate a few frames of a yet unseen future: to foresee the next movements of vehicles in a self-driving situation (Lotter, Kreiman, and Cox 2017), or to envision the implications of the movements of a robotic arm in a room full of objects (Finn, Goodfellow, and Levine 2016). Video prediction *augments* the actual workings of machine vision: by inferring the future position of nearby vehicles, the self-driving car acquires information that may affect its decisions in real time. This is also broadly speaking why autonomous vehicles are such an interesting case for media studies: they are a condensation of machine vision and visualisation techniques, calculation and machine-learning techniques, and cloud-based operations in urban (and non-urban) environments with multiple other agents (traffic) (Sprenger 2019, pp. 384–397).

Defined as a set of techniques aimed at the procedural continuation of videos with future frames, video prediction is an activity aimed mainly at the generation of images. That is, it is not about the prediction of events alone, but about the *generation* of *visual appearances*. This imaging ability, addressed in the technical literature as a "visual imagination of different futures" (Finn, Goodfellow, and Levine 2016, p. 64) or as a "visual hallucination of probable events" (Walker, Gupta, and Hebert 2014, p. 3302), is a central aspect of what we wish to emphasise here. While other (video) machine-learning developments are meant to extract data in terms of classification, identification of objects, places, or gestures within video streams,[4] Next Frame Prediction is an operation focused on the generation of new images, to be used as plausible futures frames. In other words, NFP produces images in relation to motion and movement in real space, however, motion and movement are calculated in the microtemporal computational space. Hence, there is something interesting going on in the status of these images. The epistemology of images relating to classification and identification (e.g. from satellite imagery) is complemented by this particular video 'art' of prediction, the hypo-real regime of images – images that could be, might be, and in that case are valuable hallucinations of the future. Of course, the haphazard use of 'hallucination' in technical literature can be seen as an interesting rhetorical gesture. But it is also part of the lineage of technical media – at least since film and cinema – as a particular psychotechnical manipulation of movement, change, and visibility that catches the physiological potentials (and limitations) of the human perceptual apparatus. To quote Holl:

> Since cinema itself has once and for all left its classical setting in movie theatres to spread across electronic meshes and across individual or shared screens, its specific entanglement of physical cultures and wishful hallucination returns as an issue with ever more insistence.
>
> *(Holl 2017, p. 13)*

But in machine learning, hallucination is less about tricking the human perceptual apparatus than about the projective potential of automated cognition that imagines, even hallucinates, on our behalf, modeling (yet) non-existent futures as real and existent patterns, as hypo-realistic hypotheses of sorts (Chun 2015). In

"Visual hallucination of probable events" **53**

order to work, machine-learning-based video prediction relies on a computational object – the model – that, given a sequence of frames as input, is able to produce, as an output, a subsequent set of frames. As this occurs characteristically in the context of artificial intelligence, the predictive model is built recursively in a so-called training process. First, an initially randomised instance is provided. Then, a data set of similar-looking videos is fed into the process – for example, different traffic videos of the same road in order to initiate archive searches on the basis of which prediction tests are performed. Prediction tests used in training are based on sequences with a known (or real) next frame. The predicted frames are subsequently compared to the so-called "ground truth", an actual video image; the differences between the two are used to automatically modify the evolving model. This procedure is repeated an appropriate number of times, so that the differences between next-frame predictions and the ground truth are minimised. In this way, the model is tuned to its function, resulting in what is usually referred to as a machine-learned model.

To better understand the imaging abilities of video prediction models, we will next consider two significant preconditions the model relies on. First, NFP is based on the calculability of video frames. In order to be able to track and register differences between frames, these differences need to be processed as digital objects. Frame difference is not just one of the possible numerical operations between frames, but the fundamental one that grounds the video encoding software, codecs, allowing the circulation and streaming of digital video (Mackenzie 2008; Cubitt 2014; Ernst 2016). In digital video, frames are encoded in relation to their differences from their immediate past and future "neighbours". They are not images in the sense of a classical optical photographic picture but aggregates of different moments of time that the decoding player assembles for the human eye (Ernst 2016, p. 156). Digital video relies on a microtemporal architecture where even the future is structurally anticipated. While there would be a lot more to discuss in relation to the frame, suffice it to note in this chapter that a key aspect relates to the expression of movement as actual and virtual. Frames contain worlds, actual and virtual. As Cubitt notes "[t]he actual always contains in itself the virtual: every motion contains in itself the possibility of unforeseen development, only one of which becomes actual in the next frame, but all of which lie latent in the first" (Cubitt 2016, p. 3). While the frame has become a key reference point in philosophical understanding of movement and cinema (see, for example, Deleuze 2013), it has also become a way to understand the *movement* of moving images as related to data compression, network culture, as well as to our broader argument, namely, prediction issues.

In addition, motion becomes embedded in the calculated workings of the frame. To make the predictive disposition of video encoding techniques even more explicit, a standard and ubiquitous compression algorithm relies on "motion prediction", a block-based technique that replaces most of the visual data by motion vectors (Mackenzie 2008, pp. 52–54). Taking this into account, machine-based video prediction – a technique built on the escalation of frame differences – follows the predictive condition of codecs.[5] As a matter of fact, one of the typical

54 Abelardo Gil-Fournier and Jussi Parikka

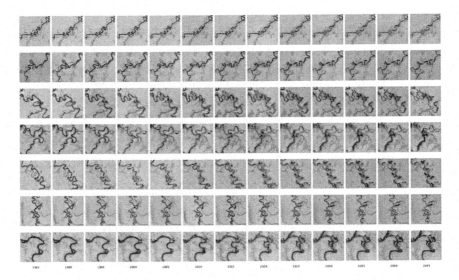

FIGURE 3.2 Abelardo Gil-Fournier, *An Earthology of Moving Landforms*, 2018 [workshop documentation]. A series of predictions of the movements of the fast meandering Ucayali River in Perú.

Source: © Abelardo Gil-Fournier

approximations of this type of video prediction is the so-called "encoder-decoder" (Lotter, Kreiman, and Cox 2017, p. 5) pair, where encoding is used as a reference to the activity performed by the algorithm. A common ground of temporal architectures underlies encoding and video prediction; both are future-making techniques that stem from the calculational image. The second requirement of NFP is data sets with sequences that unfold in a temporally patterned and replicable way. Videos derived from traffic cameras or simple procedural animations are examples of these. A neural network makes sense of data by approaching it as a set of training examples, then adjusting its internal model (Mackenzie 2017, p. 27). In the case of video prediction, the model is said to "capture the motion" (Shi et al. 2017, p. 5619) that videos display by training its predictive capabilities across sequences in the data set. Aptly enough, "motion capture" has its own media archaeological reference point in the early experiments with moving images; note, for instance, Muybridge's late nineteenth-century techniques for stop-motion and extracting data from images and their intervals (Muybridge 1979 [1887]). Of course, in the context of data images in contemporary culture, the extractive process occurs as a generalisation from examples, which is related to a different sort of media historical lineage than the one concerned solely with images. Here, we are also dealing with the legacy of statistical society as it emerged in the nineteenth century, according to Hacking and Desrosières: from mathematics to probability to state institutions to the more recent developments in computational analysis and synthesis. Machine learning, sometimes also referred to as statistical learning (Mackenzie 2017, p. 30), is located at the intersection of computer science and statistics (van Otterlo 2016; Strauß 2018), which would, in itself, be a further media archaeological theme to investigate, considering the roots of this mode of truth production (Amoore 2013, p. 44). Statistical methods are essential to the workings of these algorithms, whose ability to recognise behavioural patterns relies on a form of inductive inference linked to the data mining contexts (41). Future frames in video prediction are inferred in a similar way as products are recommended to buyers by predictive analytics, following local correlations between individual items rather than global averages of historical data. Small bits of motion – a swerve of a moving car or the enlargement of a street – are seized as recognisable patterns. The moving environment becomes a part of the environment of images that are part of predictive calculation environments. The calculated images, generated along a microtemporally structured axis of time, piece together the inferred blocks of motion drawn from the data set. Any temporal sequence of frames is therefore split by the model into a chained aggregation of recognised behaviours, and advanced as such – even if some of these behaviours don't actually exist, practising apophenia when needed (Amoore and Plotukh 2016, p. 6; Steyerl 2016). Worlds are created from statistical data and from controlled hallucination that, as we mentioned briefly above, should be seen as a function of technical media: a machine-created synthesis of perceptual content; however, also automated simulation of potential future events, or chains of events.

From Next Frame Prediction to Numerical Weather Prediction

In order to further elaborate on the implications of the statistical contexts of the time-calculated image, we will address one of the first-known environmental applications of these techniques – weather nowcasting. So far, we have argued that image-based machine learning has extended what Virilio called 'environment control' as a form of temporal manipulation related to both photographic and moving images. Video prediction includes the technical – even aesthetic – form of approaching environmental changes, whether short or longer term. It is related to the question of hypo-reality (Chun 2015), hypothetical modelled futures, and as such, also, to the politics of uncertainty in data cultures. While the space imaging industry is already offering machine-learning services fed with satellite imagery to forecast crop figures, retail sales, and oil reserves information,[6] the generation of future images as performed by video prediction is still an experimental practice when it comes to dealing with environmental monitoring and forecasting. A significantly advanced context of application of these, however, is meteorology, where ongoing research has shown that NFP outperforms other technologies. In particular, when faced with the task of forecasting the immediate evolution of clouds in a specific location, video prediction has produced the most accurate predictions to date (Shi et al. 2017). This pilot application of environmental monitoring will allow us to expand on the argument with which we closed the previous section: image environments structure the temporality of the predicted image, too. The accidental appearance of recognisable cloud formations in aerial photographs obtained with V-2 rockets spurred the meteorological interest in orbital imagery. Until the emergence of computing in the context of the Cold War, the meteorological now-moment had been produced by data maps reliant on a technical infrastructure for managing information, from individual technologies such as barometers to the telegraph networks over vast geographical areas. Meteorological forecasts relied on the circulation of the readings of these measurement instruments in communication networks (Edwards 2013, p. 40). In contrast, the orbital imaging infrastructure allowed to picture, from above and at once, large-scale systems such as storms and other patterned structures. Additionally, orbital photomosaics attained greater detail when compared to "the detection threshold of the data network" (Grevsmühl 2014, p. 179) – the geographical distance between two contiguous measuring stations – giving rise, as Grevsmühl has argued, to a new visual language to address cloud formations and dynamics (176). In Paul Edwards' words, meteorologists started to "literally see large-scale weather systems, instead of laboring to construct maps and mental images from instrument readings alone" (Edwards 2013, p. 219). Since then, the weather has been embedded in the planetary-scaled imaging infrastructure of satellites, telecommunications and processing stations. In terms of the techniques of the future, however, and despite the prominence of images as sources of information, developments in computer technology kept physics-based data and models as the central predictive tools. Recalling Galison's distinction between the epistemic traditions of the image and logic in the history of science, forecasting was dominated by logic, due to the early successes of calculative modelling (Galison 1997). As Edwards argues, Numerical Weather Prediction (NWP) was rendered objective –a 'mature science' – against the inferred-subjective predictions based on data images: "for the first time, a weather forecast could be calculated objectively (at least in principle) from basic physical laws, rather than inferred from maps on the basis of subjective experience" (Edwards 2013, p. 86). Images, Virilio's real-time interfaces, replaced sensor grids as builders of the now-moment in weather reports. They rendered weather a controllable and calculable object – but didn't actually calculate it. Until recent developments in computer vision and machine learning, forecasting belonged to the data realms of numerical modelling.

The operational modifications of the image, ushered in by machine learning, have caused meteorological changes to be not only observable but also predictable as images. As recently shown, the current experimental state of video prediction techniques has already improved the forecasting abilities of NWP (Shi et al. 2017). The evolution, movement and cloud dynamics observed and collected as sequences of images, have been used to train NFP models that are now able to produce one to six hours of visual forecasts. Cloudy skies of the near future are predicted and visualised without any reference to physics-based models or magnitudes. As observed in the literature, "precipitation nowcasting and video prediction are intrinsically spatiotemporal sequence forecasting problems in which both the input and output are spatiotemporal sequences" (3).

Nowcasting, a term familiar both to meteorology and economics,[7] is a crucially important epistemological practice for the management of large quantities of data close to real-time. The very act of monitoring and systematically registering inscribes the possibility of a calculable future that has an effect on its own material as well as financial conditions of existence. Image sequences give rise to models without the need to refer to any previous scientific diagram. Orbital monitoring operations constituted environmental imaging as a twofold operation: on the one hand, the environment was imaged; on the other hand, image environments were produced as a result. When archived, processed, and circulated, these image environments become data sets, which reveal – through machine-learning analysis – variations and modulations. Such time-critical units are, in turn, central to the practices and techniques of governing territories as well as financial markets. Inferred technically hallucinated futures, are the legacy of the contemporary calculational infrastructures of space imaging.

Conclusions

"A hallucination is neither metaphor nor imagination but the reappearance in the real of a signifier that was rejected in the symbolic", suggests Siegert (2015, p. 51), allowing us to focus on the otherwise perhaps casual engineering reference to "visual hallucination of probable events" mentioned above. As explained, hallucinations have a media archaeological context; they are produced from the moving image and cinema and 'transplanted' to machine learning; synthetic realities that do not seem to fit the symbolic categories of true or false, but are, nevertheless, entirely real. Symbolic representations of the planetary entity in real-time future projections and forms of future making have been part of the geographical and geological visualisation that plays a significant role in economic and security-related realms. Symbolically significant futures presented in genres such as science fiction are complemented by the constant – grey – operations of prediction. Our chapter has engaged with video frame prediction and nowcasting, which, as with techniques, form part of a bigger picture of calculation and the temporality of images central to contemporary data culture. An important question has emerged from this discussion: what are the potential forms of images *beyond* visual culture germane to the patterning of time and the infrastructure of calculation? How do such images operate as images? What are the extended contexts in which they operate integrated into data-intensive patterning? While images are primarily addressable as files, formats, and data, their microtemporal operations produce other times: times of projection, prediction and forecasting. It is this bundle of questions about images, time, and machine learning that we wanted to present briefly in this chapter while acknowledging that the questions are both technically much larger (in terms of the planetary infrastructures) and conceptually more far-reaching, given the variety of ways in which they deal with temporality and the techniques of geographical and geological surfaces. We started with Virilio's view of the repercussions of vision machines as a significant point of reference in earlier

Notes

1 An earlier version of this text was published as "Visuelle Halluzination von möglichen Ereignissen' oder: Über Umweltbilder und Maschinelles Lernen" in *Archiv für Mediengeschichte* 18. The research for this article has been conducted as part of the Czech Science Foundation funded project 19-26865X "Operational Images and Visual Culture: Media Archaeological Investigations".
2 Such techniques are part of a variety of data sets and contexts from agricultural monitoring and modelling to other environmental and geographical, as well as military and financial uses of visualisation techniques from large amounts of satellite data to other forms of mobilising remote sensing data.
3 Parks has also recently recalled the notion of diachronic omniscience in her approach to predictive analytics, war and satellite imagery (Parks 2018, pp. 131–136).
4 As examples, see Google Research's project on video classification, Abu-El-Haija et al. 2016. Another example is the Places data set project to allow machine learning to infer the locations where sequences were shot: Zhou et al. 2017.
5 Convolutional accounts in the context of machine learning to the mathematical sort of scanning method that allows to address the spatial arrangement of the information in the image.
6 See Planet Labs, Orbital Insight, Descartes Lab or Earth Now as examples of companies offering imaging services together with machine-learning predictive analytics. In this vein, on the implications of artificial intelligence and predictive analytics on mapping techniques, see Mattern 2017.
7 In contexts of economy and finance, nowcasting refers to "the construction of automated platforms for monitoring macroeconomic conditions in real time", including the feedback loop between the nowcast and the economic events, or series, it addresses; this

> model extracts the latent factors that drive the movements in the data and produces a forecast of each economic series 2 that it tracks: when the actual release for that series differs from the model's forecast, this "news" impacts the nowcast of GDP growth. This approach formalizes key features of how market participants and policymakers have traditionally produced forecasts, a process that involves monitoring many data releases, forming expectations about them, and then revising the assessment of the state of the economy whenever facts differ from those expectations. The model combines in a unified framework a variety of approaches developed over time for monitoring economic conditions.
>
> *(Bok et al. 2017, p. 1)*

References

Abu-El-Haija, S et al. 2016, YouTube-8M: "A Large-Scale Video Classification Benchmarking", [cs.CV]. Available from: https://arxiv.org/abs/1609.08675 [accessed 29 August 2018].

Amoore L 2013, *The Politics of Possibility. Risk and Security Beyond Probability*. Durham, NC: Duke University Press.

"Visual hallucination of probable events" **59**

Amoore L and Plotukh V (eds.) 2016, *Algorithmic Life. Calculative Devices in the Age of Big Data.* New York: Routledge.

Bok B et al. 2017, "Macroeconomic Nowcasting and Forecasting with Big Data", *Staff Report No: 830 Federal Reserve Bank of New York.* Available from: www.newyorkfed.org/ medialibrary/media/research/staff_reports/sr830.pdf [accessed 11 December 2019].

Bratton B 2013, "What We Do Is Secrete: On Virilio, Planetarity and Data Visualisation", in Armitage J and Bishop R (eds.), *Virilio and Visual Culture.* Edinburgh: Edinburgh University Press, pp. 180–206.

Chun WHK 2015, "On Hypo-Real Models or Global Climate Change: A Challenge for the Humanities", *Critical Inquiry*, vol. 41, no. 3 (Spring), pp. 675–703.

Cubitt S 2014, *The Practice of Light. A Genealogy of Visual Technologies from Prints to Pixels.* Cambridge, MA: MIT Press.

Cubitt, S 2016, *Finite Media. Environmental Implications of Digital Technologies.* Durham, NC: Duke University Press.

Cubitt S 2017, "Three Geomedia", *Ctrl-Z*, no. 7. Available from: www.ctrl-z.net.au/articles/ issue-7/cubitt-three-geomedia/ [accessed 29 August 2018].

Deleuze G 2013, *Cinema 1. The Movement-Image*, trans. Tomlinson H and Habberjam B. London: Bloomsbury.

Edwards P 2013, *A Vast Machine. Computer Models, Climate Data, and the Politics of Global Warming.* Cambridge, MA: MIT Press.

Ernst W 2016, *Chronopoetics. The Temporal Being and Operativity of Technological Media.* London and New York: Rowman and Littlefield.

Farocki H 2004, "Phantom Images", *Public*, no. 29, pp. 12–24.

Finn C, Goodfellow I, and Levine S 2016, "Unsupervised Learning for Physical Interaction through Video Prediction", *Advances in Neural Information Processing Systems*, no. 29, pp. 64–72.

Gabrys J 2016, *Program Earth: Environmental Sensing Technology and the Making of a Computational Planet.* Minneapolis, MN: University of Minnesota Press.

Galison P 1997, *Image and Logic. Material Culture of Microphysics.* Chicago, IL: University of Chicago Press.

Graham S 2016, *Vertical. The City from Satellites to Bunkers.* London and New York: Verso.

Grevsmühl SV 2014, "Serendipitous Outcomes in Space History. From Space Photography to Environmental Surveillance", in Turchetti S and Roberts P (eds.), *The Surveillance Imperative.* New York: Palgrave, pp. 71–191.

Holl U 2017, *Cinema, Trance and Cybernetics*, trans. Hendrickson D. Amsterdam: Amsterdam University Press.

Kaplan C 2018, *Aerial Aftermaths: Wartime from Above.* Durham, NC: Duke University Press.

Krapp P 2016, "The Invisible Axis. From Polar Media to Planetary Networks", in Starosielski N and Walker J (eds.), *Sustainable Media.* New York: Routledge, pp. 264–279.

Likavčan L 2019, *Introduction to Comparative Planetology.* Moscow: Strelka Press.

Lotter W, Kreiman G, and Cox D 2017, "Deep Predictive Coding Networks for Video Prediction and Unsupervised Learning", *International Conference on Learning Representations.* Available from: https://openreview.net/forum?id=B1ewdt9xe [accessed 29 August 2018].

Mackenzie A 2008, "Codecs", in Fuller M (ed.), *Software Studies. A Lexicon.* Cambridge, MA: MIT Press.

Mackenzie A 2017, *Machine Learners. Archaeology of a Data Practice.* Cambridge, MA: MIT Press.

Mattern S 2017, "Mapping's Intelligent Agents", *Places Journal*, September. Available from: https://doi.org/10.22269/170926 [accessed 29 August 2018].

Milcinski G 2018, "Multi-Year Time Series of Multi-Spectral Data Viewed and Analyzed in Sentinel Hub". Available from: https://medium.com/sentinel-hub/multi-year-time-series-of-multi-spectral-data-viewed-and-analyzed-in-sentinel-hub-5628ec4fad9c [accessed 29 August 2018].

Muybridge E 1979 [1887], *Complete Human and Animal Locomotion.Vols 1–3.*New York: Dover Publications.

Parks L 2005, *Cultures in Orbit.* Durham, NC: Duke University Press.

Parks L 2018, *Rethinking Media Coverage. Vertical Mediation and the War on Terror.* New York: Routledge.

Shi X et al. 2017, "Deep Learning for Precipitation Nowcasting: A Benchmark and A New Model", *Advances in Neural Information Processing Systems*, no. 30, pp. 5617–5627.

Siegert B 2015, *Cultural Techniques. Grids, Filters, Doors, and Other Articulations of the Real*, trans. Winthrop-Young G. New York: Fordham University Press.

Sprenger F 2019, *Epistemologie des Umgebens.* Bielefeld, [transcript].

Steyerl H 2016,"A Sea of Data.Apophenia and Pattern (Mis-Recognition)",*e-flux* 72.Available from: www.e-flux.com/journal/72/60480/a-sea-of-data-apophenia-and-pattern-mis-recognition/ [accessed 29 August 2018].

Strauß S 2018,"From Big Data to Deep Learning.A Leap Towards Strong AI or 'Intelligentia Obscura'?", *Big Data and Cognitive Computing*, vol. 2, no. 16.

van Otterlo M 2016,"The Libraryness of Calculative Devices", in Amoore L and Plotukh V (eds.), *Algorithmic Life. Calculative Devices in the Age of Big Data.* New York: Routledge, pp. 35–54.

Virilio P 2000, *Polar Inertia.* London,Thousand Oaks, CA and New Delhi: Sage.

Walker J, Gupta A, and Hebert M 2014, "Patch to the Future: Unsupervised Visual Prediction", *Computer Vision and Pattern Recognition*, March, pp. 3302–3309.

Yusoff K 2013, "The Geoengine: Geoengineering and the Geopolitics of Planetary Modification", *Environment and Planning* A, no. 45, pp. 2799–2808.

Zhou B et al. 2017, "Places: A 10 million Image Database for Scene Recognition", *IEEE Transactions on Pattern Analysis and Machine Intelligence*, vol. 40, no. 6, pp. 1452–1464.

Zylinska J 2017, *Nonhuman Photography.* Cambridge, MA: MIT Press.

PART II
Patterning use and extraction

4
BIOMETRIC DATAFICATION IN GOVERNMENTAL AND PERSONAL SPHERES

Btihaj Ajana

Introduction

A few months ago, when visiting my local gym after an absence of several weeks, I was surprised to see that my access card no longer worked. A member of staff informed me that access cards had been replaced by a facial recognition system (Figure 4.1), and that, in order to continue using the gym, I would have to enrol my face scan. I refused and insisted on using my card, not least because that was what I had signed up to when I joined the gym.

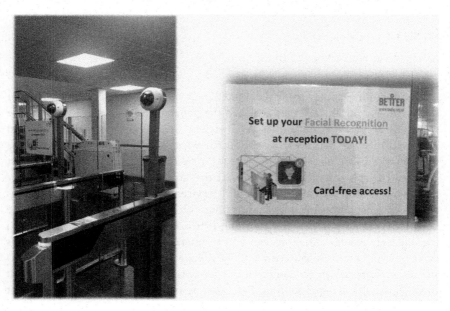

FIGURE 4.1 Gym turnstiles with facial recognition cameras, 2019.
Source: Photo: Btihaj Ajana. © Btihaj Ajana

64 Btihaj Ajana

Infuriated by the lack of prior customer consultation, I decided to share a post about this on my neighbourhood's Facebook page in the hope of mobilising more voices against such intrusive developments. Here are some of the responses I received (Figure 4.2):

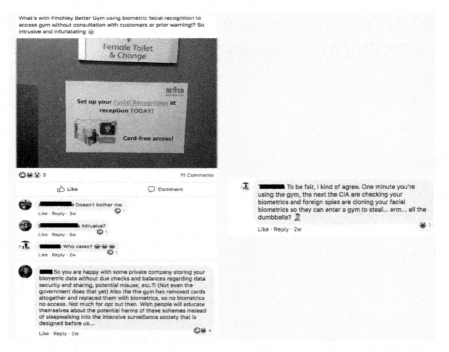

FIGURE 4.2 Facebook responses, 2019.

Source: Photo: Btihaj Ajana. © Btihaj Ajana

Disappointing as they were, these indifferent and dismissive comments did not surprise me at all. In fact, they reflected the general attitude towards surveillance technologies today: complacency. As a society, we have become so accustomed to surveillance that we no longer see it for what it is. Surveillance[1] has become so normalised that the critical distance we may have had in the past has almost disappeared. This is partly due to the fact that surveillance technologies are now embedded in our *everyday* products and services. We use biometric fingerprints and facial recognition to unlock our phones or log into our bank accounts; we use MobilePay to purchase our morning coffee; fitness trackers, such as Fitbit, to log our daily exercise; voice recognition to interact with virtual assistants such as Amazon's Alexa and Google Assistant. Technologies that would have seemed intrusive a few years ago are so commonplace today that it can seem paranoid to resist them, as the above responses from Facebook users testify. Who needs the 'thought police' *à la* Orwell when people are now happily sharing their data, unquestionably subjecting their bodies to biometric control, and broadcasting every thought to whomever cares to listen or read?[2] Initially, the use of biometrics was consigned to spaces of 'exception' such as prisons and detention centres. Increasingly now, biometric techniques are part of the 'normal' and routine functioning of contemporary societies. They are in schools, at the workplace, in gyms, bars, casinos, supermarkets, on mobile phones and smart watches. Biometrics has spilled from the specificity of certain governmental practices and spaces, such as immigration control, to the totality of everyday life and the general body of the population. By infiltrating the *consumer* sphere, it has become normalised and accepted as a convenient technology of everyday identification and a security mechanism for public safety.

As a technology of identity, biometrics involves the scanning and matching of a person's physical and behavioural characteristics – iris, face, fingerprint, voice, or hand geometry – to determine or verify identity. It relies on biology (use of the body), digitisation (use of algorithms), and datafication (use of databases and data analytics). Combined with big data techniques, such as machine learning, pattern recognition, and association analysis, biometrics has become a popular solution for law enforcement agencies and commercial entities alike. Retailers use facial recognition to gain insights into the consumer shopping experience and identify known shoplifters. Big data makes it possible to process faces in real time and often without the customers' awareness (Scott 2016). Carlo, the director of Big Brother Watch, a non-profit civil liberty campaigning organisation, describes the widespread use of facial recognition in the UK as an "epidemic", calling for more robust regulations (Carlo, cited in Gayle 2019). Biometrics is also used in blockchain technology, a form of distributed ledger system that provides un-editable digital transaction records, increasingly used for identity management and authentication.

Some years ago, Agamben warned against this spillover and normalisation of biometric technology, a process he referred to as "bio-political tattooing" (Agamben 2004). Agamben famously cancelled a course he was scheduled to teach at New York University, refusing to travel to the United States where new security measures requiring foreign nationals to submit fingerprints had been introduced. What Agamben took issue with was how the body itself had become both the *object* and the *means* of control and intervention; his main objection being that the "bio-political tattooing", imposed by the US, could very well be the precursor of 'acceptable', 'normal' practices of identity registration and verification in the future. Agamben's prophecy seems to have come true: many countries have, since then, adopted compulsory biometric border identification and use biometrics in commercial spheres, too. It is, for this reason, hard to imagine how long one could meaningfully resist biometrics, increasingly the default identification technology without which it may be impossible to access vital services, products, and spaces. We are complicit when it comes to product development. Facial recognition, for instance, has become more sophisticated thanks to Facebook users tagging each other in photographs and using applications such as FaceApp. Facebook can recognise faces about 97 per cent of the time already, building on its vast network of users (Scott 2016). Despite these warnings, people choose to feed such developments with their volunteered data. The current culture of biometric control and dataveillance is not entirely imposed from above. It relies on customer consent and participation, on the earlier-mentioned "participatory surveillance".

One thing to remember is that this seemingly 'totalising' spillover of biometrics across various societal domains and practices does not affect everyone in the same way, nor is it about technology alone. Rather, the biometric spillover is highly polysemic, multifaceted, context-based, and reflective of existing social structures and political rationalities. It is therefore important to attend to the diverse uses of biometrics and the multiplicity of spaces within which it is deployed, so as to understand its manifold meanings and functions, and how and why biometrics has emerged as a popular data-driven medium of identity and biological measurement. This chapter attempts to do precisely that. It draws on a series of examples and domains where biometrics is either used in a governmental/security context or in the personal sphere, and, at times, at the criss-crossing of both. These domains are border management, humanitarianism, and personal self-tracking. In each, there is an increasing convergence of body and data for the purpose of control and monitoring. Every day, thousands of people crossing borders have their fingerprints, eye scans, photographs, names, and nationality recorded and verified on various interoperable and networked databases, such as EURODAC and the Visa Information System. Border officials, governments, and security contractors use this data to monitor individuals crossing borders, while aid workers use it to administer vital services to refugees. Examples of humanitarian programmes such as the ID2020 project and ProGres Database are taken up in this chapter to show how techniques of biometric control and monitoring are becoming humanitarianised and couched in the language of care. By critically reflecting on these developments, the chapter raises some important ethical questions vis-à-vis power and agency, and the interplay between care and control. These issues are further addressed in relation to self-tracking, which provides a different perspective on the generation and use of biometric data. In this context, data sharing, commercialisation, and the shifting of health responsibilities from the state and medical institutions to individuals are raised and addressed. These different domains are considered as expressions of the current big data trends, each revealing a context where the abstraction, digitisation and datafication of the body is the prerequisite of identification, securitisation and (self-)management. Together, they constitute thematic perspectives, which demonstrate the spread and proliferation of dataism in contemporary societies (van Dijck 2014), and in the different spheres of everyday life.

Biometric borders

Over the years, technology has increasingly occupied a central place in the discussions, strategies, and policies concerning the management of borders and immigration. "Monitoring mobility and migration have changed drastically in the digital age

Biometric datafication **67**

[…] Data from various different sources are broken down into bits and bytes and reassembled in databases that have become a cornerstone of modern migration policy" (Broeders and Dijstelbloem 2016, p. 244). Borders are no longer simply physical frontiers that separate states. They have become ubiquitous, dispersed and invisibly embedded in everyday administrative processes, ranging from ostensible practices, such as stop-checks 'inside' the territory, or at its shifting periphery, to more subtle mechanisms such as access to public health services and social benefits, applying for a National Insurance Number, or any other activity that requires proof of identity as a prerequisite for access to services. These activities function as an *inner border* and a filter of legitimacy. At the same time, recent years have witnessed an increase in 'outsourced' control strategies that act as an *outer border* in that they allow control over borders to be performed *at a distance*. E-border schemes and stringent visa systems in consulates located in the third countries are some of the mechanisms that seek to keep the poorest foreigners and potential asylum-seekers as far as possible from the frontiers of developed countries (Yuval-Davis et al. 2005, p. 518). Such mechanisms are turning physical borders into portable, omnipresent and virtual borders. Yet, 'physical borders' still play a strong role in the political imaginary (e.g. Trump's obsession with building a 'wall' between the US and Mexico) while the actual process of 'bordering' itself is increasingly conducted through digital, biometric, and data-driven technologies.

This quantitative and qualitative transformation in the nature, ontology, and function of borders has been made possible through the continuous evolution of monitoring techniques, and surveillance technologies. In Europe, for instance, since the establishment of Schengen for the purpose of abolishing internal borders between participating EU member states, a host of surveillance mechanisms and automated control systems has been unleashed to support the monitoring of non-EU travellers, migrants, and refugees. A series of European-wide databases has been implemented including the Schengen Information Systems (SIS I and SIS II), EURODAC, and the Visa Information System (VIS). These databases are all cross-referenced by border authorities and rely on the registration of biometric details. The SIS is a large-scale information system that supports the management of external border control in Europe and law enforcement cooperation in the Schengen States. Through this system, participating states upload information (also called 'alerts') to the SIS database on travel bans, wanted and missing persons, and lost and stolen property. The information is directly accessible to all authorised police officers and other law enforcement authorities. EURODAC is an EU-wide database containing the biometric fingerprints of all asylum applicants in the EU. Its aim is to detect multiple asylum claims made by the same applicant and chart the distribution of asylum seekers across Europe, while the VIS database is a system containing information, including biometrics, on visa applications by third-country nationals requiring a visa to enter the Schengen area. It globally connects the immigration authorities of the EU member states with their consular posts, providing aggregate information on trends in visa applications and mobility. As such, these systems act as a 'digital border' primarily targeted at asylum seekers, irregular migrants, and visitors on short visas. What they all have in common, in terms of technicality and purpose, is their interest in identity and identification, and their management through data analytics and biometric technologies. Together they represent a sophisticated platform for "abstracting" information from circulating bodies and fitting it into "neat categories and definitions" (Adey 2004, p. 502), while enabling the distribution of collected data across a multitude of searchable databases. These systems have the technical ability to create various profiling mechanisms and deductive classifications in order to systematically "sort among the elements to formulate what and who must be surveyed" (Bigo 2006, p. 39). In fact, one of the primary functions of these systems is to codify, categorise and profile in order to manage the (perceived and constructed) risks associated with global mobility, including the mobility of refugees. In this way, the identity of the person attempting to cross an international border is established, encoded, and profiled prior to reaching the physical border itself through the digital traces of applying for a visa, purchasing an air ticket, using a bank card, and conducting a Google search. As argued elsewhere, the person's data and digital identity travel "in advance" through the various information networks, circuits, and databases, and wait for the physical referent (the body) to arrive (Ajana 2015, p. 73). On arrival, sometimes even before, the person's identity is matched with their body through biometric techniques and screened against other profiling data associated with behavioural patterns and risk levels. Border access is then either granted or denied.

Data-driven techniques of monitoring provide endless possibilities for control and surveillance. Not only do they institute and manage the conditions of access to borders and services, they also intensify the culture of sorting, prediction and pre-emption that has become the norm in border security policies and practices. Through these techniques, governments are increasingly able to target "undocumented migrants with an unheard of ease, prevent refugee flows from entering their countries, and track remittances and travel in ways that put migrants at new risks" (Lee 2013, np.). Worth mentioning here is that developments in border management and surveillance are increasingly driven by private actors and the lucrative security industry, which play an important role in defining the refugee and migration experience in Europe and elsewhere. Following the recent refugee crisis, a growing number of corporations have seen financial opportunity in the most vulnerable people. In 2014, Air Berlin PLC was paid some US$350,000 to operate charter flights to deport rejected asylum seekers on behalf of the government. In Sweden, the government paid a language-analysis firm US$900,000 to verify asylum-seekers' nationality. And, in Greece, a Western Union branch has been disbursing €20,000 a day to migrants, reaping fees on each transaction (Troianovski et al. 2015, p. 1). What is also interesting about these developments is that governments, military agents, and private security contractors are not the only actors using data collection to monitor and control the movement of refugees. Humanitarian organisations, too, make use of a host of sophisticated techniques to administer aid and manage the identities of refugees. Ultimately, humanitarianism becomes implicated in forms of control that often end up stripping refugees of their agency and subjecting them

Biometric datafication **69**

to imposed techniques of identification. The next section examines examples of 'humanitarian technologies' and their deployment in response to the refugee crisis.

Biometric humanitarianism

Recently, aid agencies have started using similar techniques to those used by border agencies in order to register refugees and provide them with the necessary support. As Favell puts it, in the context of Syrian refugees, "[f]orget the stereotype of the aid worker with the clipboard, the Syrian aid effort is digital – registration with biometric verification, smartcard-based aid, smart device data collection, mobile communications and telemedicine" (Favell 2015, np.). Favell goes on to explain that without registration on the United Nations High Commissioner for Refugees (UNHCR) ProGres Database, a Syrian in a host country is not officially recognised as a refugee and thus not entitled to protection and aid from UN agencies and other NGOs. ProGres was launched in 2004 to improve the collection, sharing and use of information on refugees and other individuals of concern. It is now in use in more than 70 countries. Commenting on the ProGres system, Dona Tarpey from UNHCR states that

> [b]efore, we had dozens of databases that were not necessarily compatible [...] with ProGres, we now have one unified database that caters for a wide range of UNHCR operations and situations, from camp-based to urban refugees, from repatriation to resettlement.
>
> *(Tarpey cited in Goldstein-Rodriguez and Tan 2004, np.)*

Designed to capture and store an extensive range of bio-data, ProGres creates a digital global record for every refugee, containing their personal details, contact information, place of origin, time of arrival, education, occupation, and names of family members. In addition, iris scans are performed on refugees during the registration process where a digital capture of the individual's iris is taken and stored on the database to be later used as a method of identity verification. According to IrisGuard Inc, the provider of this biometric system, there are now more than 1.6 million Syrian refugees in the region who have been registered in this way (O'Carroll 2015). The iris database is used to deliver a variety of vital services to refugees including food, financial aid, and health assistance. Increasingly, the traditional approach to delivering aid in physical form (tents, blankets, food, and household goods) is being replaced by digital financial aid where beneficiaries can use biometrically enabled systems, such as smart cards, to access their allocated cash-based assistance and purchase products at designated retailers. But as Favell points out, digital aid programmes vary considerably between the different host countries and aid agencies, depending on local conditions and regulations. At the moment, Lebanon has the largest implementation of digital aid where more than one million refugees are using either the World Food Programme's smartcard to buy goods at participating supermarkets, and/or UNHCR-backed ATM cards to withdraw money instead of receiving physical goods. Jordan has reportedly the most sophisticated aid delivery methods; at designated bank ATM machines, refugees can withdraw their cash entitlement from UNHCR by placing their eye against an IrisGuard scanner without using a card. The World Food Programme has also been piloting the use of a similar biometric system to allow refugees to purchase food in participating supermarkets using their irises. Praising the accuracy and speed of its biometric technology, IrisGuard Inc argues that "refugees are currently able to walk up to an IrisGuard enabled ATM on the street, present one eye only (no card or pin) and effortlessly withdraw their cash allocated financial subsidy immediately" (O'Carroll 2015, np.). This biometric method is promoted as a faster, simpler and more 'dignified' way of delivering aid to displaced refugees than the more traditional methods of 'in-kind aid'. It is also promoted as a way of combating fraud. The UN reported that, since implementing this scanning system, the number of Syrians requesting aid has reduced by 30 per cent (O'Donovan 2015).

But despite the seemingly convenient features of biometric-based aid delivery solutions, such as IrisGuard, these systems raise many issues that are at once ontological and political. The fact that access to refugee aid is made contingent on the imperative of submitting one's biometric information to the ProGres database, strips refugees of any sense of agency and places them at the mercy of these systems and the administrating agencies. Refugees are thus left with no other choice but to enrol one of their most intimate aspects: their bodies. Here, the refugee body becomes a forensic stabiliser of identity, functioning increasingly as a passcode, as a lie detector that can condemn or exonerate. Through these biometric procedures, the refugee body becomes abstracted and broken down into a series of data, which then defines the person's legitimacy and right to access vital services. Agamben argues that humanitarian organisations, despite themselves, "maintain a secret solidarity with the very powers they ought to fight" insofar as they can only grasp human life in the figure of "bare life" (Agamben 1998, p. 133), a naked form of life bereft of political rights and reduced to its purely biological existence. Only as such, according to Agamben, does the human life of refugees become the object of aid and protection. Similarly, Žižek contends that "the privileged object of the humanitarian biopolitics [...] is deprived of his full humanity through the very patronising way of being taken care of" adding that the refugee camps and the delivery of humanitarian aid "are the two faces, 'human' and 'inhuman', of the same socio-logical formal matrix" (Žižek 2002, p. 91). Fassin uses the term "compassionate repression" to refer to the dual and paradoxical practices whereby force and humanitarianism dialectically entwine, oscillating between "a politics of pity and policies of control" (Fassin 2005, p. 366) where care and repression are profoundly linked. In this sense, the compulsory registration of refugees on the ProGres database, and their biometric enrolment and scanning, create a form of humanitarian governance which exchanges "aid for discipline" (Schram 2006, p. 175) by forcing refugees, at their moment of vulnerability and need, to submit their bio-data and subscribe to the imposed biometric processes. This way, humanitarian organisations become the "perfect supplement" (Schram 2006, p. 175) to the sovereign power of modern states and a complicit agent in the surveillance of vulnerable groups, such as refugees and irregular migrants. In this governmental order, refugees and their bodies are caught in the middle of what Lyon refers to as the "continuum between care and control" (Lyon 2007, p. 3) where they are obliged to endure various forms of surveillance in the name of support and rescue. In this continuum, contested and problematic technologies of control, such as biometrics, become 'humanitarianised' and couched in a rhetoric of care, which, in turn, imbues them with a humane value giving them normative and scientific validation. In fact, refugees and their bodies have long acted as the testing ground for various technologies and interventions, be it compulsory biometric surveillance, experimental vaccine testing, or the provision of food considered unsafe by Western standards. As Chandler rightly contends,

> humanitarian subjects can easily be seen as less valued as their lives and liberties are placed in jeopardy while humanitarian practices test and develop new technologies. The distinction between humanitarian aid and the new exploitation of humanitarian subjects seems to be a fine one.
>
> *(Chandler 2016, p. x)*

Chandler's statement brings to mind a project recently launched under the name ID2020. The project is described as a "call for action" which seeks to provide identity solutions for the estimated 1.1 billion people, including refugees, who are living without a legally recognised identity in order to help them access basic services such as healthcare and education. It responds to one of the aims of the 2030 Sustainable Development Goals, adopted by world leaders at the United Nations on 25 September 2015: To provide legal identity for all, including birth registration by 2030 (United Nations 2015). As a UN-supported public–private partnership, ID2020 brings together government representatives, humanitarian agencies, NGOs, charities, technology businesses, and experts on digital and legal identity. Technology features quite prominently in this initiative, particularly with regard to the potential of blockchain technology and biometrics to provide identity solutions. Indeed, ID2020 represents a marketing opportunity for the tech industry to promote some of the most recent developments in digital technologies and discuss their relevance to the question of identity. While its aims are couched primarily in 'humanitarian' terms, this is also a project about 'security', as is evident from the level of interest it has received from the banking sector (anti-money laundering) and the various security-related actors (police, border control agencies, and social services). Discussions around ID2020 have also quickly shifted from the narrative of helping refugees and the 'unidentified' to security and monitoring narratives in the banking sector and the like. ID2020 is, as such, another clear example of where the discourse of care and the will to control converge. It is also an example of how the misery of vulnerable groups, such as refugees and the poor, is often used to advance an agenda that is (or at least has the potential to become) essentially about surveillance and control at a larger scale – if only as an unintended consequence of the development of mass global identity systems. As Agamben has extensively argued (Agamben 1995, 1998, 2005), refugees, and the mechanisms of control they are subjected to, can be seen as precursors to how the whole of humanity will be treated in the future. The UN's goal of establishing a legal identity 'for all' is a case in point; it raises the question as to whether a universal biometric identity card will eventually be required for everyone to access vital services and whether those who refuse to submit their biometrics might risk being outcast or disqualified from receiving healthcare or education, holding a job, or opening a bank account. In countries such as Denmark, it is already impossible to fully function in society and conduct everyday activities without having a *Det Centrale Personregister* (usually referred to as the CPR number), a national registration mechanism that assigns a unique identity number to each Danish citizen and resident without which one cannot access any services. A 'cashless' society is also being designed in which all economic activity will have to go through banks where transactions can be tracked, watched, and monitored. As Snyder warns, "[w]hat the elite want to do is to make sure that everyone is 'in the system'. And it is a system that they control and that they manipulate for their own purposes" (Snyder 2015, np.). In terms of biometrics, we can already see its function creep through the example of biometric passports and ID cards that some countries have adopted, not only for foreign nationals but also for their own citizens.

Another issue is the very essence of the question driving the UN's 2030 Sustainable Development Goals and the ID2020 project, namely *how* to provide a legal identity for *all*. Underlying this question is the assumption that *everyone* on the planet wants and needs an identity in the form *prescribed* by the authorities, and that all that is required is a system to provide it. This assumption ignores that some populations, such as nomadic groups and remote tribes, may not wish to subscribe to the ideology of legal identity, and that, in fact, a lack of official identity may be convenient in certain circumstances, for certain groups and individuals whose identifiability may cause them more harm than good, as in the case of fleeing persecution. This assumption also rationalises the very bureaucratic and technocratic machinery that reduces people to numbers on a database or a piece of ID, without which the person becomes a 'nobody'. Diop, the World Bank Vice President for Infrastructure, argues that "identification provides a foundation for other rights and gives a voice to the voiceless" (Diop 2016, np.). But the increasing emphasis on legal identity as a *prerequisite* for exercising basic rights could very well result in strengthening or even creating further forms of exclusion. The 'humanitarian question' must therefore be reframed in a way that challenges the supremacy of legal identity rather than affirms it. Instead of asking how to provide a legal identity to all, the question that needs to be raised is: how can access and entitlement to relevant services and programmes be *disassociated* from the tyranny of legal identity, so that access to basic rights – education and healthcare – is not made contingent on birth registration, and identity documentation, but based on the mere fact of existing? In other words, *everyone should enjoy rights regardless of their lack of legal identity and identification documents*. Undermining the validity, authority, and importance of legal identity and identification technologies is a necessary step towards freeing the human from the juridico-political shackles of identity and legality. For, after all, identity and its technologies have long been a powerful tool of state control – from the use of identity to administer welfare and classify populations to more extreme practices of ethnic cleansing, as in the historical cases of Rwanda and Nazi Germany.

Biometric selves

In the preceding sections, I examined border management and humanitarianism as examples where techno-mediated control is *imposed* on vulnerable bodies, such as refugees and asylum seekers. In the remaining section, I turn to a different context in which body datafication is performed *voluntarily*, that is, the context of self-tracking. Self-tracking represents another expression of big data development and a striking example of what I call 'self-inflicted biometrics', a phenomenon indicating how individuals are now willingly quantifying and tracking themselves more than ever before and actively turning themselves into projects of (self-)governance and surveillance.

Over the last few years, we have witnessed a rapid development in digital tracking devices, accompanied by the emergence of techno-social movements, such as the Quantified Self, which promote data-driven forms of self-analysis and monitoring. Intended to motivate users by encouraging a healthy lifestyle through daily monitoring, such devices and apps record a wide range of biometric data, health indicators, and vital signs. This is achieved through inbuilt sensors for automated data collection as well as self-reporting whereby users log the food consumed and the activities undertaken. To be sure, the idea or desire to monitor the body and its activities is by no means new. Athletes have long been required to record their nutritional intake, and track and document their performance. Women have long relied on menstrual cycles for family planning and contraception. Nevertheless, the development of new digital personalised and mobile technologies has made it easier than ever for people to collate and analyse their personal data. The availability and relative affordability of self-tracking devices and apps made it possible for the average person, especially in Western countries, to effortlessly generate large statistical data deploying quantitative analytical methods akin to those found in science and business. As a result, the traditional professional health-monitoring devices and techniques are now becoming increasingly accessible to the general public, while sensors are being transformed into smaller, cheaper, and ultimately more manageable pieces of equipment fit for everyday use.

In economic terms, measuring the body has always been a profitable industry. The personalisation of biometric devices also meant an increase in consumers of these technologies and thereby an increase in the profit made by the manufacturers of such devices. According to a recent report by Mordor Intelligence (2018), the wearables market was valued at US$181.51 million in 2018 and this figure is anticipated to grow by 19.10 per cent by 2024. The rapidly increasing market value of wearable tracking devices and apps is, indeed, indicative of the growing interest

74 Btihaj Ajana

in such technologies and the notable shift towards self-quantification and performance monitoring in general.

Critics argue that this increasing focus on numbers and their potential for self-analysis and improvement is not driven by technology alone but is reflective of a larger shift towards the 'neo-liberal' ethos of self governance and health management, whereby individuals are increasingly expected to take charge of their own health and well-being, at a time when state support for social and health programmes is in decline. Lupton, for instance, argues that data-driven and technologically mediated practices of health management and self-tracking conform to a neo-liberal politics which focuses on citizens' personal behaviour and self-responsibility, shifting the management of health away from institutions towards individuals themselves (Lupton 2014). Similarly, De Souza suggests, with reference to the Quantified Self, that this movement "conforms to the ideal neoliberal citizen: the self-optimizing individual who voluntarily monitors, measures, regulates and collects biometric data on their own health, wellbeing and fitness; taking control of their own bodies on a minute and detailed level" (De Souza 2013, np.). This conceptual linking of self-tracking with neo-liberalism has do with the fact that they both incite individuals to regard themselves as "projects", as "mini-corporations" (Martin 1999), in need of constant self-development, improvement, and investment. The following statement by Wolf, the co-founder of the Quantified Self movement, captures this project-like approach to the self: "[w]e use numbers when we want to tune up a car, analyze a chemical reaction, predict the outcome of an election. We use numbers to optimize an assembly line. Why not use numbers on ourselves?" (Wolf 2010, np.). We can see this metric attitude promoted not only in the domain of personal health and fitness management but also in other spaces including the home, leisure, and work, especially given the increasingly blurred boundaries between these spheres and the gamification of life (Whitson 2013), which turns everyday tasks into games in order to increase motivation. For instance, companies are now sponsoring 'wellness programmes' to encourage their employees to lead healthy lifestyles; leisure time is becoming increasingly integrated into the sphere of labour (Till 2014). The retail company, Target, offered 335,000 Fitbit devices to its US employees (Bloomberg 2015). More recently, Fitbit has introduced a new activity and sleep tracker called Fitbit Inspire, which is only available through corporate wellness schemes and health plans (Farr 2019). Health has become "a corporate concern" (Till 2016).

Within self-tracking practices and their overall philosophy, the body and its physical activities occupies centre stage. Data emerging out of bodily quantification are believed to reveal some kind of "objective truth" about the self-tracker that was previously not achievable through techniques of self-analysis and introspection. Such practices establish a direct relation between the body and the self, between biology and knowledge, between technology and truth. This is obviously not the first time that technologically mediated developments have attempted to establish such a strong link between body, technicity, and forms of knowledge. For instance, as I argue above and elsewhere (Ajana 2013), the deployment of biometrics in security and border control has redefined the relationship between body and identity. By laying claim to the idea that identity can "objectively" be determined through the body (Ajana 2010), biometrics has given the body unprecedented significance, casting it as a source of "instant truth" (Aas 2006, np.). This is encapsulated in the expression "the body does not lie", the marketing slogan of the biometrics industry.

The will to knowledge is never a neutral pursuit. For knowledge, as Bacon reminds us, *is* power (Bacon cited in Garcia 2001, p. 109). The body is often a site of power as much as it is a site of knowledge, be it in terms of the regulatory systems it is subjected to (e.g. biometric identification that renders the body as 'password'; scanning technologies at the border; work-related health checks; dietary regimes) or the self-inculcated habits and practices of which self-tracking is a prominent example. At the heart of self-tracking, is, in fact, a desire for 'control'. As Rowse argues, "quantification provides a means for understanding the self that seems to enable a certain feeling of control. One can change a behavior, and see a direct response in the numbers" (Rowse 2015, p. 39). Control, in this context, is not so much about *explicit* coercive discipline, but follows the neo-liberal modality of free choice, the rhetoric of agency and the promise of reward; the reward for exercise and self-regulation in line with the set norms, and with the promise of a healthier life or a better-looking body.

Moreover, although the 'self' is often an over-emphasised part of the self-tracking culture, there is also a collective dimension to such practices. Increasingly, personal self-tracking data are integrated into social media platforms and dedicated forums that enable users of self-tracking technologies to share and compare data and results, and compete with each other. The Fitbit website, for instance, has a community section comprising various discussion boards which allow Fitbit users to share health tips, seek advice about Fitbit products, and chat about nutrition or sleep. The forum also encourages users to share their fitness achievements on social media networks and compete with friends and colleagues. This social trend of participating in online communities, established for the purpose of sharing health-related information and experience, echoes Rabinow's concept of "biosociality" (Rabinow 1996), a type of connection between individuals centred on bio-logically based forms of socialisation. Biosociality gestures towards the interface between developments in biotechnologies, social practices, and individual and col-lective subjectivities. The emergence of social media has undoubtedly provided new opportunities for building web-based communities where individuals can share information about their health, fitness, and diseases. Increasingly, however, various actors other than users themselves are interested in harvesting the self-tracking data. These range from public health institutions and private insurance companies to employers and product developers. In the healthcare sector, self-tracking practices are looked up to as a means of realising the aspirations of par-ticipatory, preventative, and personalised healthcare models. This is insofar as these practices can enable the capturing of quantifiable health data that can feed into decision-making vis-à-vis one's lifestyle, diet options, exercise activities, perform-ance, and habits.

The passage from 'small data' (individual self-tracking data) to big data is now part of the discussions about how personal data can usefully contribute to collective health goals (Lupton 2016). Both the public and the private health sectors are interested in how self-tracking data generated by individuals can feed into a larger big data ecosystem. The belief is that when ensembles of individuals' data are combined, a collective social picture will emerge, that of the population, its health, finances, and productivity. It is about the move from the micro to the macro level, from the Quantified Self to the "Quantified Us" for the purpose of prediction, control, risk analysis, and decision-making on a larger scale (Jordan and Pfarr 2014, np.).

To this end, self-trackers are encouraged to embrace data donation and sharing as a way of enacting good bio-citizenship (see the example of Patients Like Me and its *Data For Good* campaign). There is, in fact, a certain moral economy at work, which underpins data sharing practices and prescribes these as a form of biosociality, altruism, and civic duty, all of which are often packaged under the rubric of "data philanthropy" (Ajana 2017). But there remains a great tension between the notion of data philanthropy and issues of data commercialisation. While many users of self-tracking technologies operate under the assumption that the data they generate belong to them, the reality is that companies providing the technology often own the data. Some tracking platforms and device manufacturers sell data back to users and charge them a fee to download their own records. Service providers often leave users with no choice as to whether to save the data on the company's server or on their own devices. As such, users have hardly any control over how their data is stored and processed (Mulder 2019). The technically savvy members of the Quantified Self community tend to circumvent such issues by building their own tracking tools so that their data remains their own property. But that is not the case with the majority of everyday self-trackers who rely on commercial devices and apps to track their activities. There is, indeed, a delicate dance between commercial goals and the aim of "self-knowledge through numbers" (Fotopoulou 2018, p. 3).

Conclusion

This chapter discussed three expressions of big data trends related to the application of biometric technologies, namely border control, digital humanitarianism, and self-tracking. What is apparent in such trends is the growing extraction of data from the body itself for the purpose of monitoring and dataveillance, leading not only to the intensification of control but also to the redefinition of identity and selfhood. In big data culture, identity is increasingly regarded as an asset from which value and knowledge can be extracted, or as a forensic trail for securitisation processes. At the same time, expressions and understandings of selfhood are increasingly data-driven as is the case with the Quantified Self movement. What is also apparent is the intertwinement of care and control. Biometric humanitarianism provides a clear example of how, in the name of care and help, the bodies of refugees and asylum seekers are subjected to various forms of technologically mediated control. With the rapid spread of data technologies in everyday life, it is important to be more vigilant about the kind of future that is being designed through the normalisation of biometric tracking practices and the datafication of life itself.

Notes

1 Some scholars favour the use of dataveillance instead of surveillance to indicate the increasingly important role of data and digital technologies in monitoring and policing processes and differentiate these from traditional modes of closely observing individuals and groups. I personally regard surveillance as an umbrella term that subsumes dataveillance practices and see the latter as a "remediation" (Bolter and Grusin 1999) of traditional forms of surveillance (e.g. facial recognition as a remediation of CCTV cameras). Therefore, in this chapter, I use the term surveillance more frequently than dataveillance. When the term 'dataveillance' is used here, it is for the purpose of emphasising the digital and datafied aspects of the discussed surveillance mechanisms.
2 Anders Albrechtslund (2008) locates such changing attitudes in the rise of 'participatory surveillance', a form of surveillance that relies on the voluntary participation of individuals.

References

Aas KF 2006, "'The Body Does Not Lie': Identity, Risk and Trust in Technoculture", *Crime Media Culture*, vol. 2, no. 2, pp. 143–158.

Adey P 2004, "Secured and Sorted Motilities: Examples from the Airport", *Surveillance & Society*, vol. 1, no. 4, pp. 500–519.

Agamben G 1995, "We Refugees", *Symposium: A Quarterly Journal in Modern Literatures*, vol. 49, no. 2, pp. 114–119.

Agamben G 1998, *Homo Sacer: Sovereign Power and Bare Life*. Stanford, CA: Stanford University Press.

Agamben G 2004, "No to Bio-Political Tattooing". Available from: www.egs.edu/faculty/giorgio-agamben/articles/no-to-bio-political-tattooing/ [accessed 10 January 2006].

Agamben G 2005, *State of Exception*. Chicago, IL: University of Chicago Press.

Ajana B 2010, "Recombinant Identities: Biometrics and Narrative Bioethics", *Journal of Bioethical Inquiry*, vol. 7, no. 2, pp. 237–258.

Ajana B 2013, *Governing through Biometrics: The Biopolitics of Identity*. Basingstoke: Palgrave Macmillan.

Ajana B 2015, "Augmented Borders: Big Data and the Ethics of Immigration Control", *Journal of Information, Communication and Ethics in Society*, vol. 13, no. 1, pp. 58–78.

Ajana B 2017, "Digital Health and the Biopolitics of the Quantified Self", *Digital Health*, vol. 3, no. 1, pp. 1–18.

Albrechtslund A 2008, "Online Social Networking", *First Monday*, vol. 13, no. 3. Available from: https://firstmonday.org/article/view/2142/1949 [accessed 1 September 2009].

Bigo D 2006, "Globalized (In)Security: The Field and the Ban-opticon", in Bigo D and Tsoukala A (eds.), *Illiberal Practices of Liberal Regimes – The (In)security Games*. Paris: L'Hartmattan.

Bloomberg. 2015, "Target to Offer Fitbits to 335,000 Employees". www.bloomberg.com/news/articles/2015-09-15/target-to-offer-health-tracking-fitbits-to-335-000-employees [accessed 1 September 2016].

Bolter JD and Grusin R 1999, *Remediation: Understanding New Media*. Cambridge, MA: MIT Press.

Broeders D and Dijstelbloem H 2016, "The Datafication of Mobility and Migration Management: The Mediating State and its Consequences". Available from: www.researchgate.net/publication/290194722_The_Datafication_of_Mobility_and_Migration_Management_the_Mediating_State_and_its_Consequences [accessed 1 September 2017].

Chandler D 2016, "Forward", in Jacobsen KL (ed.) *The Politics of Humanitarian Technology*. London: Routledge.

De Souza P 2013, "Self-tracking and Body Hacking: The Biopolitics of the Quantified Self in the Age of Neoliberalism". Available from: https://bodycartography.wordpress.com/2013/06/11/self-tracking-and-body-hacking-the-biopolitics-of-the-quantified-self-in-the-age-of-neoliberalism/ [accessed 1 October 2016].

Diop M 2016, "African Partners, World Bank Commit to Provide Identification to Millions". Available from: www.worldbank.org/en/news/press-release/2016/04/14/african-partners-world-bank-commit-to-provide-identification-to-millions [accessed 1 September 2017].

Farr C 2019, "Fitbit has a New Health Tracker, but you can only get it through your Employer or Insurer". www.cnbc.com/2019/02/08/fitbit-releases-insprire-for-employers.html [accessed 1 August 2019].

Fassin D 2005, "Compassion and Repression: The Moral Economy of Immigration Policies in France", *Cultural Anthropology*, vol. 20, no. 3, pp. 362–387.

Favell A 2015, "How Technology is Helping Deliver Aid to Syrian Refugees in the Middle East". Available from: www.computerweekly.com/feature/How-technology-is-helping-deliver-aid-to-Syrian-refugees-in-the-Middle-East [accessed 1 September 2017].

Fotopoulou A 2018, "From Networked to Quantified Self: Self-tracking and the Moral Economy of Data", in Papacharissi Z (ed.), *A Networked Self: Platforms, Stories, Connections*. New York: Routledge.

Garcia, JMR 2001, "Scientia Potestas Est – Knowledge is Power: Francis Bacon to Michel Foucault", *Neohelicon*, vol. 28, no. 1, pp. 109–121.

Gayle D 2019, "Privacy Campaigners Warn of UK Facial Recognition 'Epidemic'". Available from: www.theguardian.com/technology/2019/aug/16/privacy-campaigners-uk-facial-recognitin-epidemic [accessed 16 August 2019].

Goldstein-Rodriguez R and Tan V 2004, "UNHCR Seeks ProGres in Refugee Registration". Available from: www.unhcr.org/news/latest/2004/9/4135e9aa4/unhcr-seeks-progres-refugee-registration.html [accessed 1 September 2017].

Jordan M and Pfarr N 2014, "Forget the Quantified Self. We need to Build the Quantified Us". Available from: www.wired.com/2014/04/forget-the-quantified-self-we-need-to-build-the-quantified-us/ [accessed 1 September 2016].

Lee C 2013, "Big Data and Migration: What's in Store?". Available from: http://noncitizensoftheworld.blogspot.co.uk/ [accessed 1 October 2014].

Lupton D 2014, "Quantified Sex: A Critical Analysis of Sexual and Reproductive Self-Tracking Using Apps", *Culture Health & Sexuality*, vol. 17, no. 4, pp. 1–14.

Lupton D 2016, *The Quantified Self*. Cambridge: Polity Press.

Lyon D 2007, *Surveillance Studies: An Overview*. Cambridge: Polity Press.

Martin M 1999, "Mind–Body Problems". Available from: http://havenscenter.wisc.edu/files/mind_body.pdf [accessed 1 October 2016].

Mordor Intelligence. 2018, "Smart Wearable Market – Growth, Trends, and Forecast (2019–2024)". Available from: www.mordorintelligence.com/industry-reports/smart-wearables-market [accessed 1 August 2019].

Mulder T 2019, "Health Apps, their Privacy Policies and the GDPR", *European Journal of Law and Technology*, vol. 10, no. 1, pp. 1–20.

O'Carroll J 2015, "IrisGuard – EyeBank® Cash Payment – Serving Syrian Refugees Daily". Available from: www.prlog.org/12461828-irisguard-eyebank-cash-payment-serving-syrian-refugees-daily.html [accessed 4 July 2020].

O'Donovan C 2015, "Tracking Refugees puts a Vulnerable Population at Risk". Available from: www.buzzfeed.com/carolineodonovan/tracking-refugees-puts-a-vulnerable-population-at-risk?utm_term=.jrGP4beVx#.gfmMNY7lb [accessed 1 September 2017].

Rabinow P 1996, *Essays On the Anthropology of Reason*. Princeton, NJ: Princeton University Press.

Rowse LM 2015, "Statistics of the Self: Shaping the Self Through Quantified Self-Tracking". Available from: http://scholarship.claremont.edu/cgi/viewcontent.cgi?article=1656& context=scripps_theses [accessed 1 September 2016].

Schram SF 2006, *Welfare Discipline: Discourse, Governance and Globalization*. Philadelphia, PA: Temple University Press.

Scott J 2016, "Big Data: Facial Recognition and the Biometrics Movement". Available from: https://mapr.com/blog/big-data-facial-recognition-and-biometrics-movement/ [accessed 1 August 2019].

Snyder M 2015, "The UN Plans to Implement Universal Biometric Identification for All of Humanity by 2030". Available from: www.activistpost.com/2015/11/the-un-plans-to-implement-universal-biometric-identification-for-all-of-humanity-by-2030.html [accessed 1 September 2017].

Till C 2014, "Exercise as Labour: Quantified Self and the Transformation of Exercise into Labour", *Societies*, vol. 4, no. 3, pp. 446–462.

Till C 2016, "Why do Companies want us to be Healthy? Corporate Wellness, Self-tracking and Philanthrocapitalism". Available from: https://christopherharpertill.wordpress.com/2016/04/06/why-do-companies-want-us-to-be-healthy-corporate-wellness-self-tracking-and-philanthrocapitalism/ [accessed 15 January 2017].

Troianovski A et al. 2015, "The Growth of Refugee Inc". Available from: www.wsj.com/articles/in-european-refugee-crisis-an-industry-evolves-1442252165 [accessed 15 September 2017].

United Nations. 2015, "Transforming our World: The 2030 Agenda for Sustainable Development". Available from: www.un.org/ga/search/view_doc.asp?symbol=A/RES/70/1&Lang=E [accessed 1 September 2017].

van Dijck J 2014, "Datafication, Dataism and Dataveillance: Big Data between Scientific Paradigm and Ideology", *Surveillance and Society*, vol. 12, no. 2, pp. 197–208.

Whitson J 2013, "Gaming the Quantified Self". Available from: http://ojs.library.queensu.ca/index.php/surveillance-and-society/article/view/gaming [accessed 1 December 2015].

Wolf G 2010, "The Data-driven Life". Available from: www.nytimes.com/2010/05/02/magazine/02self-measurement-t.html?_r=0 [accessed 1 October 2015].

Yuval-Davis, N et al. 2005, "Secure Borders and Safe Haven and the Gendered Politics of Belonging: Beyond Social Cohesion", *Ethnic and Racial Studies*, vol. 28, no. 3, pp. 513–535.

Žižek S 2002, *Welcome to the Desert of the Real*. London: Verso.

5

DIGITAL BIOPOLITICS AND THE PROBLEM OF FATIGUE IN PLATFORM CAPITALISM

Tim Christaens

Advances in big data analytics and information control have caused a paradigm shift in the field of work, propelling it towards a 'gig economy' where stable employment is replaced with short-term 'gigs'. The so-called 'platform companies' – Uber, Deliveroo and Amazon Mechanical Turk, among others – use specialised software to coordinate 'gigs', creating new digitised markets to crowdsource workers, promising a steady income with the flexibility befitting a twenty-first century entrepreneur. However, the reality is often less exalting. In 2017, *The New Yorker* reported the story of a nine-month pregnant woman Mary. One day, Mary, who was contracted by Lyft, Uber's main competitor, feels mild contractions and decides to drive herself to hospital. However, on the way, she receives a ride request and takes a detour to pick up a costumer. When she finally gets to the hospital, doctors tell her she is already in labour and has taken a great risk in not coming in earlier. The story eventually ends well, but shows how harmful platform gigs can be for low-income workers,[1] who, instead of being entrepreneurially independent, jeopardise their health – perhaps even their child's life – for a few bucks.

Stories like these are at odds with our moral compass but it is hard to pinpoint what exactly is at stake here on the basis of the existing critiques of capitalism. Discussions of contemporary capitalism have tended to centre on exploitation (Terranova 2000; Hardt and Negri 2001; Moulier Boutang 2011) and alienation (Sennett 1998; Jaeggi 2014; Virno 2015). Employing Franco 'Bifo' Berardi's critique of the problem of fatigue in techno-capitalism, I analyse a key contradiction of twenty-first century capitalism: new digital technologies demand more energy from human bodies than the latter can actually deliver. There are limits to how much work a human being can perform, yet the biopolitics underlying the platform business model *exceed* those limits. To acquire profits, platform companies must exhaust their main resource: human mental energy. The advent of big data has introduced a widening gap between abstract software that steers workers according to the profit motive, and concrete bodies reduced to the status of living appendages of the platform. The speed of the platform's algorithms exceeds the capacities of human bodies. The unsustainability of this contradiction recalls the exhaustion workers experienced in the nineteenth-century factories described by Marx in chapter 15 of *Capital Volume I* on "Machinery and Modern Industry". There, too, the rhythm of the industrial factory outpaced the physical constitution of the workers' bodies. Despite the fact that the social situation has drastically changed since the nineteenth century, the problem of fatigue returns in a new guise. To overcome this contradiction, I argue for the need to redesign platforms as 'open objects' and make their algorithms available to, as well as alterable by, workers to enable them to co-write the platform economy's rules.

The weaponisation of big data

According to Marx, one should read the history of modern technology as the progressive invention of weaponry against working-class resistance (MacKenzie 1984, pp. 487–488; Wendling 2009, p. 68). "It would be possible to write quite a history of the inventions, made since 1830, for the sole purpose of supplying capital with weapons against the revolts of the working class" (Marx 1996, p. 439). In section 3 of chapter 15 on "The approximate effects of machinery on the workmen", Marx clarifies three ways in which industrial machinery impacted workers (Dyer-Witheford, Kjösen, and Steinhoff 2019, pp. 16–17). (1) It transformed women and children into direct competitors for increasingly fewer, deskilled jobs. Machinery caused mass redundancies, while simultaneously making the remaining jobs easier to perform. Resistant workers could thus easily be replaced with more docile ones. (2) Machines prolonged the workday. Because machinery had to operate as much as possible to constitute a profitable investment, factory owners mobilised their workforce for longer stretches of time. (3) The factory system also intensified the workday. Machines accelerated the work rhythm, so workers were obliged to work harder to keep up with their equipment.

In our current age of immaterial labour, traditional industry has predominantly moved to non-Western countries. The service sector has become increasingly important. One of the key advantages for this sector is that it enables a mode of production centred around "the soft tyranny of interactivity" (Massumi 2011, pp. 47–48). Instead of, first, producing commodities, then selling them, today's service companies first incite consumers to interact with the service provider then tailor products to fit the individual customer's desires. By calibrating their services and customer expectations, service providers produce the commodity as well as the consumer for the commodities they produce. Digital technologies have vastly amplified the possibilities for such provider-consumer "co-creation" projects (Prahalad and Ramaswamy 2000). One of the main novelties in this field are platform companies (Scholz 2017, p. 159; Srnicek 2017, pp. 43–44) – Google, Amazon, Uber, Facebook – which create a digital space where individuals can easily exchange commodities with fewer practical obstacles than ever. Building a bookshop with all the world's books is impossible, however Amazon provides a website where publishers can directly present their books to a global audience. Discovering our most intimate desires is too costly for advertisers, however Google sells information about our search entries to help companies create individually targeted advertisements. These corporations make profits by extracting and analysing the behavioural data generated on digital platforms (Bastani 2019, p. 84; Zuboff 2019, p. 96), which can either be sold to third parties or used to optimise the platform's own services. As different as this world of big data might seem from industrial machinery, the effects on workers are strikingly similar.

(a) Just as working men in industrial times were out-competed by women and children, who, at the time, were a cheaper and more docile workforce, leading to worsening conditions for all, the platform economy constantly undermines workers' rights by minimising job vacancies and maximising competition. Data analytics make it possible to determine exactly how many workers the company needs at any hour of the day (O'Neil 2012, p. 124; Ciccarelli 2018, p. 39). Amazon, for example, processes the data from shipment orders to determine the minimal number of staff required for any particular task with great precision, eliminating superfluous workers from the balance sheets. Digital technologies, however, not only diminish the number of job vacancies but also expand the number of prospective employees (O'Neil 2012, p. 128; Srnicek 2017, pp. 22–23; Ciccarelli 2018, p. 55). For example, Amazon Mechanical Turk (AMT) is a digital marketplace where companies can hire workers from all over the world to perform small, easy digital tasks for a few cents per task, like recognising captchas or filling in research surveys. The platform relies heavily on cheap Asian freelancers and unemployed Americans (Scholz 2017, p. 29). The effect is clear: while this is beneficial for disadvantaged workers previously excluded from Western labour markets, platform technology minimises opportunities for steady employment, while the globalisation of the labour supply also undermines Western workers' bargaining position, leading to a steady decline in jobs, wages, and social benefits.

(b) Platform technology prolongs the workday. Digital technologies are used to keep workers on platforms longer than they originally intended. Uber, for example, uses "means of behavioural modification" (Zuboff 2019, p. 8) that incentivise drivers to "choose" to prolong their workday of their own free will (Kessler 2018, p. 103; Rosenblat 2018, p. 78). It sends push notifications to encourage drivers to meet arbitrary daily goals to induce them to work more. These targets have no inherent meaning, however Uber knows that simply communicating a target is enough to seduce people into trying to reach it. At a more fundamental level, the workday is also prolonged because more activities are included in the sphere of work as value-creation; activities that would previously have been considered leisurely are increasingly captured in the cycle of capital accumulation (Scholz 2017, p. 156; Mezzada and Neilson 2019, p. 145; Zuboff 2019, pp. 99–100). Whereas one may previously have asked a friend to drive one to the airport, Uber precludes the need to bother a friend. Free time is increasingly captured in the economic system (Terranova 2000).

(c) Work is not only prolonged, but also intensified. Platform companies endow their algorithms with surveillance systems that augment labour productivity. Like prisoners in Bentham's panopticon, workers do not know how or when their data is being tracked, so they internalise the surveillance mechanism (Berardi 2009, p. 192; Hardt and Negri 2017, 116; Rosenblat 2018, p. 91). "The flesh and bone boss no longer exists. The new boss would be an algorithm" (Ciccarelli 2018, p. 56, my translation). Uber, for instance, tracks how drivers brake and accelerate to compose safe-driving reports about individual drivers (Rosenblat 2018, p. 139). The app sends messages to drivers such as "Several harsh brakes detected" or "Great work". Actions like these make drivers suspect that Uber is collecting much more information so they work as if Uber were always watching (138). Since the exact machinations of Uber's algorithm that links drivers to clients is a mystery to workers, the latter are lured into a potentially infinite loop of self-improvement (Lazzarato 2014, p. 53; Ciccarelli 2018, p. 41; Rosenblat 2018, p. 149). Whatever activity Uber is measuring, they have to improve their data to acquire further gigs. Systems like these establish a "mental subsumption" (Berardi 2017, p. 106) forcing workers to internalise the platform's profit motive. "Obligations [become] internalized and social control [is] exercised through a voluntary, albeit inevitable, subjugation to chains of automatisms" (Berardi 2011, p. 35).

The digital biopolitics of the platform

In the aforementioned chapter on modern industry, Marx emphasises the fact that workers' conduct had to be tailored to the requirements and speed of the factory's machinery, not the other way around.

> In handicrafts and manufacture, the workman makes use of a tool; in the factory the machine makes use of him. There the movements of the instrument of labour proceed from him; here it is the movements of the machine that he must follow. In manufacture the workmen are part of a living mechanism. In the factory we have a lifeless mechanism independent of the workman, who becomes its mere living appendage. [...] By means of its conversion into an automaton, the instrument of labour confronts the labourer, during the labour process, in the shape of capital, of dead labour, that dominates, and pumps dry, living labour power.
>
> *(Marx 1996, pp. 425–426)*

Modern industry turned workers into living appendages of a mechanical *perpetuum mobile* over which they had no control. As workers would not allow themselves to be "pumped dry" (426–427), Marx stressed the necessity of discipline on the work floor, which subjugated labourers to the rule of machines. That is, supervisors had

84 Tim Christaens

to *forcefully* implement factory discipline for the industrial system to function. Today, computers and smartphones have largely replaced the factory superintendents (Dyer-Witheford, Kjösen, and Steinhoff 2019, p. 2). Digital technology has automatised work surveillance: "[a] system of algorithms […] serves as a virtual 'automated manager'" (Rosenblat 2018, p. 3). For Berardi (2011, p. 40; 2012, p. 123; 2017, pp. 109–110), the result is a network of "connections": "an operative concatenation between previously formatted agents of meaning (bodies or machines) that have been […] formatted according to a code" (Berardi 2015a, pp. 21). Connection is the mode of subjectivation in which human beings are adapted to a digital format geared towards maximising the platform's profits. A digital code renders bodies compatible with machinic operations in the service of capital accumulation. Human beings are first disassembled into data streams that algorithms can subsequently reconnect according to the platform's needs. Uber, for instance, often tricks its drivers with misleading push notifications about future price surges to ensure profits at the cost of the workers' incomes (Rosenblat 2018, pp. 131–132). Whenever demand in a particular geographic area is significantly higher than the number of Uber drivers available, a price surge automatically occurs where drivers get a higher percentage of the client's payment. However, Uber keeps data records of past price surges; its algorithms can predict future demand and prevent price surges by pre-emptively notifying drivers *en masse* of upcoming opportunities. The push notification here turns into a self-defeating prophecy: the mere announcement of higher revenues makes so many drivers flock to the scene that the price surge never materialises. Otherwise put, Uber automates Althusserian interpellation (Althusser 1995) to manage its workforce addressing workers with a personalised 'Hey, you there' to subject them to market imperatives. However, these platforms use big data not to govern individual workers directly, but rather, as databanks of statistical evidence *about* workers. Algorithmic biopolitics "literally abstracts specific tasks and activities from the embodied experience of a single worker, inserting him or her into a workflow that obscures any subjectivity" (Mezzadra and Neilson 2019, p. 83). Uber and other platforms do not see workers with their integral biography, but as abstract flows of data that can be connected to benefit the company's financial flows (Berardi 2018, p. 21; Ciccarelli 2018, pp. 62–63). Its algorithms track GPS locations, consumer ratings, and average driving speeds to link the most suited driver to a particular request. The app augments overall efficiency by disassembling workers into equivalent atoms of abstract labour-time that can be rearranged according to present or future market requirements.

> Connection requires a prior process whereby the elements that need to connect are made compatible. Indeed, the digital web extends through the progressive reduction of an increasing number of elements to […] a code that makes compatible different elements. […] The leading factor of this change is […] the proliferation of artificial devices in the organic universe, the body, communication, and society.
>
> *(Berardi 2012, pp. 124–125)*

Lazzarato argues that this form of digital biopolitics operates predominantly with "machinic subjugation" rather than with "social subjection" (Lazzarato 2014, pp. 23–29; 2015, pp. 183–185; Christiaens 2016, pp. 2–3). In social subjection, consciously rehearsed linguistic representations inform social conduct. To orientate themselves in the world, human beings need discourses and images to tell them what their social roles are. For example, Catholic discourses and imagery portray humankind as a community of sinners in need of divine grace. This portrayal subsequently interpellates Catholics to consciously relate to their own conditions of existence as sinners. Platform companies use social subjection only sparsely. Uber attracts new drivers by representing Uber as a company of and for young and successful entrepreneurs (Rosenblat 2018, pp. 75–77), but the effects of these advertisement campaigns are minimal.

Digital biopolitics operates far more successfully through machinic subjugation. Some languages are not meant for communicating ideas. They issue commands in a network of flows, similarly to how traffic lights use "red" and "green" to manage traffic (Deleuze and Guattari 1972, p. 290). The 1s and 0s of computer code are not the carriers of poetic meaning; they regulate electrical circuits by establishing or cutting links between different network nodes. Computer software can thus be understood as a series of coordinated commands that manage flows of electricity in order to generate information flows. Code does not represent a reality out there to which human beings could relate. It is a direct "producer of the real" (Kitchin 2014, p. 23); it issues commands that alter reality without the mediation of human consciousness. Establishing a human-machine 'connection' here entails rendering human brains compatible with the electrical circuits of a particular piece of software. Video games, for example, immerse players in the game in such a way that the players' mental attention, the movements of their fingers, and the endorphin levels in their brains all align with the flow of the gameplay (Väliaho 2014). Instead of addressing individuals' capacity for conscious reflection, machinic subjugation targets their pre-conscious, bodily, affective interaction with their milieu.

A sector that has been perfecting this form of control for decades is digital finance (Lazzarato 2014, pp. 96–101; Christiaens 2016). Traditionally, the stockbroker has been seen as a *homo oeconomicus*, rationally calculating the costs and benefits of transactions. However, the volatile dynamics of the stock market contradict this portrayal. In reality, the traders' conscious minds are, in the algorithmic age, too slow to perform the necessary calculations, the nanosecond pace too fast to make rational decisions. The typical financial trader today no longer takes part in the shouting matches in the trading pit, but is more likely a 'tech nerd' staring at multiple computer screens, automatically responding to graphs moving up, lights turning red, buzzers going off (MacKenzie 2009; Zaloom 2010). Traders have inserted their brains into a human-machine assemblage where the originating source of decision-making is no longer the human being. Conscious elaboration is here replaced by pre-conscious, instinctive automatisms embedded in the digitised assemblage. Traders are trained to automatically react in pre-determined ways. If a light turns red, they *unthinkingly 'know'* they have to click on the sell button. The decision to sell comes not from the autonomous human subject but from a network of machinic and human elements and interactions. Machinic subjugation eventually creates a network of flows (muscular movements, nervous impulses and electric currents) channelled through circuits that can select, distribute, and transform disparate flows into money flows. If traders succeed in inserting their brains into the global financial network, they acquire an instinctive "feeling for the market" (Knorr Cetina and Bruegger 2002, p. 179). They learn to automatically 'know' how to react to the ebb and flow of financial markets. Buying and selling become a matter of intuition and split-second decisions where traders strike a connection with the market through the automated interactions between their bodily movements and computer algorithms (Borch, Hansen, and Lange 2015).

Platform companies, too, employ machinic subjugation to connect their workforce to their business operations. For a company like Uber, the world is a series of data streams to which its drivers have to respond correctly. As the only line of communication between the company and its users is an app, the app needs to have "an addictive interface design" (Scholz 2017, p. 162) to insert drivers' brains directly into the data flows visible to Uber's algorithms. Zuboff hence argues that contemporary businesses

> declare their right to modify others' behavior for profit according to methods *that bypass human awareness*, individual decision rights, and the entire complex of self-regulatory processes that we summarize with terms such as autonomy and self-determination.
>
> *(Zuboff 2019, p. 297; emphasis mine)*

Uber's app is endowed with nudge systems that pre-consciously steer drivers' behaviour (Rosenblat 2018, p. 135), exploiting psychological biases for company profits (Morozov 2017; Scheiber 2017; Kessler 2018, p. 103). Uber's forward dispatching system, for instance, is inspired by Netflix's automatic queuing system (Scheiber 2017), which encourages viewers to binge watch films by automatically suggesting and playing new material whenever the viewer finishes watching something. Because human brains are governed by inertia, it takes more effort for people to actively stop watching Netflix than it does to continue. Uber uses the same tactic with its drivers: by automatically suggesting new requests even before a driver has finished a job, the company wields the power of inertia to induce drivers to work longer. The forward dispatching system allows drivers to smoothly flow from one task to another like an inert object in a vacuum. The time for reflection and critical thought is here diminished. Human beings are consequently slowly transformed into automatised nodes in an assemblage of cars, customers, and traffic, governed by the platform's algorithms. "Technology has acquired an all-pervading potency, up to the point of its ability to grow independent from its human creators, and of deploying itself as a system of automatisms" (Berardi 2017, p. 58).

Human limits to growth

Given that machinic subjugation occurs in fields as diverse as gaming, finance, and the platform economy, it is not immediately obvious that it is politically problematic. However, Berardi's critique of connection, which emphasises the overburdening of the human brain, is an important contribution to this debate (Berardi 2011, p. 45; 2017, p. 53). The human mind and today's global assemblage of digital networks are fundamentally incompatible. With its abstract algorithmic modes of governance, platform capitalism is blind to human finitude. It slowly depletes the mental energy that fuels its operativity. Contemporary discourse celebrates the high-pace lifestyle of creative flexibility, entrepreneurial independence, and the passionate work ethic (Boltanski and Chiapello 2011; Rosa 2013; McRobbie 2016), but the reality of burnout and depression breaks through this ideological screen.[2]

One discerns an uncanny return of the problem of fatigue Marx identified in large-scale modern industry (Rabinbach 1992, p. 74; Wendling 2009, p. 78; Hardt and Negri 2017, pp. 131–132).

> In the first place, in the form of machinery, the implements of labour become automatic, things moving and working independent of the workman. They are henceforth an industrial *perpetuum mobile* that would go on producing forever, did it not meet with certain *natural obstructions in the weak bodies and the strong wills of its human attendants*. The automaton, as capital, and because it is capital, is endowed, in the person of the capitalist, with intelligence and will; it is therefore animated by the longing to reduce to a minimum *the resistance offered by that repellent yet elastic natural barrier, man.*
>
> *(Marx 1996, p. 406; emphasis mine)*

Marx suggests that industrial machinery would keep production running to infinity, were it not for the resistance from workers' weak bodies and strong wills. Most commentators focus on the latter, identifying resistance with workers becoming "a potentially powerful collective political force" of contestation (Harvey 2010, p. 226). But the weak bodies are not to be neglected. The "resistance" suggested in this passage has less to do with a confrontation of wills and more with the friction between a force and its medium. Just as physical objects can resist the conductance of electricity, human bodies can resist the self-propelling *élan* of large-scale production. Once bodies start dropping out, the automatic system must replace them with fresh bodies, or slow down the production process. The depletion of human potentiality puts a *physical limit* on the growth curve of industrial capitalism.

In the platform economy, the problem of fatigue returns in a new guise, as lasting mental exhaustion (Moulier Boutang 2011, p. 74; Crary 2013, p. 17; Scholz 2017, p. 67). It takes workers years to recover from a burnout or depression, if they ever do. Suicide from overwork has become a global phenomenon (Berardi 2015b, p. 167). Berardi rightly distances himself from authors like Negri, who mistakenly present the human potentiality for social cooperation as an infinite resource (2011, p. 46; 2017, p. 8). "Even if the general intellect is infinitely productive, the limits to growth are inscribed in the affective body of cognitive work: limits of attention, of psychic energy, of sensibility" (Berardi 2012, p. 77). If human potentiality is not replenished in due time, it runs out like most other natural resources. As long as there are enough people to replace the current workforce, however, platform companies are under no obligation to render the production process sustainable for their workers (Srnicek 2017, p. 77). They can burn through human potentiality like the global economy burns through its oil supply, as if there were no tomorrow. At Deliveroo, for instance, bikers sometimes try to make more money by cycling faster (Van Nieuwenhove 2017). They are paid per delivery, so completing more deliveries should equal higher pay. However, the algorithm takes the bikers' higher average speed for granted and sends them on longer trips. They have to keep cycling at this accelerated speed if they want to avoid an income decline. Doing one's job well is, in other words, 'rewarded' with more work for the same pay.

Not only physical energy but primarily mental well-being is depleted through platforms' connective biopolitics. To stay connected to the platform, workers continuously check their phones or computers. They are permanently "on call" for new tasks (Rosenblat 2018, p. 37) leading to generalised sleep deprivation (Crary 2013, 11; Scholz 2017, p. 120; Rosenblat 2018, p. 67). AMT workers report not daring to leave their computer for fear of missing out on profitable micro-tasks (Kessler 2018, pp. 75–76). They have to constantly pay attention to their computer screen to catch good gigs, even if "it is possible to contract a single worker anonymously for two or three minutes, paying her one or two cents or even nothing at all, and fire her right after a given task is done" (Scholz 2017, p. 114). The computer and smartphone become tools to fragment people's time into microscopic bits that the company mobilises at will (Berardi 2011, p. 35; 2015a, p. 206; 2015b, p. 140; O'Neil 2012, p. 123; Ciccarelli 2018, p. 23). Srnicek calls the platform economy a "market for day labourers" (Srnicek 2017, p. 78) but the situation is worse. Most workers are not hired for a full day, only for the performance of small, low-skilled tasks. "Workers offer their entire day to capital and are paid only for the moments when their time is made cellular" (Berardi 2009, p. 90). The entire notion of a preplanned day becomes impossible; instead, one is constantly in a state of alertness to quickly move in when the platform requires it (Berardi 2015a, p. 205; 2015b, p. 139). In infolabour, "[c]apital no longer recruits people, but buys packets of time, separated from their interchangeable and occasional bearers" (Berardi 2011, p. 90). Eventually however, workers can no longer keep up with the incessant pressure from push notifications, text messages, subconscious nudging, and the ultimately disappointing revenues. Machinic subjugation

> welcomes data on the behaviour of our blood and shit, but it has no interest in soiling itself with our excretions. It has no appetite for our grief, pain, or terror, although it eagerly welcomes the behavioural surplus that leaches from

our anguish. It is profoundly and infinitely indifferent to our meanings and motives.

(Zuboff 2019, p. 360)

If the platform economy's algorithmic infrastructure is indifferent to human needs and desires, while pushing for ever-more profits, the connection between humans and machines breaks down. "Cybertime (the time of attention, memory, and imagination) cannot speed beyond a limit. If it does, it cracks. And it is actually cracking, collapsing under the stress of hyperproductivity" (Berardi 2011, p. 55). Some individuals temporarily suppress this exhaustion with pills that fight fatigue and boost productivity, like Ritalin, Aderall, painkillers, or antidepressants (Scholz 2017, p. 114), which keep the human body inserted in the digital network of the platform. For the post-industrial *perpetuum mobile* to keep moving, its human elements need medical support. Ultimately, however, when the pressure to perform breaks through the "repellent yet elastic natural barrier" (Marx 1996, p. 406) of human mental potentiality, the mind devolves into a catatonic state commonly known as burnout. Mental resources have been depleted and what is left is a barren wasteland. At this point, the contradiction between finite concrete bodies and abstract algorithms' imperative toward infinite growth reaches its depressing climax.

Coda: toward the open platform

Fortunately, the dominance of digital biopolitics is not an inescapable fate, but a contingent and changeable affair (Berardi 2009, p. 63; Lazzarato 2015, p. 207; Hardt and Negri 2017, p. 221; Bastani 2019, p. 186). Just as platform companies have weaponised big data against their workforce, workers should not fear or hope, but look for new weapons. "We create technologies and suffer from them, renovate them and go beyond them. Instead of rejecting technology, then, we must start from within the technological and biopolitical fabric of our lives and chart from there a path of liberation" (Hardt and Negri and 2017, p. 107). One opportunity here lies with cooperative platforms owned, not by corporations in Silicon Valley, but by workers themselves (Scholz 2017, p. 2; Srnicek 2017, p. 128) where big data can be used to empower workers' collective autonomy (Scholz 2017, p. 181). A more emancipatory mobilisation of big data uses data extraction and analysis to allow workers to coordinate their actions more efficiently. There is nothing inherently wrong with an app like Uber allotting drivers to people looking for a ride. Problematic are the surreptitious means of behavioural modification managing workers' behaviour by bypassing their conscious awareness and mobilising their neurological and psychological weaknesses against them. In cities like Denver and Newark, taxi drivers and unions have started developing their own apps to undermine Uber (Scholz 2017, p. 178). This allows them to optimise the efficiency of their service without sacrificing their own mental and physical well-being.[3] In the vocabulary of Simondon, initiatives like these imagine platforms as "open objects"[4]

90 Tim Christaens

(Simondon 2014, pp. 312–313). Simondon uses the priory of Sainte-Marie De La Tourette near Lyon, designed by Le Corbusier, as a paradigm. The priory was built as a set of concrete blocks, but the exact contours of the building are permanently revisable. Le Corbusier designed the priory, according to Simondon, as an open platform for human creativity and the autonomy of its inhabitants. He only provided 'a starters' package'; it is up to future generations to adapt the building to their own needs. While buildings are usually designed as 'closed objects', where the architect fixes the contours and layout of the building, Le Corbusier's priory of Sainte-Marie De La Tourette is an open space for the creative self-organisation of its inhabitants, up for continuous democratic renegotiation.

Likewise, in *The Role of the Reader*, Eco observes that contemporary composers write music that leaves considerable freedom to its performers (Eco 1984, pp. 47–66). Beethoven's symphonies or Bach's fugues may have been open for multiple interpretations, but the works themselves are fixed. Berio's *Sequence for Solo Flute*, on the contrary, predetermines the sequence and intensity of the musical notes, but not their duration. Berio's work renders composition a collaborative effort between the composer and a multitude of performers. Every time Berio's *Sequence for Solo Flute* is played, it is not just a different interpretation of the same composition, but an essentially new and unique composition. There is no 'primordial' composition that acts as an anchor to the infinite iteration of its performances. There is only the 'starters' package', so to speak.

Digital technologies, and algorithms in particular, are too often designed as 'closed objects'. Just as in traditional music, the original programmer writes the score while users execute pre-established commands. We cannot reconfigure an Apple iPhone, Uber's pricing algorithm, Google's PageRank software, or even Facebook's terms and conditions. However, the algorithms underlying the operations of platform companies could and should become vehicles for workers' collective self-organisation. Instead of delivering finished products, platform providers should produce basic protocols that allow people to code their own work schedule. "Not only must the code be accessible to the workers so that they can understand the parameters and patterns that govern their working environment, the software also needs to be developed in consultation with the workers from day one" (Scholz 2017, p. 187). Examples like the taxi apps in Denver and Newark provide a paradigm for this operation. Instead of allowing their work to be organised via Uber's algorithms according to Uber's standards, they use open-source protocols to create a taxi company according to their own needs and goals. If platform companies made their software open source, platform software could become a vehicle for social emancipation instead of machinic subjugation. Allowing workers to govern their own platforms will not only deliver the entrepreneurial freedom today's platforms misleadingly promise, it will also provide a safety valve against the irremediable depletion of human potentiality.

Notes

1 Most platforms call their providers 'independent contractors' instead of employees, to avoid labour regulations (Scholz 2017, p. 44; Kessler 2018, p. 7; Mezzadra and Neilson 2019,

p. 81). It is, however, hard to see how individuals could be independent entrepreneurs if they cannot set their own prices, cannot decline requests without punishment, can be instantly 'deactivated' without the possibility of appeal. Platform workers are rather 'para-subordinate workers' (Moulier Boutang 2011, p. 142). The power-relation between employer and employee does not disappear but is depersonalised by a seemingly neutral digital infrastructure.

2 Different kinds of platform workers ought to be distinguished here. Whereas university students or middle-class families are hardly inconvenienced by digital biopolitics (Rosenblat 2018, p. 52) and migrant, disabled, or transgender workers could even be considered empowered by new income opportunities (Scholz 2017, p. 29; Rosenblat 2018, p. 54), research suggests that the more dependent individuals are on irregular gig work and the longer their hours, the higher the chances of overwork, mental stress, and the illnesses that sometimes follow (Gross et al. 2018; Wood, Graham et al. 2019). Rosenblat (2018, p. 50) hence distinguishes between three types of platform workers: hobbyists, part-time workers, and full-time workers, to locate most of the problems associated with platform capitalism in the third type.

3 The challenge for these open source initiatives would obviously be to avoid what Paolo Virno calls "the communism of capitalism" (2004, p. 110), that is, the initial promotion and subsequent capture of bottom-up instances of workers' self-organisation by platform companies. Google, for instance, released its Android operating system in 2008 as an open source platform where individual users could independently create and diffuse their own apps (Dyer-Witheford, Kjösen, and Steinhoff 2019, pp. 54–56; Zuboff 2019, pp. 132–134). The underlying motivation for Google's generosity was, however, that the corporation secretly collected data generated on these apps. Seemingly autonomous users were hence unknowingly creating supply routes for Google's private databanks.

4 I owe this comparison to Johannes Schick.

References

Althusser L 1995, *Sur la Reproduction*. Paris: Presses Universitaires de France.
Bastani A 2019, *Fully Automated Luxury Communism*. London: Verso Books.
Berardi 'Bifo' F 2009, *The Soul at Work*, trans. Cadel F and Mecchia G. Los Angeles, CA: Semiotext(e).
Berardi 'Bifo' F 2011, *After the Future*. trans. Bove A, Cooper M, Empson E, Enrico, Mecchia G, and Terranova T. Edinburgh: AK Press.
Berardi 'Bifo' F 2012, *The Uprising: On Poetry and Finance*. Los Angeles, CA: Semiotext(e).
Berardi 'Bifo' F 2015a, *And: Phenomenology of the End*. Los Angeles, CA: Semiotext(e).
Berardi 'Bifo' F 2015b, *Heroes: Mass Murder and Suicide*. London: Verso Books.
Berardi 'Bifo' F 2017, *Futurability: The Age of Impotence and the Horizon of Possibility*. London: Verso Books.
Berardi 'Bifo' F 2018, *The Second Coming*. Cambridge: Polity Press.
Boltanski L and Chiapello E 2011, *Le Nouvel Esprit du Capitalisme*. Paris: Gallimard.
Borch C, Hansen CB and Lange A-C 2015, "Markets, Bodies, and Rhythms: A Rhythmanalysis of Financial Markets from Open-Outcry Trading to High-Frequency Trading", *Environment and Planning D: Society and Space*, vol. 33, no. 6, pp. 1080–1097.
Christiaens T 2016, "Digital Subjectivation and Financial Markets: Criticizing Social Studies of Finance with Lazzarato", *Big Data & Society*, vol. 3, no. 2, pp. 1–15.
Ciccarelli R 2018, *Forza Lavoro*. Rome: DeriveApprodi.
Crary J 2013, *24/7*. London: Verso Books.

Deleuze G and Guattari F 1972, *L'Anti-Oedipe*. Paris: Editions de Minuit.

Dyer-Witheford N, Kjösen AM, and Steinhoff J 2019, *Inhuman Power: Artificial Intelligence and the Future of Capitalism*. London: Pluto Press.

Eco U 1984, *The Role of the Reader*. Bloomington, IN: Indiana University Press.

Gross S-A et al. 2018, *Well-Being and Mental Health in the Gig Economy: Policy Perspectives on Precarity*. London: University of Westminster Press.

Hardt M and Negri A 2001, *Empire*. Cambridge, MA: Harvard University Press.

Hardt M and Negri A 2017, *Assembly*. Oxford: Oxford University Press.

Harvey D 2010, *A Companion to Marx's Capital*. London: Verso Books.

Jaeggi R 2014, *Alienation*, trans. Neuhouser F and Smith AE. New York: Columbia University Press.

Kessler S 2018, *Gigged*. London: Penguin.

Kitchin R 2014, *The Data Revolution*. London: SAGE Books.

Knorr Cetina K and Bruegger H 2002, "Traders' Engagement with Markets: A Postsocial Relationship", *Theory, Culture & Society*, vol. 19, nos. 5–6, pp. 161–185.

Lazzarato M 2014, *Signs and Machines*, trans. Jordan JD. Los Angeles, CA: Semiotext(e).

Lazzarato M 2015, *Governing by Debt*, trans. Jordan JD. Los Angeles, CA: Semiotext(e).

MacKenzie D 1984, "Marx and the Machine", *Technology and Culture*, vol. 25, no. 3, pp. 473–502.

MacKenzie D 2009, *Material Markets*. Oxford: Oxford University Press.

Marx K 1996, *Capital, Volume 1*, trans. Moore S and Aveling E. London: Lawrence & Wishart.

Massumi B 2011, *Semblance and Event*. Cambridge, MA: MIT Press.

McRobbie A 2016, *Be Creative*. Cambridge: Polity Press.

Mezzadra S and Neilson B 2019, *The Politics of Operations: Excavating Contemporary Capitalism*. Durham, NC: Duke University Press.

Morozov E 2017, February 19, "So you Want to Switch off Digitally? I'm Afraid that Will Cost you", *The Guardian*. Available from: www.theguardian.com/commentisfree/2017/feb/19/right-to-disconnect-digital-gig-economy-evgeny-morozov [accessed 13 April 2020].

Moulier Boutang Y 2011, *Cognitive Capitalism*, trans. Emery E. Cambridge: Polity Press.

O'Neil C 2012, *Weapons of Math Destruction*. London: Penguin Books.

Prahalad C and Ramaswamy V 2000, "Co-opting Costumer Competence", *Harvard Business Review*, vol. 78, no. 1, pp. 79–87.

Rabinbach A 1992, *The Human Motor*. Berkeley, CA: University of California Press.

Rosa H 2013, *Social Acceleration: A New Theory of Modernity*, trans. Trejo-Mathys J. New York: Columbia University Press.

Rosenblat A 2018, *Uberland*. Oakland, CA: University of California Press.

Scheiber N 2017, "How Uber Pushes Drivers' Buttons", *New York Times*, April 3. Available from: www.nytimes.com/interactive/2017/04/02/technology/uber-drivers-psychological-tricks.html [accessed 13 April 2020].

Scholz T 2017, *Uberworked and Underpaid*. Cambridge: Polity Press.

Sennett R 1998, *The Corrosion of Character: The Personal Consequences of Work in the New Capitalism*. New York: Norton.

Simondon G 2014, "La Mentalité Technique", in Simondon G (ed.), *Sur la Technique*. Paris: Presses Universitaires de France, pp. 295–313.

Srnicek N 2017, *Platform Capitalism*. Cambridge: Polity Press.

Terranova T 2000, "Free Labor: Producing Culture for the Digital Economy", *Social Text*, vol. 18, no. 2, pp. 33–58.

Väliaho P 2014, "Video Games and the Cerebral Subject: On Playing Call of Duty: Modern Warfare 3", *Body & Society*, vol. 20, nos. 3&4, pp. 113–139.

Van Nieuwenhove J 2017, "Zo is het Werken voor Deliveroo", *VRT NWS*, 20 November. Available from: www.vrt.be/vrtnws/nl/2017/11/20/zo-is-het-werken-voor-deliveroo–hoe-sneller-ik-fiets–hoe-verd/ [accessed 13 April 2020].

Virno P 2004, *A Grammar of the Multitude*, trans. Bertoletti I, Cascaito J, and Casson A. Los Angeles, CA: Semiotext(e).

Virno P 2015, *When the Word Becomes Flesh*, trans. Mecchia G. Los Angeles, CA: Semiotext(e).

Wendling A 2009, *Karl Marx on Technology and Alienation*. Basingstoke: Palgrave Macmillan.

Wood A, Graham M et al. 2019, "Good Gig, Bad Gig: Autonomy and Algorithmic Control in the Global Gig Economy", *Work, Employment and Society*, vol. 33, no. 1, pp. 56–75.

Zaloom C 2010, *Out of the Pits*. Chicago, IL: University of Chicago Press.

Zuboff S 2019, *The Age of Surveillance Capitalism*. London: Profile Books

6

APPRECIATING MACHINE-GENERATED ARTWORK THROUGH DEEP LEARNING MECHANISMS

Lonce Wyse

Introduction

Understanding art involves far more than engaging with the surface level representation. Our appreciation is enriched by situating a work historically as well as by interrogating the process, methodologies, and intentions of the artist, even if we never arrive at definitive interpretations. These ideas have been theorised in many different ways and contexts (from Plato's notion of art as mimetic representation of nature to Dickie's valuation through institutional structures and Gel's theorisations of artworks as social mediators), all of which explore the ways in which meaning making extends beyond the artwork *per se*. The rich connections an artwork has beyond itself are exactly what is severed by Turing test derivatives applied to art. Turing devised the famous 'imitation game', now commonly referred to as the Turing test, as a way to approach the question: can machines think?, a question impossibly complicated by the different ways people understand what it means to think. Turing replaced that question with a close proxy, which asks whether the difference between a human and a computer can be recognised by a human judge communicating with the two agents through written messages. An obvious critique of this operationalisation is that the connection to the original question is lost due to the hermetic communication channel. In the context of art and creativity, the Turing test has been recast to identify a programme as creative if a human cannot tell the difference between human- and machine-generated artwork (Boden 2010). However, this approach is not helpful for understanding machine art as it severs the rich connections beyond the artefact itself that contribute to the usual process of artistic meaning making.

Figure 6.1 is an image that we may interpret aesthetically. However, our understanding and appreciation of the image depends on knowing whether it was created by nature, painted by an artist, or photographed for an exhibition of found

FIGURE 6.1 *Woman in Wood* 2017.

Source: Photo by Lonce Wyse. © Creative Commons

objects. We are impressed when we find out that the work was not created by a human and perhaps even more so if we have botanical knowledge of how trees live and grow. In this chapter, I explore deep learning systems that generate art and demonstrate qualities that, when recognised in humans, are thought of as creative. The emergence of art-making behaviour through machine learning rather than explicit programming invites anthropomorphic interpretation. However, my goal is to shed light on the *mechanisms* responsible for this behaviour rather than on their status relative to human creativity. In other words, the goal is to deepen the set of conceptual tools at our disposal to understand and appreciate a work of art at the nexus of the context from which it emerges rather than how it appears. The question is thus not whether machines possess authentic human creativity (they do not), but, rather, why and how they can seem to.

Five different types of generative process will be examined. Each makes its own connection to what we think of as creative, however a few related themes run through the analysis of all of them that help establish this connection. For example, one is that with neural networks, behaviours emerge from the interaction of simple units rather than being explicitly programmed. The analogy from brain to machine suggests the mapping of human qualities. Another theme is that the machinery considered here is built for purposes other than the creative characteristics it exhibits; repurposing at the mechanistic level plays a key role in generating the novelty associated with machine creativity. Yet another theme woven through the generative processes explored below is the critical dependence of generative capabilities on sensing and categorical perception, a dependence that is prevalent in human creativity as well.

Computational creativity

Deep Learning neural networks are notorious for their opacity. We know exactly what is happening at the level of activations and weighted connections between the millions of nodes that may comprise a network, but we are lacking in the analytical tools that would provide human-understandable explanations for decisions or behaviour at the macro level. With neural networks, complex behaviours emerge out of the simple interaction between potentially millions of units that are loosely analogous to brain cells. Only the interaction between cells is programmed, not the high-level behaviour such as recognising a cat in an image. The architectures and unit-level learning algorithms in combination with exposure to data for training allow the networks to configure themselves to exhibit behaviours ranging from classification to media generation. The architectural configurations, such as the connections between units and the behaviours comprised of equations for the activity level of cells, are the mechanisms that will be used to explain capabilities that appear akin to human creativity. When behaviours are emergent rather than explicitly programmed, then their 'hidden' nature is not just a methodological choice for framing a definition or establishing criteria for creativity. Understanding how they work requires scientific investigation and is less likely to diminish our appreciation of their behaviour than the unveiling of a piece of computer code that explicitly generates a specific creative behaviour.

The emergent nature itself of neural network mechanisms is relevant to current trains of thought in the Computational Creativity community of researchers, theorists, and artists. Bodily and Ventura suggest that an autonomous aesthetic, not programmed by a designer, is fundamental to creative systems (Bodily and Ventura 2018). Neural networks also foreground the relationship between perception and generation that has deep roots in psychology. Flowers and Garbin, for example, explore connections between the way scientists and artists organise and analyse sensory information and its relationship to the novelty they produce (Flowers and Garbin 1989). This has sometimes been neglected in classical AI approaches to programming generative systems that focus primarily on *output processes*. Generative neural networks create media based on the same mechanisms that are configured during training on input data from the same domain. That is, the very same cells whose behaviour was modified by learning in response to perceptual input – images of a cat, for example – participate in determining the output during creative generation – of, say, cat-like beasts. Mechanisms are also interesting in complex systems because of the way a particular mechanism can play a role in different kinds of behaviour. The mechanism that allows a system to see edges across luminance contrast – between squares on a checkerboard – may also cause illusions in response to particular stimuli, such as 'imagining' edges where there are none. Similarly, learning mechanisms that support generalisation from scant evidence might enable taking reasonable novel action under unseen conditions in one context, such as never biting into another lemon after that first time, but be recognised as biased decision-making when deployed in an inappropriate context, such as depriving yourself of great musical experiences because of that one experimental piece that tortured you. In this chapter, mechanisms in deep learning architectures that give rise to the following five characteristics associated with creativity are explored: transformative perception; synthesis of different domains; sentiment recognition and synthesis; analogic and metaphorical reasoning; and abstraction. No definition of creativity is attempted or necessary, nor are any claims made about whether the mechanisms discussed are authentically creative in the human sense of the word. Instead, anthropomorphic terms are given mechanistic explanations.

Fundamentals

A brief review on the basics of neural networks will provide useful reference points for discussions of various mechanisms of machine creativity. Neural network units are loosely modelled on biological neurons. They have an activation level analogous to a firing rate in a neuron, and connections to other neurons, analogous to neural synapses, as can be seen from Figure 6.2. The activity of a neuron contributes to the tendency of another to fire through a function of the strength of the connection, commonly referred to as the weight. Learning in neural networks is nothing but the adjustment of these weights.

In deep learning network architectures, neurons are arranged in layers, and are connected through synaptic weights to neurons in the next (deeper) layer (Figure 6.3). Layers can be 'fully connected' so that every unit in one layer connects to every unit in the next layer, or, as in the standard convolutional neural network (CNN), take input from a localised region of the previous layer.

The input (an image, for example) is connected to the first, or shallowest layer, and the output is connected to the deepest layer. When an input is presented, the

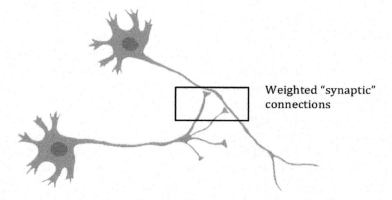

FIGURE 6.2 In a simplified model of neurons, units have activation levels that influence others through weighted connections. Changing the weights constitutes learning.

Source: Figure by Lonce Wyse. © Creative Commons

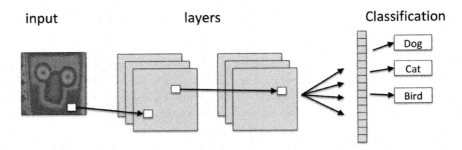

FIGURE 6.3 Each layer is connected to a region of cells in the previous layer and specific cells in the last layer are associated with categories.

Source: Figure by Lonce Wyse. © Creative Commons

network layers multiply the units in the image or previous layers by the weights of their connections, and take on an activation level as a (typically non-linear) function of the weighted connections. With classification networks, for example, we can interpret each output unit to represent a different class, and identify the maximally activated unit as the class assigned to the input by the network. During supervised training, the output of the network is compared to what is referred to as the 'true' class label. If the network output is different from the training label, we compute the difference as an error, and go back through the network, changing the weights to make the true label a little more likely the next time the same input is presented, in a process called back propagation. Networks can have anywhere from a few to hundreds of layers, billions of connections (weights); large networks can classify millions of images into thousands of categories with almost perfect accuracy.

Transformative perception

"Make it new" is a phrase poet Pound canonised (Pound 1935), referring to a transformative way of seeing that emerged at the heart of the Modernist artistic process. Can neural networks see the world in a unique way based on their own individual exposure and interaction with the world and share their vision with others? In an attempt to understand and characterise what the units and layers are actually computing in terms of the input, a procedure known as activation maximisation has been developed (Erhan et al. 2009; Nguyen et al. 2016). This method is very similar to those used to probe human neural response characteristics. Hidden units are monitored, and the input images are manipulated in order to amplify the response patterns of particular individual or ensembles of units. Systematic exploitation of this idea yielded one of the most prominent image-generating deep-learning systems to attract widespread attention beyond the research community – the DeepDream network (Mordvintsev, Olah, and Tyka 2015). The manipulated images produced in the service of understanding response characteristics of network units turned out to be striking for their hallucinogenic and dream-like character, and thus an artistic generative technique was born.

Architectures such as the DeepDream network also afford a systematic way to 'parametrically' control certain characteristics of the images generated in this way. It turns out (again in a loose analogy to the way the human brain is structured), that peripheral layers tend to respond to 'low level' features such as edges, while units in deeper layers tend to respond to 'higher-order' features such as spatial relationships between lower level feature patterns. As deeper layers are probed, the nodes respond to what we recognise as semantic features. When images are manipulated to maximise the activation level of a particular hidden unit (or ensemble), the results are dependent on the specific nodes and layers being probed. Images manipulated to maximise activity in peripheral layer nodes yield edge (and other low-level feature) enhancements (Figure 6.4, row 1), while images manipulated to maximise the response of units in deeper layers reveal patterns related to the objects that the networks were trained to categorise at their output (Figure 6.4, row 2). This example illustrates the close relationship between the perceptual and generative capabilities of this kind of deep learning architecture. The novelty in the generated image arises from the technique of exploiting the knowledge in weighted connections learnt during perceptual training on input images in order to 'read into' the peripheral image during generation. This machinic process of apophenia – seeing patterns where there

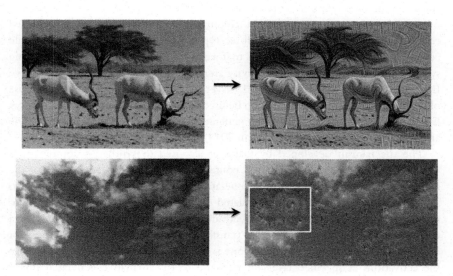

FIGURE 6.4 Top: One of the original images presented to the DeepDream network, and the image systemmatically transformed to enhance highly activated nodes in a peripheral layer. Bottom: An original and a transformed image that enhance highly activated nodes in a deep layer. Inset: A zoomed section of the transformed image.

Source: Images by Mordvintsev et al. 2015, modified with inset. © Creative Commons

are none – has been cast as a pathological tendency of neural nets to be biased by interpreting their environments based on their previous exposure to data rather than interpreting them objectively (Apprich 2018). Steyerl recognises the creative dimension of apophenia, which can be seen as a cross-domain synthesis between a specific input image and images previously seen and learned (Steyerl 2018).

Cross-domain synthesis

In many works of art across a variety of genres, there is a recognisable distinction between content and style. Content is identified with the subject matter, semantics, or indexical referencing while style refers to the choice of media and techniques reflective of the process of production or individual perspective. Style is further associated with time periods, art movements, and individual artists. Vermeer's 1665 *Girl with a Pearl Earring* and Picasso's 1937 *Portrait of Dora Maar* may both be portraits, but each brings a unique perspective to the subject matter through the styles associated with each painter and their times. Likewise, the Beatles' song *Yesterday* has been adapted thousands of times, and although the lyrics, chords, and melody are essentially the same, the crooning of Presley and the *a cappella* version by Boyz II Men afford entirely different musical experiences with their different renderings. Content and style (in certain, albeit not all, art genres) are independent in the sense that any style can be combined with any content, and their combination considered a 'synthesis' across domains. Synthesis is considered as a component of creativity across numerous fields including visual psychology. Boden identified combinational creativity as one of three types of creativity (Boden 2004) while conceptual blending is an approach to formal computational models addressing synthesis in the computational creativity arena (Pereira and Cardoso 2003). Gatys, Ecker, and Bethge showed that the 19-layer VGG-Network, trained to recognise objects, learns representations that can be used to separate content from style (Gatys, Ecker, and Bethge 2016) and for the generation of arbitrary combinations of style and content (Simonyan and Zisserman 2014).

The mechanism developed by Gatys et al., used to synthesise combinations of style from one specific image, and content from another, is reminiscent of the DeepDream network. During the generative process, an image is presented to the network and then slowly manipulated through the back propagation of error through the network until it causes activations of the hidden layers to achieve a certain objective. In the case of style transfer, however, the objective function for computing error comes in two parts: one is the content objective, which is to have the activations at specified layers in response to the formative generated image match the values of those same units in response to the original content image; and the second is the style objective. However, rather than trying to achieve a match with actual activation levels of specific hidden layers resulting from the style source image and the generated image, the input is manipulated until there is a match of a statistical measure derived from patterns of activation. The objective based on this second order measure – known as a Gram matrix – maintains correlations between

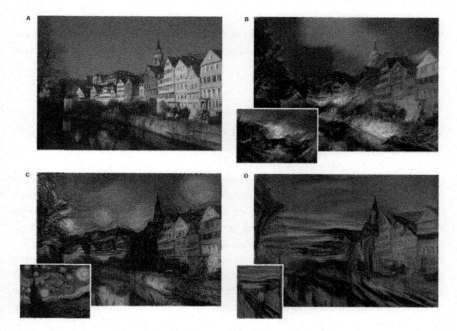

FIGURE 6.5 (A) Original photo by Andreas Praefcke rendered in the styles from (B) *The Shipwreck of the Minotaur* by J.M.W Turner, 1805, (C) *The Starry Night* by Vincent van Gogh, 1889, and (D) *Der Schrei* by Edvard Munch, 1893.

Source: © Gatys, Ecker, and Bethge 2016. Courtesy of Gatys, Ecker, and Bethge

features but is independent of their spatial location in the 2D representation of the image at the given layers. This measure of statistical correlation between features aligns very closely (although not always completely) with our sense of painterly style, as can be seen in the images in Figure 6.5.

Similar architectures have been shown to work on audio represented as a 2D spectrogram image (Ulyanov and Lebedev 2016[1]) although the results are not as compelling in the audio domain as they are in the visual domain (Shahrin and Wyse 2019). Both Ustyuzhaninov et al. (2016) and Ulyanov and Lebedev (2016) have reported a fascinating aspect of this technique of cross-domain synthesis: it makes little difference whether or not the network was trained before being used for generation. A shallow network with untrained (randomised) weights can achieve similarly convincing blends of style and content from different spectral images. That is, the architecture itself, along with the statistical style measure, and the dual style-plus-content objective function, are sufficient for this process of cross-domain synthesis. Note that the link between perceptual (input) process and generation is still present in this architecture because image generation is achieved through the back propagation of error through the same network that responds to image input. Although we might not recognise the process as apophenia without the influence

Sentiment

While sentiment, emotion, and affect are not generally considered as defining creativity (Forgas 2000; Boden 2004) they are certainly associated with motivations, processes, and reception of creative artistic works. Human social communication is not merely an exchange of information. Emotion and sentiment are sometimes communicated explicitly – through emojis, for example – but more often implicitly through the tone of voice or nonverbal cues such as facial expressions. Computational perceptual systems can perform like humans if they can read those cues in faces, tone of voice, and language usage. The automatic or parametric control of systems to induce particular emotional responses has been the focus of some generative games (Freeman 2004), and music (Livingston et al. 2007). Picard's approach to affective computing was about imbuing computers with the ability to express, recognise, and exhibit emotional behaviour such as happiness, anger, fear, and surprise (Picard 2000). One way to make deep neural network (DNN) architectures capable of both categorisation and generation of affect would be simply to start with a massive data set tagged with affective labels of emotions and sentiment – happy, sad, bored, or apprehensive – for supervised training, and hope that there is statistical consistency in the data that the machine can detect. There are systems that develop a sensitivity to emotional cues in language without being explicitly trained to do so. One such story starts with a Recurrent Neural Network (RNN) trained to generate natural language reviews of products based on images. RNNs lend themselves to learning and generating sequential data such as speech (Graves, Mohamed, and Hinton 2013), music (Eck and Schmidhuber 2002), and text (Karpathy 2015). Data is typically streamed as input to the network one token at a time – for example, characters from the text of a product review – possibly along with 'conditioning' input, such as data from images of products, and the system learns to predict the next character in a sequence.

An RNN can be run in two phases. The first is training with the target output provided by the 'teacher' while the network adjusts weights (along each of the arrows in Figure 6.6), and the other is generation when, after learning, the system produces the next token (in this case a character) in the sequence at the output. During generation, each output token is in turn fed back into the network as the input for prediction at the next step. Karpathy interpreted creative capabilities of character-generating RNNs (Karpathy 2015) while Radford, Jozefowicz, and Sutskever were interested in studying what kinds of internal language representations an RNN learns in order to accomplish its predictive task (Radford, Jozefowicz, and Sutskever (2017). Specifically, they wondered if the learnt representation would disentangle high-level concepts such as sentiment – emotional valence

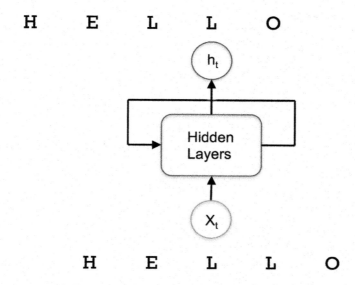

FIGURE 6.6 An RNN with recurrent connections training to predict a sequence of characters. The output (top) predicts the next character given the input (bottom), one character per time step.

Source: Figure by Lonce Wyse. © Creative Commons

and semantic relatedness – connections between concepts based on their meaning. They approached the problem as a 'transfer learning' paradigm where training on one task, such as character prediction, is used as a starting point for learning a different task, for example, sentiment identification. Radford et al. first trained their predictive system on Amazon product reviews. After training, the RNN can be run in generative mode using each predicted character output in the sequence as input at the next time step. It thereby learns to spin text resembling product reviews. They then considered the trained network as a language model. To test whether the language model internally represents recognisable high-level concepts, a separate linear classifier was trained on the state of the penultimate hidden layer activations during and after processing a product review. Taking sentiment as a particular example, a linear classifier was trained to map this input to the externally provided (supervised) 'positive' or 'negative' assessment, where 'positive' indicates that the language used in the review reflected the reviewer's favourable impression of the product, and 'negative' indicates language reflecting an unfavourable impression. The performance of the linear classifier is interpreted as the measure of how well the concept, or in this case, sentiment was captured by the original predictive RNN in the representation of the review. It was discovered that not only was the network able to achieve state-of-the-art performance on rating reviews as positive or negative (compared with networks that had been fully trained specifically for that task), it was also noticed that a single node in the representation was responsible

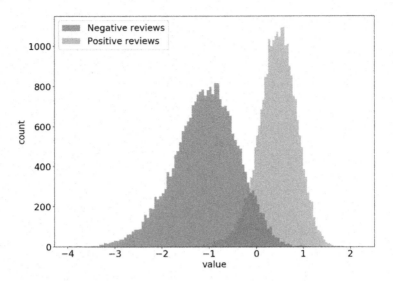

FIGURE 6.7 The activation of a single unit in the penultimate layer of a predictive RNN shows a clear bimodal activation pattern corresponding to the sentiment of the review.

Source: © Radford, Jozefowicz, and Sutskever 2017. Courtesy of Radford, Jozefowicz, and Sutskever 2017

for the decision about sentiment. That is, the RNN that was trained only to generate successive characters in a review learnt its own 'model' of sentiment as the value of a single node in the network. The activation response of that node shows a very clear bimodal distribution, depending on the actual sentiment of the review, as can be seen from Figure 6.7.

The unsupervised character-level training also provides insight into another important dimension of creative computation in deep learning architectures – the ability of such systems to learn for themselves what aspects of an unstructured environment are significant. The system discovered the value of the sentiment representation, or learning node activation patterns, for this purpose, the meaning of which is grounded only in its own predictive learning task that was separate from an explicit sentiment detection task. Furthermore, the sentiment node can be utilised parametrically in the generative phase of the RNN. By 'clamping' it to a value representing the negative or positive assessment and letting the RNN run its character-by-character review synthesis, the reviews it constructs can be clearly recognised as having the desired sentiment characteristic despite all the other variations in a product review. This can be seen from the excerpts of sentences generated by the same trained network while holding the identified 'sentiment node' fixed at its positive value: "Just what I was looking for …", and at its negative value: "The package received was blank and has no barcode. A waste of time and money" (Radford, Jozefowicz, and Sutskever 2017, np.).

Analogy and metaphor

As early as 1725, philosopher Vico recognised, in *The New Science*, the role of metaphor as the foundation of language, reasoning that figurative language precedes literal language and that the meaning of words only becomes fixed through convention (Vico 2000 [1725]). Metaphor and the kindred analogical reasoning are creative because they involve constructing new meaning out of established knowledge – understanding and experiencing one thing in terms of another (Lakoff and Johnson 2008). Some three hundred years after Vico, word2vec models (Mikolov et al. 2013) took a bold step in the field of language modelling to represent words based only on the context (consisting of other words) in which they appear in language use. The representation itself has a structure with geometrical properties that support analogical reasoning. Some sort of vector representation of words is typically used to feed input to neural networks. One way to motivate and understand the word2vec strategy is to start from a 'one-hot' baseline representation. A one-hot representation is a vector with a length equal to the number of possible different items to be represented. In this case, that length is equal to the number of words in the vocabulary. Each word is represented with a '1' in its unique position in the vector, and '0's elsewhere. For example, for two particular words we might have:

scary: ... 0, 0, 0, 0, 0, 0, 0, 0, 0, 0, 0, 0, 0, 0, 1, 0, 0, 0, 0, 0, ...
dog: ... 0, 0, 1, 0, 0, 0, 0, 0, 0, 0, 0, 0, 0, 0, 0, 0, 0, 0, 0, 0, ...

The advantage of one-hot coding is the direct dictionary-like mapping between the vector and the word. However, two issues are immediately apparent. One is the inefficiency of a vocabulary-length vector for each word. The other issue is that the representation does not capture any of the structure that might be inherent in the data, such as semantic relatedness or syntactic similarities. To address at least the first problem, a "distributed" code would be much more memory efficient, decreasing the length of each vector, but having more non-zero values in the vector for each word. A typical way to reduce the dimension of a representation for neural networks is to train an 'autoregressive' neural network to learn a reduced representation. An autoregressive neural network simply learns to reproduce its input at the output, but has a hidden layer that is of a much lower dimension than the input and output dimensions. By training the network to reproduce all the one-hot representations, the activations in a hidden layer (usually referred to as an 'embedding' in the literature) can be interpreted as a new compact distributed representation for the words. The autoregressive network can then function as the encoder (mapping one-hot to distributed representations) to produce the code for use in other neural network tasks and architectures, and as a decoder (mapping the distributed representation back to the one-hot representation to retrieve the human-readable word).

If it were possible to additionally endow the compact distributed codes with some sense of the meanings of the words, then the representation might further assist the networks that will be doing the language processing. The word2vec 'Continuous

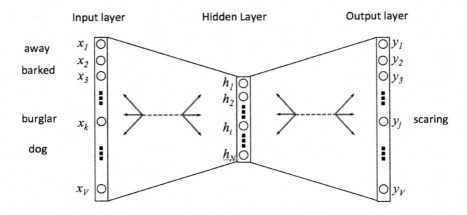

FIGURE 6.8 Training a compact distributed representation (the hidden layer) of the word "scaring" using contexts in which the target word appears.

Source: Figure by Lonce Wyse. © Creative Commons

Bag of Words' (CBOW) technique uses the same idea as the autoencoder for reducing dimension, but instead of learning to map just the single word to itself, it learns to map all n-word sequences in a database that surround the target word to the word itself at the output (Figure 6.8). For example, 'The dog barked scaring the burglar away' and 'The child enjoyed scaring neighbours on Halloween' would be two of the (very many) contexts containing 'scaring' that would be used to learn to produce the word 'scaring' at the output. It is easy to construct the input to train the representations just by adding the one-hot vectors of the context words together. No sense of ordering is preserved, hence the derivation of the name of the CBOW technique from 'bag of words'.

The encoding and decoding function is preserved by this training strategy. However, now the hidden layer code for a given word not only indexes the individual word, but also embeds information about how the word is used in the language. This representation is beneficial for training neural networks on a wide variety of natural language tasks. But one of the most impressive demonstrations of the elegance of the representation comes from Mikolov et al. (2013). As an m-dimensional vector, the distributed representation of a word is a point in an m-dimensional space where m is much lower than the size of the vocabulary. The question is: does the data have interesting structure in this space, and if so, what kind of structure is it? It is probably of no surprise that words with similar semantics occupy nearby points in the representation space based on their similar usage patterns. For example, 'frightening' and 'scaring' show up in many of the same usage patterns. We can substitute one word for the other in the above example without drastically changing the meaning of the sentences. Because the contexts are similar, the hidden layer learns similar embedding representations. Simple vector mathematics can be used to explore whether vector operations have any interpretation in terms of the language. For example, taking the vector difference between the points that represent 'puppy' and 'dog' yields a vector that connects the two points and in some sense 'defines' their relationship. What Mikolov demonstrated is that these different vectors do have semantic meaning. It turns out that if we take the same vector that represents the difference between 'dog' and 'puppy', and place one endpoint on the point representing 'cat', the other endpoint lands near the point for 'kitten' (Figure 6.9). This ability of vector relationships to capture semantic relationships provides the means for having the system fill in the blanks for A::B as C::? (read 'A is to B as C is to what?') – a kind of analogical reasoning that provides a way to 'understand one thing in terms of another' in order to discover or create new meaning.

The network was not trained for this purpose explicitly, but it self-organises the given task of learning word representations based on usage context. Ha and Eck have done the same kind of vector math on latent vector representations for analogical generation in the domain of drawing images (Ha and Eck 2017). The Google Magenta group has also carried out similar work in the domain of music (Roberts et al. 2018).

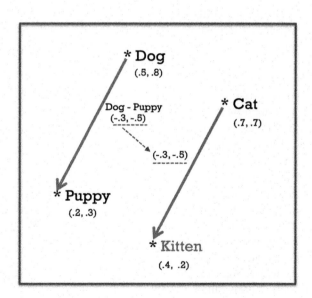

FIGURE 6.9 The vector between points representing Dog and Puppy, (-.3, -.5), when taken from the point representing Cat, points to the neighbourhood of Kitten.

Source: Figure by Lonce Wyse. (© Creative Commons)

Abstraction

Philosopher Buckner's study of deep convolutional neural networks (DCNN) mechanisms produced a notion of "transformation abstraction" (Buckner 2018). Buckner invites us to see that the layers, convolutions, and pooling mechanisms of DCNNs (as shown in Figure 6.3)

> jointly implement a form of hierarchical abstraction that reduces the complexity of a problem's feature space (and avoids overfitting the network's training samples) by iteratively transforming it into a simplified representational format that preserves and accentuates task-relevant features while controlling for nuisance variation.

For Bruckner, classification in DCNNs is thus identified as a process of abstraction.

In the realm of art, there are at least two types of images we call abstract. One is comprised of shapes, lines, and colours that are not readily identifiable as any real-world object. Examples include the cube and line 'neoplastic' paintings of Mondrian. A second kind of abstract image (not associated with the historical genre of Abstract Art) is comprised of some features that form the basis for an identification as a real-world object, but includes others that are generally not associated with the real-world object, and lacks many that are. Duchamp's 1912 painting *Nude Descending a Staircase No. 2* can be considered of this type. White's 2018 *Perception Engine* foregrounds the notion of abstraction as well as the role of perception in the generative process. One component of *Perception Engine* is an image generator constrained to generate combinations of curved lines and blobs. The other is a pre-trained classification network trained on many thousands of example images, each belonging to one of a large collection of labelled categories (e.g. electric fan, golf cart, basketball). The generator starts with a random combination of the shapes it is constrained to draw. It then iteratively manipulates the blobs and lines in the image in such a way as to increase the activation strength of a specific category in a classification network. Figure 6.10 shows an image generated in this way to maximise the 'hammerhead shark' category.

One interesting aspect of this work is that the generated images are very different from the images that were used to train the classification networks for a given category, such as hammerhead shark. The categories a network learns can be large or even infinite, as long as they separate the training examples properly. White's system explores and exposes regions of learned categories in the classifiers where no training examples were provided. The potentially infinite spaces of possible images that the categoriser classifies together are not apparent, given the typical means of testing networks with images 'similar' to the data it was trained on. The shapes of learned categorical regions can be surprising, and often confront researchers with serious challenges. For example, most trained classifiers, even those that appear to be accurate and generalise well on natural images, are subject to being fooled (Nguyen et al. 2016). The so-called adversarial examples (Szegedy et al. 2013) are derived

Machine-generated artwork 109

FIGURE 6.10 Tom White's, *Perception Engine* that gets classified as a hammerhead shark.
Source: Courtesy of Tom White. © Tom White

from images that would be classified correctly, but that are modified slightly in a way typically imperceptible to a human, sometimes by only a single pixel (Su et al. 2019), causing misclassification of the modified image. Adversarial image research focuses on images very near to classification boundaries – as little as one different pixel away – and reveals that the formation of categories with neural networks is very different from that of humans. White's system, on the other hand, explores the strange and wonderful high-dimensional spaces far from boundaries that the system has learned by generalising during training. The *Perception Engine* starts with an unidentifiable 'abstract' image (by virtue of its pallet and the randomness), and finishes with an abstract image that contains some local and/or structural features sufficient to generate strong categorical responses in the classifier, while entirely lacking others that real-world objects, including those used to train the networks, have. White states that "the system is expressing its knowledge of global structure independent of surface features or textures" (White 2018, np.) which aligns with the use of the term 'abstraction'. He has also shown that it is sometimes possible for humans to identify the same classification label as do the neural networks, or at least to be able to recognise features in the image that might have caused the neural network classification after its selection is known (as we do for the hammerhead shark example).[2] One of the most remarkable features of this system becomes apparent when the resulting generative works are shown to many different deep-learning classifiers that have been trained on the same real-world data. Despite their different network architectures, the different systems tend to make the same classifications on White's abstractions. That is, if one network classifies the *Perception Engine* blob-and-line drawing as a 'fan', then the image tends to strongly activate the same 'fan' category in other classifiers. Generalisation patterns in neural networks appear to be

110 Lonce Wyse

general. The synthetic images can sometimes even achieve category scores greater than human-labelled natural objects that were not used for training.

It is also interesting to consider the *Perception Engine* as a 'style' machine. The constraints, or 'artistic discipline' of the generator define a style in terms of the types of shapes and lines the system will use to construct images. The target categories – hammerhead shark, fan, cello, hair dryer – can be considered 'content', while a series of different drawings by the same *Perception Engine* generator would clearly be recognisable as having a consistent style due to the constrained palate of shapes and lines from which it draws.

Conclusion

Taken together, the mechanisms supporting the five different examples of behaviours associated with creativity reveal certain patterns. The behaviours exhibited by deep learning neural networks are not explicitly programmed, but, rather, *emerge* from the simple interaction programmed at the level of nodes and weights. Furthermore, many of the emergent mechanisms identified that serve creative purposes in generative networks arise during training on entirely different and often non-generative tasks: a classification task produced generalising capabilities exploited for abstract image synthesis (the *Perception Engine*); a prediction task led to a sentiment representation that afforded parametric control over affect in text generation (the product review system); and a representational efficiency lent itself to the ability to discover semantic relationships and construct analogies (word2vec). Although a wide variety of network types were considered here, they all use machinery designed for the perceptual processing of media. Some networks generated output using the exact same substrate used for perception, such as the DeepDream network, while others used separate, but intimately collaborating perceptual and generative systems, as did White's *Perception Engine*. Blaise Agüera y Arcas interprets Michelangelo's observation, that every block of stone contains a sculpture, to mean that "we create by perceiving and that perception itself is an act of imagination and is the stuff of creativity" (Blaise Agüera y Arcas 2016). The kinship between human and machinic creativity at this level of description is striking and motivates further research into the distinctly non-human mechanisms that can give rise to such activity, as well as new ways of appreciating their creations.

Acknowledgements

This research was supported by a Singapore MOE Tier 2 grant, "Learning Generative and Parameterized Interactive Sequence Models with Recurrent Neural Networks", (MOE2018-T2-2–127), and by an NVIDIA Corporation Academic Programs GPU grant. This chapter is a modified version of the paper, "Mechanisms of Artistic Creativity in Deep Learning Neural Networks", presented at the International Conference on Computational Creativity, 2019.

Notes

1 Audio examples can be found here: https://dmitryulyanov.github.io/audio-texture-synthesis-and-style-transfer/.
2 See https://medium.com/@tom_25234/synthetic-abstractions-8f0e8f69f390 for more examples generated by White's Perception Engine.

References

Agüera y Arcas B 2016, "How Computers are Learning to be Creative". [Video]. Available from: www.ted.com/talks/blaise_aguera_y_arcas_how_computers_are_learning_to_be_creative? [accessed 24 November 2019]

Apprich C 2018, "Data Paranoia: How to Make Sense of Pattern Discrimination", in Apprich C et al. (eds.), *Pattern Discrimination*. London and Minneapolis, MN: Meson Press and University of Minnesota Press.

Boden MA 2004, *The Creative Mind: Myths and Mechanisms*. London: Routledge.

Boden MA 2010, "The Turing Test and Artistic Creativity", *Kybernetes*, vol. 39, no. 3, pp. 409–413.

Bodily PM and Ventura D 2018, "Explainability: An Aesthetic for Aesthetics in Computational Creative Systems", in *Proceedings of the Ninth International Conference on Computational Creativity*, Salamanca, Spain, pp. 153–160.

Buckner C 2018, "Empiricism without Magic: Transformational Abstraction in Deep Convolutional Neural Networks", *Synthese*, vol. 195, no. 12, pp. 5339–5372.

Eck D and Schmidhuber J 2002, "Finding Temporal Structure in Music: Blues Improvisation with LSTM Recurrent Networks", in *Proceedings of the 12th IEEE workshop on neural networks for signal processing*, Martigny, Switzerland, IEEE, pp. 747–756.

Erhan D et al. 2009, "Visualizing Higher-layer Features of a Deep Network", *Dept. IRO, Université de Montréal, Tech. Rep. no. 4323*.

Flowers JH and Garbin CP 1989, "Creativity and Perception", in Glover A et al. (eds.), *Handbook of Creativity*. Boston, MA: Springer, pp. 147–162.

Forgas JP 2000, *Feeling and Thinking: The Role of Affect in Social Cognition*. Paris: Cambridge University Press.

Freeman D 2004, "Creating Emotion in Games: The Craft and Art of Emotioneering™", *Computers in Entertainment* (CIE), vol. 2, no. 3, pp. 15–16.

Gatys LA, Ecker AS, and Bethke 2016, "Image Style Transfer using Convolutional Neural Networks", in *Proceedings of the 2016 IEEE Conference on Computer Vision and Pattern Recognition*, Las Vegas, USA, IEEE, pp. 2414–2423.

Graves A, Mohamed AR, and Hinton G 2013, "Speech Recognition with Deep Recurrent Neural Networks", in *Proceedings of the 2013 IEEE International Conference on Acoustics, Speech and Signal Processing*, Vancouver, Canada, IEEE, pp. 6645–6649.

Ha D and Eck D 2017, "A Neural Representation of Sketch Drawings", *arXiv preprint*. Available from: https://arxiv.org/abs/1704.03477 [accessed 17 November 2019].

Karpathy A 2015, "The Unreasonable Effectiveness of Recurrent Neural Networks", [Blog post]. Available from: http://karpathy.github.io/2015/05/21/rnn-effectiveness/ [accessed 17 November 2019]

Lakoff G and Johnson M 2008, *Metaphors We Live By*. Chicago, IL: Chicago University Press.

Mikolov T et al. 2013, "Efficient Estimation of Word Representations in Vector Space", *arXiv preprint*. Available from: https://arxiv.org/abs/1301.3781 [17 November 2019].

Mordvintsev A, Olah C, and Tyka M 2015, "Inceptionism: Going Deeper into Neural Networks", [Blog post]. Available from: https://ai.googleblog.com/2015/06/inceptionism-going-deeper-into-neural.html [accessed 13 November 2019]

Nguyen A et al. 2016, "Synthesizing the Preferred Inputs for Neurons in Neural Networks via Deep Generator Networks", in *Advances in Neural Information Processing Systems*, pp. 3387–3395. Available from: https://arxiv.org/abs/1605.09304 [accessed 17 November 2019].

Pereira FC and Cardoso A 2003, "Optimality Principles for Conceptual Blending: A First Computational Approach", *AISB Journal*, vol. 1, no. 4, pp. 351–369.

Picard RW 2000, *Affective Computing*. Cambridge, MA: MIT Press.

Pound E 1935, *Make it New*. New Haven, CT: Yale University Press.

Radford A, Jozefowicz R, and Sutskever I 2017, "Learning to Generate Reviews and Discovering Sentiment", *arXiv preprint*. Available from: https://arxiv.org/abs/1704.01444 [accessed 17 November 2019].

Roberts A et al. 2018, "A Hierarchical Latent Vector Model for Learning Long-term Structure in Music", *arXiv preprint*. Available from: https://arxiv.org/abs/1803.05428 [accessed 17 November 2019].

Shahrin MH and Wyse L 2019, "Applying Visual Domain Style Transfer and Texture Synthesis Techniques to Audio: Insights and Challenges", *Neural Computing and Applications*, pp. 1–15.

Simonyan K and Zisserman A 2014, "Very Deep Convolutional Networks for Large-scale Image Recognition", *arXiv preprint*. Available from: https://arxiv.org/abs/1409.1556 [accessed 17 November 2019].

Steyerl H 2018, "A Sea of Data: Pattern Recognition and Corporate Animism (Forked Version)", in Apprich C et al. (eds.), *Pattern Discrimination*. London and Minneapolis, MN: Messon Press and University of Minnesota Press.

Su J et al. 2019, "One Pixel Attack for Fooling Deep Neural Networks", *IEEE Transactions on Evolutionary Computation*, vol. 23, no. 5, pp. 828–841.

Szegedy C et al. 2013, "Intriguing Properties of Neural Networks", *arXiv preprint*. Available from: https://arxiv.org/abs/1312.6199 [accessed 17 November 2019].

Ulyanov D and Lebedev V 2016, "Audio Texture Synthesis and Style Transfer", [Blog post]. Available from: https://dmitryulyanov.github.io/audio-texture-synthesis-and-style-transfer/ [accessed 24 November 2019].

Ustyuzhaninov I et al. 2016, "Texture Synthesis using Shallow Convolutional Networks with Random Filters", *arXiv preprint*. Available from: https://arxiv.org/abs/1606.00021 [accessed 17 November 2019].

Vico G 2000 [1725], *New Science*. Reprint, Penguin Classics.

White T 2018, "Perception Engines", [Blog post in Medium]. Available from: medium.com/artists-and-machine-intelligence/perception-engines-8a46bc598d57 [accessed 18 November 2019].

PART III

Patterning cultural heritage and memory

7

DATA TO THE NTH DEGREE

Zooming in on *The Smart Set*

Craig J. Saper

Images of wide scope

In an influential essay, cognitive psychologist Gruber explains that Darwin's use of the tree image helped Darwin generate the principle of natural selection. Darwin had struggled to find an image – seaweed was one of his earlier choices – to explain a set of data and a perplexing mass of details. Gruber uses Darwin as an example to illuminate that "images of wide scope" are not used to explain to the general public difficult scientific research findings but to articulate, for the scientist, the complex relationships between perplexing data sets (Gruber 1978, p. 131; cf. Gruber and Davis 1988). Images generate ways of thinking. Like Darwin, researchers still use *metaphoric images* to conceptualise relationships between data points, evidence, details, and information. Metaphoric images work particularly well when they suggest visual and semantic analogies and conceptual puns. Darwin's image of the family tree gave him, and future students of evolutionary biology, a pun on the words 'family' and 'descendants'. Humans and horses are literally descended from biological parents, and figuratively descended from other species, genus, and order. The problem with reading big data sets (distantly, closely, or through dynamic pattern recognition) is that it is easy to forget that these are metaphors or *models of reality* that use aesthetics in order to illuminate the same data differently. To better understand big data and the mechanisms used to read big data sets, this chapter considers a cinematic image of the zoom shot, represented by the headings below, beginning with 10 to the zero power, then 10 to 1st power (or 10^1), 10^2, 10^3, attempting to script precisely that dynamic metaphoric image of zooming out and zooming in. This chapter advocates using this metaphor for researchers to better pose problems when analysing big data.

Decades ago, Sternberg and Okagaki argued that school tends to frame knowledge so it only seems "relevant for doing the kinds of problems that are found in

116 Craig J. Saper

school", outside of school "problems and problem solving are not neat [...] Non-academic problems are messy, ill defined, and sometimes unanswerable. With non-academic problems, even identifying that there is a problem is crucial" (Sternberg and Okagaki 1998, p. 9). I begin with an existing academic project described in the next paragraph that seeks to identify quantitative evidence of change over time of a magazine's circulation; a neat and unsullied problem that has an obvious solution: the circulation changed. If we read the data from a distance, it quickly corrects some of the misconceptions involved in the close, detailed information about the magazine's circulation. Zooming in we see that what looks clear and distinct in the graph becomes a fuzzy set. I use this single example of a magazine's circulation to make a much larger argument, applicable to science, art, and the humanities, about how we read and interpret big data and small details. The significance of this essay for most readers is not its particular findings about an early twentieth-century magazine, serendipitously named *The Smart Set*, but in the image of wide scope introduced here. My model allows for newer ways to delineate data sets, challenge the boundaries between big and small types of data, and question the distinction between conceptual models and the specific evidence of *The Smart Set*. My implicit argument is that the model of smart sets of data and the historical details and evidence about *The Smart Set* are imbricated one upon the other just as Darwin's family tree of evolutionary biology is inextricably engaged with the specific evidence and circumstances. Of course, Darwin's work sought to explain a set of perplexing evidence with a well-known, familiar, and personally important image of the descent of every Victorian man and woman: the lineage of the family tree.

10^0

The above graph (Figure 7.1) illustrates the changes in the circulation of the magazine *The Smart Set*, published between 1900 and 1935. Circulation, which, in this context includes subscribers, news-stand sales, and other copies distributed, increased from a few thousand at the beginning to a peak of over 400,000 readers in 1926. This particular graph appears in a big data project "Circulating American Magazines: Visualization Tools for U.S. Magazine History" that, by 2021, will have

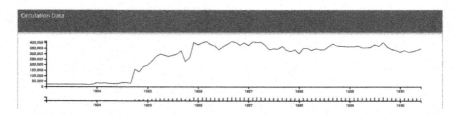

FIGURE 7.1 An excerpt from the "Circulating American Magazines: Visualization Tools for U.S. Magazine History" big data project 2020.

Source: Used with permission from BE Hefner, James Madison University

short entries to explain and contextualise the raw data in terms of the history of those magazines.

10[1]

The chart of *The Smart Set*'s circulation above appears to demand what Moretti calls a "distant reading" (Moretti 2013) of the circulation for every year of the magazine's publication. Moretti's phrase, first proposed in 2000 and more fully explained in his 2013 book *Distant Reading*, alludes to big data's opposite, the small details found in literary studies' 'close readings' of texts, in which a literary, media, or cultural studies scholar reads the textual information starting with each word, sometimes even a seemingly stray mark on the page, for its overdetermined meanings and etymologies both specifically and in the syntagmatic meaning in a larger text. In a close reading, one might read a magazine like *The Smart Set* in terms of its influence on literary history, by looking closely at the contributors' names, and finding the later famous contributors. One might look at the editors' names, and determine the editorial direction by reading the stories, squibs, essays, and editorials. In a distant reading, one would discuss those circulation numbers diachronically as they rise and fall over time.

10[2]

Reading the magazine's circulation data obviously looks like a "distant reading" because you see the changes over 35 years in a chart that looks like a distant landscape. Mandell calls this type of reading "distributed" (Mandell 2015); Barnett expands the phrase into a more complete methodology (Barnett 2018), which seeks to discover abstract patterns by visualising sets in charts, graphs, and data landscapes, in this case of all American magazine circulation numbers. This type of reading is distributed, rather than merely distant, because it does not zoom into specific magazines or texts. Rather, it draws conclusions and finds meanings in the changes to the distribution of magazines graphed over time. One immediately notices, from the graph above, that in late 1924 the magazine's circulation changed dramatically, reaching its peak around 1926 and levelling off at around 400,000 for the remainder of its publication. Given the big data sets alone, we cannot say more.

10[3]

The question my use of the big data sets asks is can one find "the smart set" lurking in, near, or beyond the big (dumb) data sets of the "Circulations of American Magazines" project? One approach is to use historical, textual, and archival research to supplement the big data sets or vice versa to use the abstract and distant reading to supplement the fine-grained research. In that case, one can try to explain the dramatic change in the magazine's reach, starting in late 1924. Founded in 1900 by d'Alton Mann, *The Smart Set* became culturally important when first Wright, from

1913 to 1914, then Mencken and Nathan, from 1914 to 1923, edited the magazine, with the latter adding a series of new subtitles, that changed frequently, but beginning with the subtitle that the previous editor had used, *A Magazine of Cleverness*.

Wright's innovation was to invite important avant-garde writers such as Pound, Lowell, and Yates to contribute. Even among scholars of the magazine, the mythology surrounding Wright's short-lived editorship was that his publishing of those avant-garde writers and poets left the magazine near bankruptcy in the year after the infamous Armory Show in which avant-garde modernism, including work by Duchamp, arrived in New York. As can be seen from the graph, there was little noticeable change in those years. Later explanations of why the publishers switched editors make it seem like they thought that Nathan and Mencken would steady the revenue stream and increase the readership, and remove the 'perfume of pornography' from the magazine's reputation for risk-taking decadence. In fact, Wright, Nathan, and Mencken were already working together to form the editorial direction even if not formally, and when the publisher Thayer sought to replace Wright both Nathan and Mencken declined, again at least formally, for eight months, before officially taking the helm in October 1914 when Thayer offered them a 25 per cent stake each in the magazine rather than regular salaries. Unofficially, they had really been determining the editorial direction and choosing contributors since around the June issue in 1914. The new editors soon established the magazine's literary legacy in a lineage of literary and culturally sophisticated magazines including *The New Yorker*. The magazine's circulation during those years had a relatively, and perhaps intentionally, modest reach.

10^4

Pulling back further, under the Mencken and Nathan editorial leadership the magazine continued to struggle to increase circulation. That magazine had a very small audience, but the lack of financial success led Mencken and Nathan to cynically start popular pulps, including the well-known *Black Mask*, to fund their real interest in publishing works with lasting literary and aesthetic value. Mencken's model was to use popular magazines to fund other types of writing – political or literary – that might not find a large audience. Mencken, famously contemptuous of genre fiction and popular tastes, was a successful pulp publisher who fed those popular tastes even as he and Nathan explicitly sought a much more aesthetically discerning and politically suspicious audience, that nevertheless sought a light satirical touch and wisdom in the wise-crack more than in the solemn story.

10^5

When Hearst bought the magazine and took complete editorial control around 1924, he changed the smart literary and culture magazine to a women's magazine more like *Cosmopolitan*, and almost instantly its circulation went up sevenfold. With market share and constantly expanding circulation as the singular goal, the

New Smart Set, that dropped both the subtitle and the focus on 'cleverness', eventually closed even with about five years of nearly 400,000 circulating copies during Hearst's reign as publisher. This magazine's circulation data suggests that its lasting cultural value is in inverse proportion to the bottom line and market share; the greater the reach of the magazine, the less lasting the cultural memory and value, suggesting that cultural memory exists on a completely different networked or *rumorological* plane than in the marketplace of ideas. Intimate publications with low circulations might spread their influence and impact our memories through the literary networks even as the audience for the popular version of the same magazine eclipsed, at the time, any importance of the earlier publication, *The Smart Set*. In other words, in the idiom of the first quarter of twenty-first-century political discourse, too much winning is a losing proposition: insipid and forgettable. Likewise, the dominance of algorithmic reading practices from a distant scale eclipses other possible scales of reading. One thing that is readily available, and archived online, is the full colour paintings of women's faces in the Hearst version of the magazine. The covers are collectors' items speaking to the surface skin-deep value of the new version of the magazine, or to the stress on visually appealing cover art. The inside content of the new version of the magazine is not archived in the Hathi Trust Digital Library collection or in Brown University's Modernist Journals Project (MJP). Both Hathi and MJP include issues until 1923. Further, we do not know whether Hearst's circulation numbers were driven simply by the company's ability to place copies more widely or by genuine demand because of its change in focus. If the latter, then the data seems to be demeaning to women readers who seem to have cared less about reading great works of literature than they cared for superficial beauty advice; and it also has an implicit bias against beauty advice as feminine and therefore excluded from the canon of literature. With access to the big data alone, we do not know – nor can we know – whether the same authors wrote for both Hearst's and the Mencken and Nathan version, as authors often hid their identities for reasons such as not wanting to be associated with a popular low-brow magazine printed on cheaper paper and produced like pulp paper pouring out of a metaphoric machine.

10^6

This type of smart or clever reading of the big data sets might require a bit more specificity. In fact, what I am proposing here is best described by an analogy, or image of wide scope, using *The Powers of Ten* film, made by The Offices of the Eames in 1977 for the American Physics Society, as a metaphor of how one might read big data. The film begins with a title card that reads in all capital letters, "A FILM DEALING WITH THE RELATIVE SIZE OF THINGS IN THE UNIVERSE" with a line space and then, "AND THE EFFECT OF ADDING ANOTHER ZERO". The nine-minute long film's clever construction moves the view out with an indicator of the scale and distance in the margins of the frame. It begins with a view of a lakeshore picnic in Chicago, Illinois, at 1 metre or

10^0 metres scale until reaching into distant space, 10^{24} or 100 million light years away from Earth). For our purposes, the accuracy of the Eames' "technoscientific, cosmological artwork" is of less concern than its simulation of the cinematic zoom using an "animated collage" of the imagined views (Woods 2017, pp. 62–63). Of course, it is the 10^4 to 10^7 global views, as an analogy, that most scholars consider the scale of digital humanities in conceptualising big data. Intervening in the model of distant, close, or patterned readings of data requires recognising a *disjunction* between these scales that is an effect of the metaphoric model, not of any quantitative or qualitative information. Of course, my analogy, which seeks to illuminate aspects not recognised in dominant models of reading, has its own metaphysical problems: it requires one to imagine a smooth continuity between data on a linear progression rather than spreading out in an assemblage of lateral connections. For example, the zoom-in from 10^0, the human scale including the skin on one hand, to 10^{-15} metres at the atomic level might be, following this analogy, an area of digital humanities that we have mostly ignored. My proposal for data to the Nth degree, zooms out from the machinations of one magazine's publication to the yearly change in that magazine's circulation or scale of distribution. Digital humanities readings typically stop there.

The "smart set" of data first zooms in to explain the change at the business level and the ensuing dramatic change in circulation when the Hearst company bought the magazine. It zooms further in to describe what the editors published before the magazine shifted its focus and audience. From that scale, one might zoom in to the first issue of the Mencken and Nathan version of the magazine, then to one author, then to the difficulties in recognising any author when we look more closely at the attributed authors' names in each of the issues, then move to a distributed reading of other biographical, literary, publishing and cultural issues that inform the circulation numbers. We can describe these small and intimate details not as an entirely separate style of interpretation, not as a close reading, but as a spectrum that includes big data and intimate minutia, in a lateral constellation.

10^7

There have been other versions of the same idea portrayed in the Eames film, starting with the 1968 Szasz's "Cosmic Zoom", and, more recently, with the astrophysicist Obreschkow's 2018 "Cosmic Eye", a video viewed over 200 million times. Like the earlier Eames film, "Cosmic Eye" zooms up to unimaginably large scales of the universe, and then back into the most minute pre-atomic particles. There are many other examples all showing relative scale of objects and distances. In my analogy, we should not think of data as static at one scale, but rather dynamic as we change the scale of analysis. Big data is small data and vice versa. One is not limited to studying data to one, and only one, scale or proportion. Counter to Moretti, and the critics of digital humanities alike, there is no close reading or distant reading: one can zoom in or zoom out on all data in the same readings.

10^8

These questions open out to the conceptualisation of modes and platforms for information organisation, retrieval, and archiving, suggesting the need for a new spatialised notion of knowledge. Some have proposed entirely new platforms and we might think of this chapter as a blueprint for how a new presentational platform or structure of research might work. Ideally, one would be able to visually zoom into the data sets to find the dynamic "smart set" and to challenge "dumb" information that might have viral power with evidence supporting claims.

The layout of the page, and the entire regime of the flat-page interface, would change as we begin to think of information in depth, distance, and spatial relationships all at once: zoomable configuration of powers of ten. The co-founder of a new platform, named Foam, describes it as fitting nicely with my problem-posing visualisation model of reading. Foam embodies what Sloterdijk calls a "sphereological" model of spacialised and "atmospheric" knowledge production (Sloterdijk 2016). Using the Foam space, readers and writers gather information, data, and media within multidimensional bubble-worlds. In these bubble-worlds, curation, mnemonics, historiography, narratology and visualisation are imbricated together with montage editing techniques. Those techniques also include zooming, sequencing, and weaving. The reader, writers, and users deploy foam space in order to create novel powers of storytelling and contextualisation (Greco 2020, np.). In the Foam platform, one might have the opportunity to conceptualise data on a timeline as in the graph above, but then zoom-in on one year, one date, as I have demonstrated in this chapter, one magazine issue, one name, and, on into the materiality of the page. The Foam platform has the same goals as other efforts to spatialise knowledge and to consider the scale of reading practices central to debates and issues confronting text analytics, data analysis, and the digital humanities, especially in discussions of distant or close readings, anonymised or named data, algorithmically or rhetorically parsed texts.

10^9

The notion of distant reading did not begin with computational means of collecting and sorting data, and has, as Underwood explains, "a largely distinct genealogy stretching back many decades before the advent of the Internet – a genealogy that is not for the most part centrally concerned with computers" (Underwood 2017, np.). In terms of the examination of a literary magazine's circulation data, Underwood suggests that we appreciate distant reading of big data as "a conversation between literary studies and social science" (np.); it is precisely that "conversation", in which literary analysis cedes ground to the social scientific quantitative analysis, that worries humanities scholars. Pressman had noted a similar challenge to literary studies and asks: "What constitutes literary data, and what is the role of the literary in the digital humanities?" (Pressman 2013, para. 1).

One can recover what Pressman calls "literary", or what Schor calls the "aesthetic detail" (Schor 2008), by studying the "different levels of interpretive process" which, like the proposal in this chapter, asks for a "recognition that modelling operates within relational and dynamic" processes and includes "close and distant reading, symbolic/syntagmatic and semantic/paradigmatic levels of text analysis" (Ciula and Marras 2016, para. 6, np.). In this interpretive sliding scale, one avoids "stupid data" (Walker 2014, np.). Walker suggests that analyses tend to "find more 'statistically significant' relationships in larger data sets, where

> "Statistically significant" means a statistical assessment of whether observations reflect a pattern rather than just chance and may or may not be meaningful. The larger the data set, the more "statistically significant" relationships will have no meaning – creating greater opportunity to mistake noise for signal. Thus, "Big Data" produces more correlations and patterns between data – yet also produces much more noise than signal. The number of false positives will rise significantly. In other words, more correlations without causation leading to an illusion of reality.
>
> *(Walker 2014, np.)*

10^{10}

What began as one entry about one magazine's circulation in section 10^0 now touches on epistemological questions about how best to illuminate an elusive reality of unimaginably big and complex data sets. McCosker and Wilken, in an article on big data as visual knowledge, note that visualisations, whether graphs, charts, word-clouds, or spread-sheets "never" fully capture "the totality of the object, and in its dynamism", and always include a "gap between the extraction and abstraction of data" (McCosker and Wilken 2014, p. 157). Quoting Derrida, McCosker and Wilken note that by cleaning data and stressing the eloquent and beautiful simplicity and neatness of the visualisations, scholars pursue a "total knowledge, which seeks to 'objectivize with no remainder'" (Derrida 1996, p. 68; McCosker and Wilken 2014, p. 158). The remainder are all the details that do not fit in the imaging of big data sets. Instead, there is "a kind of aesthetic engagement with big data" in which one is tempted to "fetishize" the clean beauty and neatness of the visualisation rather than the dynamism of the data (McCosker and Wilken 2014, p. 156). However, rather than dismiss big data analysis, in their case for the social sciences, McCosker and Wilken argue, citing De Landa, that "the visualization [...] does not stand as the final stage in a process of problem-solving", but, similar to Gruber's argument, is "better understood as the actualisation of new ways of problem posing" (De Landa cited in McCosker and Wilken 2014, p. 163). What digital humanities to the Nth degree offers is to metaphorically zoom in on the data points as a conceptualisation of how we perform research, analyse data sets, and visualise relationships between these sets.

10^9

Zooming back down, closer to the main issues of digital humanities and big data, Flanders examines the turn to "big data" and "the comparative insignificance of any individual item in the research landscape"; after discussing Moretti, she returns to ponder

> the many potential valences of the relation between individuals and systems: for instance, a "collective" logic through which the meaning of individual cases is most effectively realized or a "system" logic of industrial management in which individual distinctiveness and locality is set aside because it cannot be thought.
>
> *(Flanders 2013, np.)*

This is precisely the issue involved in big data versus what I am calling intimate data. The one should not be thought of in subordination to the other but rather on a Möbius strip continuum in which the smallest data opens to the biggest big data and vice versa. Flanders asks us to consider big data that studies the "statistical aggregation—the large corpus, the visualization, the database—as a coordinated plane populated by data points, each of which carries its tiny payload of information (metadata, word frequency, demographics, and so forth)" in terms of the "connection between each data point [...] a text or an artwork or a human being or a linguistic transaction" (Flanders 2013, np.) or, in this case a magazine, its readers, writers, editors, publishers, and its circulation numbers.

10^6

As Schnapp notes,

> [b]ig data, however defined, are built out of small data, and even the smallest of data are hardly given or captured (as the Latin *datus* and *captus* misleadingly suggest). Rather, data are constructed; and, when captured, it is these constructs that are seized.
>
> *(Schnapp 2018, p. 424)*

The magazine circulation data are constructed by parsing the copies printed, sold, and distributed to subscribers, and subsequently placed on a graph, which, in this case, does not include enough detailed distinctions in the x-vertical axis between the magazine's founding and 1924, when Hearst bought the magazine. One could easily imagine constructing the data differently, as I have already hinted above by finding a metric that organises details and constructs data according to lasting cultural influence. Although I do not know what that metric might focus on or measure, the example explains that the data and the representation of the data are contrived. It is an idealised version of raw data. Schnapp makes a similar argument

124 Craig J. Saper

by recognising that it is "not big or small" but rather "the webs of interconnection, the zooming spaces, between different scales and points of entry" (424). Kuhn, too, challenges the usual binary construction "of quantitative versus qualitative methods, or even formal analysis versus critical theory" (Kuhn 2018, p. 301). She correctly worries that "criticisms of close reading have alienated many humanists", and, instead offers a "strategic" mixed methods approach that chooses the "appropriate methods for a particular project rather than simply denouncing any particular one *a priori*" (301). The very distinction between big and small or close and distant is an inadequate construction mapped on to a mass of details. In the digital humanities to the Nth degree, one cannot arbitrarily discount or dismiss particular types of data, big or intimate, or approaches to reading, distant or close; all scales carry intellectual weight.

10^5

As we begin to zoom back in, it is important to note that Nathan and Mencken edited 110 issues of *The Smart Set* with 1,387 names of contributors in less than 10 years. Some 369 women writers published in the magazine during those years. Since some of the contributors published under multiple pseudonyms and often using their own name, too, it is difficult to say precisely what percentage of the writers were women, but with these numbers alone it was around 27 per cent. Prior to January 1915, the publisher was listed as Thayer Company, and afterward as The Smart Set Company; the significance of that change having to do with the deals Thayer had struck with Nathan and Mencken. Wright had edited the magazine from March 1913 (issue 39.3) until January 1914 (issue 42.1), but between February and September 1914 (issues 42.2 to 44.1) it is often less clear who was editing the magazine. When Nathan and Mencken at first declined to serve as editors, Thayer put in place a business staff to focus on placing advertisements, work on circulation, and make other management decisions outside of creative control. He also listed himself as editor, but from recollections of contributors, the new editors were already cobbling together the June 1914 issue and soliciting work from a set of reliable authors like Brown, who appeared under pseudonyms to make it look as if the magazine had more contributors than it actually did. It is clear that the Nathan and Mencken team was editing the magazine from October 1914 until December 1922, but from a distance most commentators simply say from 1914 until 1923. The big data is neater and fits into graphs and visualisations. When you start zooming in, the data points proliferate to bigger data sets; the visualisation becomes more empirically accurate and, paradoxically, also more nebulous. The "smart set" of data is always the fuzzy set.

10^4

Moving into the economic numbers of *The Smart Set*, founded in 1900 by d'Alton Mann, who had published the scandalmongering rag *Town Topics*, not dissimilar to today's *Daily Mail* in the UK, or the *National Inquirer* in the US, and made a fortune printing stories about the wealthy and powerful or extorting money to kill those same stories. *The Smart Set* never made the huge profits of *Town Topics*, and Mann sold the magazine in the spring of 1911 to Thayer for $100,000. *The Smart Set* became culturally important when Huntington Wright (1913–1914) started including modernist avant-garde works like poetry by Pound, but apparently suffered from a declining circulation. Mencken and Nathan were already working on the magazine as contributors, and according to at least one knowledgeable commentary by Roscoe, they were contributing *editors*. Roscoe, who chronicled the magazine and collected stories that appeared in *The Smart Set* by "world famous authors" called the editorial team a "triumvirate" of editorial decision-making (Rascoe 1934, xxiii). Others, like Thayer and later Mencken, portrayed Wright as a disaster as an editor who nearly bankrupted the magazine by focusing on a smaller and smaller group of sophisticated readers until the circulation declined precipitously. If one studies the graph above on the magazine's changing circulation, there does not appear to be a noticeable dip in the already small circulation; the big data seems to inform the misconstruction of small details and disagreements at the human scale. The same critics who thought of Wright as crashing the magazine's finances, also thought he had brought down the magazine's reputation with the scandalous modernism considered pornographic; the publisher got nervous. Mencken and Nathan both encouraged the mythological reading in large part to secure their legacy as the editors who established the literary reputation of the magazine in the literary canon. In terms of the dire financial situation of the magazine, regardless the cause, the publisher pushed Wright out quickly. Once Wright was out, both Mencken and Nathan were approached, but they declined for eight months, continuing to contribute and offer editorial advice. It is likely that they were the unacknowledged editors between the issues in which Wright's name was listed as the editor. They finally agreed when the publisher gave them complete creative control and a 25 per cent stake each in the ownership in exchange for not drawing a full salary as editors. In 1923, when Thayer sold the magazine to Hearst for $60,000, the deal that the editors had made in 1914 paid off. Mencken and Nathan each received $15,000 and Thayer the other half. That amount would be nearly $900,000 in 2020 and for Nathan and Mencken, the equivalent of $225,000 each.

10^3

If we simply listed the names of the contributors during the Mencken and Nathan years, it would be a, now, impressive list of literary luminaries, who, at the time, were often getting their first chance at publishing stories, poems, or squibs: Fitzgerald, Anderson, and O'Neill. *The Smart Set* had previously published Lawrence's first poetry, and introduced him to an American audience. Others who appeared in the magazine include Cather, Dreiser, Lewis, Masters, Millay, Teasdale, Huxley, Joyce, Somerset Maugham, Molnar and Walpole, Burke, Hecht, Kemp, Mumford, Parker, Untermeyer, van Vechten, Abdullah, Barnes, Loos, Woodworth Reese, Walrond,

DuBois, and White. The list is striking for several reasons: how many later recognised as important writers appeared in the *Smart Set*; the ethnic and racial diversity of the group; and the inclusion of important women writers. If we look only at the big data sets, they inherently edit out precisely this diversity, and make important women writers, like Winslow or Teasdale, who won the precursor to the Pulitzer Prize in poetry, Walrond, the important Harlem Renaissance writer and journalist, or DuBois, the hugely influential founder of Black sociology, invisible.

10²

If we focus on just one issue of the magazine from June 1914, we do not see explicit evidence that Nathan and Mencken had taken over editorial control, even if they had not finalised any financial ownership or contractual deal, nor do they appear in the masthead as the editors (no one is listed). Looking at that particular issue, one can begin by listing the known contributors, besides Nathan and Mencken, who wrote multiple articles in each issue, Brown, Byrne, Saxby, Harrison, Saltus, Wilmot, Bynner, Teasdale, O'Hara, Springer, Towne, Stearns Davis, Shoemaker Wagstaff, Bridges, and Klahr. Few, if any, of these names resonate today as important writers, but at the time these were well known; some were part of the modern decadent writers comparable to Wilde and Huymanns. One could zoom in on any of these writers to illuminate how the types of works included created the readership of the time as well as discuss Abdullah's pulp magazine crime and mystery stories or his screenplays, including the one for the Academy Award-nominated 1927 *Chang: A Drama of the Wilderness*; Hibbard Kemp, known as the "Vagabond Poet" and a precursor to the Beat writers; or Bynner, an American poet, writer and scholar, now known to scholars only, if at all, for being among the modern writers in Santa Fe, New Mexico; Towne, an author, a later editor of the redone *The Smart Set* and *Harper's Bazaar*, well-known in New York's society circles; or Shoemaker Wagstaff an American poet, who deserves to find a new audience.

10³

Zooming in on Shoemaker Wagstaff, one suspects that she was likely the most famous contributor at the time. After Chartran painted her portrait in 1905, she had a certain celebrity status. Mencken liked her writing although he thought it a bit over the top when Wagstaff let "her adjectives run riot" (Mencken 2012, p. 217). Just quoting from one of her poems, *Bacchante*, published in a collection of erotic poetry in 1918, can give one a sense of the general decadent approach, in her work specifically, but also in a magazine that was still open to a more passionate and often radical sophistication: "I AM inebriate with the sunlight's golden wine, / And I would love with an insensate fury!", "Let me drain beauty even unto death!", and "Bring me a pale flower-boy, / White-limbed like a young heifer in a field" (Wagstaff 1921, p. 281). Much of her poetry is almost campy in its eroticism and gender fluidity. The myth of bacchante, the drunken female reveller involved in

Data to the Nth degree **127**

orgiastic celebrations, is difficult to imagine in contemporary poetry, let alone in the workplace of a respected publication today.

10^2

Zooming in to the scene in the office during the publication, one would be struck with an atmosphere more in keeping with the *National Lampoon* than a literary journal. The editors and writers in the office were often playing pranks reflected in the magazine, as at least 50 of the names of contributors through the Mencken and Nathan years were pseudonyms. Some names, like Owen Hatteras, were "office pseudonyms" claimed as the pen name of editors and regular contributors and there was never any definitive evidence to prove who used the name in any specific magazine issue. Seumas Le Chat was another pseudonym used by Samter Winslow or Mencken, who both claimed it – it had the typical inside joke attached to it (jokes often lost to time), suggesting the idea of a caterwauling writer named in an Anglicised version, James The Cat. In the June issue, the name O. David, a joke on the most famous short-story writer O Henry, which has no punctuation after the O, was used by Brown. The scene was a group of paid-by-the-word writers producing under various names, that obfuscated gender and identity for everyone (even for the authors who often contested who used the name); it was a party-like scene of unbelievably productive and brilliant writers, often joking around as drunken revellers. Women writers contributed as much or more than the male authors even if the names of the contributors masked identities; these details of the scene make attribution and definitive data points difficult if not impossible to pin down.

10^1

Brown also describes how, at other magazines and especially the pulps, some of the male writers' wives had to pick up the weekly check, and "sometimes substituted at the machine", to type the stories when one of those writers was "too drunk to tell the typewriter keys apart"; whether this applied to Brown, a famous beer drinker, or another *The Smart Set* writer, O'Neil, infamous for his excessive whiskey drinking, the crucial phrase in the description of the scene of someone typing up the stories was that "Nobody knew the difference. There wasn't any difference" (Brown 1932, p. 482). Even if we can track down the author of the story, when one zooms in the actual author is less clear. In a letter to Joyce about how to make money as a writer, Pound recommended sending work to *The Smart Set* magazine, which had recently advertised a call for "top-notch" work in spite of some issues filled with "one hell of a lot of muck" (Pound in Read 1967, p. 18; Earle 2009, p. 20). It is not simply that this situation existed, that someone else helped write the stories or articles, that women were doing the wash and writing the stories without credit, but that Brown states a key fact of contemporary writing: if you dig deep enough, zoom in far enough, you will find not one author, but who knows how many.

10^0

When Mencken and Nathan took over *The Smart Set*, they "bought as liberally" from Brown as *Top Notch* had. Some of those early issues contained a novelette, articles, poems, and most of the joke-like squibs and epigrams – eleven by Brown under different *noms de plume*. Years later, in 1932, when Nathan invited Brown to contribute to the first issue of the *American Spectator*, he wrote, "Mencken and I depended a lot on your versatility when we had *The Smart Set*. If it hadn't been for your material, I don't know how we'd have filled those first issues" (Nathan quoted in Curtiss 1997, p. 34). The magazine could not simply publish many stories in one issue by the same author so Brown appeared under pseudonyms and the attribution is now lost or at least a matter of argument. For *The Smart Set*, false identities helped the magazine survive through the transition; they established its lasting reputation as a venue for now 'world famous authors' even if, on close inspection, no one is certain of attribution.

The very ontology of the small data set, a list of contributors' names, for example, opens up bigger than the big data and contains multitudes; small data is bigger than the big data. Similarly, when one zooms out from the evidence to a distant reading, patterns appear that challenge or support the construal of close readings and primary research. The big data is the foundation of the small data sets. When one zooms in on the same evidence, the patterns vibrate like a moiré effect, and the close reading challenges the construal of even the most complete set of big data. The smart set of data, whether fuzzy, clear, or both (and also to varying degrees), always depends on appreciating the continuum rather than binaries between big data and intimate stories, theories of reading and epistemology, and between the practice of archival research and literary readings. The smart set is a set of data pushed in multiple directions to the Nth degree.

References

Barnett T 2018, "Distributed Reading: Literary Reading in Diverse Environments", *DHQ: Digital Humanities Quarterly*, vol. 12, no. 2. Available from: www.digitalhumanities. org/dhq/vol/12/2/000389/000389.html [accessed 12 January 2020].

Brown B 1932, "Swell Days for Literary Guys", in Mencken HL (ed.), *The American Mercury*, pp. 480–485.

Ciula A and Marras C 2016, "Circling around Texts and Language: Towards 'Pragmatic Modelling' in Digital Humanities", *Digital Humanities Quarterly*, vol. 10, no. 3, [online]. Available from: http://digitalhumanities.org:8081/dhq/vol/10/3/000258/000258.html [accessed 31 January 2020].

Curtiss TQ 1997, *The Smart Set: George Jean Nathan and H. L. Mencken*. New York: Applause.

Derrida J 1996, *Archive Fever: A Freudian Impression*, trans. Prenowitz E. Chicago, IL: University of Chicago Press.

Earle DM 2009, *Re-covering Modernism: Pulps, Paperbacks, and the Prejudice of Form*. Burlington, VT: Ashgate.

Flanders J 2013, "The Literary, the Humanistic, the Digital: Toward a Research Agenda for Digital Literary Studies", *Modern Languages Association* [online] Available from: https:// dlsanthology.mla.hcommons.org/the-literary-the-humanistic-the-digital/ [accessed 31 January 2020].

Greco M 2020, Unpublished interview transcript on 25 February 2020, from this Author's private archive.

Gruber H 1978, "Darwin's 'Tree of Nature' and Other Images of Wide Scope", in Wechsler J (ed.), *On Aesthetics in Science*. Cambridge, MA: The MIT Press, pp. 121–140.

Gruber H and Davis S 1988, "Inching Our Way Up Mount Olympus: The Evolving-Systems Approach to Creative Thinking", in Sternberg RJ (ed.), *The Nature of Creativity: Contemporary Psychological Perspectives*. New York: Cambridge University Press.

Kuhn V 2018, "Images on the Move: Analytics for a Mixed Methods Approach", in Sayers J (ed.), *The Routledge Companion to Media Studies and Digital Humanities*. New York: Routledge.

Mandell L 2015, *Breaking the Book: Print Humanities in the Digital Age*. Hoboken, NJ: Wiley.

McCosker A and Wilken R 2014, "Rethinking 'Big Data' as Visual Knowledge: The Sublime and the Diagrammatic in Data Visualization", *Visual Studies*, vol. 29, no. 2, pp. 155–164.

Mencken HL 2012, *The Collected Drama of H. L. Mencken: Plays and Criticism*, ed. Joshi ST. Lanham, MD: The Scarecrow Press.

Moretti F 2013, *Distant Reading*. London: Verso.

Pressman J 2013, "The Literary And/As the Digital Humanities", *Digital Humanities Quarterly*, vol. 7, no. 1 [online]. Available from: http://digitalhumanities.org:8081/dhq/vol/7/1/000154/000154.html [accessed 31 January 2020].

Rascoe B 1934, "Smart Set History", in Rascoe B and Conklin G (eds.), *The Smart Set Anthology of World-Famous Authors*. New York: Halcyon, pp. xiii–xliv.

Read F (ed.) 1967, *Pound/Joyce: The Letters of Ezra Pound to James Joyce, with Pound's Essays on Joyce*. New York: New Directions.

Schnapp J 2018, "The Intimate Lives of Cultural Objects", in Sayers J (ed.), *The Routledge Companion to Media Studies and Digital Humanities*. New York: Routledge.

Schor N 2008, *Reading in Detail: Aesthetics and the Feminine*. London: Routledge.

Sloterdijk P 2016, *Foams, Spheres Volume III: Plural Spherology*, trans. Wieland H. Cambridge, MA: Semiotext(e) / Foreign Agents; distributed by MIT Press.

Sternberg R and Okagaki L 1998, "Teaching Thinking Skills: We're Getting the Context Wrong", unpublished manuscript.

Underwood T 2017, "A Genealogy of Distant Reading", *Digital Humanities Quarterly*, vol. 11, no. 2 [online]. Available from: http://digitalhumanities.org:8081/dhq/vol/11/2/000317/000317.html [accessed 31 January 2020].

Wagstaff B 1921, "Bacchante", in Smith TR (ed.), *Poetica Erotica. Volume 2*. New York: Boni and Liveright.

Walker M 2014, "Big Data is Stupid Data", *Data Science Central*, 19 September [online]. Available from: www.datasciencecentral.com/profiles/blogs/big-data-is-stupid-data [accessed 31 January 2020].

Woods D 2017, "Epistemic Things in Charles and Ray Eames's *Powers of Ten*", in Clarke MT and Wittenberg D (eds.), *Scale in Literature and Culture*. Series: Geocriticism and Spatial Literary Studies. Cham, Switzerland: Palgrave Macmillan, pp. 61–92.

8

INTELLECTUAL AUTONOMY AFTER ARTIFICIAL INTELLIGENCE

The future of memory institutions and historical research

Nicola Horsley

Introduction: gatekeeping cultural heritage

Access to cultural heritage, and especially the academic pursuit of knowledge through research, has always been mediated by 'gatekeepers'; whether by privilege of ownership, as with the Medicis (who were among the first art collectors to open their private collections on request); for ideological reasons, as with the erasure of Weiwei's name from museum records (and the removal of his work after the artist was disowned by the Chinese Contemporary Art Awards); or via the process of applying for admission to venerated reading rooms by divulging one's intellectual credentials to a national library's user database. Within the cultural sector, the politics of digital knowledge and machine learning extend the conventions of the analogue and pose questions of what new routes to knowledge may be opened up – and what possibilities may be closed off. Many studies of big data in Social Science and Humanities have taken social media as their muse – an understandable response to a new wellspring of data self-identifying as social (Manovich 2011, 2014; van Dijck 2014; Ruppert et al. 2015). Less attention has been given to existing materials that may be reconstituted in the era of big data by novel uses and methods of discovering knowledge. The many forms of public knowledge, collected and preserved by memory institutions – a collective term for galleries, libraries, museums and standalone archives, which may be public or private but whose contribution to the historical record is of public interest – may be understood as data. Although the ways in which these materials are recognised, treated and behave as big data differ by degrees, their holding institutions' embrace of this new medium in their archiving systems *re-positions knowledge complexity* within the research process, and, by extension, the collective memory stored in these institutions. Much like the memory of a group is not the sum of the memories of its members, the memory of an organisation, city, region, or country is not the sum of the memories of its units but is partly based on tacit knowledge and social cohesion. Similarly, when archival information is shared with the public, it has to be formalised in order to be understandable, however, the process of formalisation does not cleanse the information of context dependence, and, in some cases, tacit knowledge. The representation of historical information of any sort includes not only the transmission and diffusion but also re-contextualisation of this representation (Confino 1997).

Archives are a sliver of social memory (Harris 2002), touchstones via which memories are retrieved as well as articulated. On the one hand, they are dependent on canons which "perpetuate what a society has consciously selected and maintains as salient and vital for a common orientation and shared remembering" (Assmann 2006, p. 221). On the other hand, archives harbour dormant memories, occluded information and knowledge. As Derrida notes, the archive affords the possibility of repetition, reproduction, re-impression (Derrida 1996, p. 11) as well as 'invention', which, in Latin, means both finding and realising or inventing. It refers to discovering what is already there and realising something new (Derrida 2010, p. 43) given that archival documents "survive in ways unintended" by their makers or initial owners to become "evidence on which other interpretations of the past can be reconstructed" (Radley 1990, p. 58). This makes archives into "active sites of constant and multiple possibilities: acquisition and destruction, cultural determinism and challenge, social conformity and opposition, opportunities gained and lost for discovery and repression" (Blouin and Rosenberg 2011, p. 160).

New technologies change the archiving process; more importantly, they also change "what is archivable" (Derrida in Derrida and Stiegler 2002, p. 46). If big data is a new medium – a new mode of organising the senses, accessing information and producing knowledge – its architectures provide new communication channels that define what may be accessed, how, and by whom. Big data has penetrated the cultural heritage sector in the form of infrastructure projects such as Digital Research Infrastructure for the Arts and Humanities (DARIAH) and Consortium of European Social Science Data Archives (CESSDA), promising to expand access to a continent of archives in the Arts, Humanities and Social Sciences, or at least, to their gatekeeping metadata – archivists' descriptions of the memory institutions' holdings. Before the advent of widespread digital communication, decisions about the classification and distribution of the knowledge contained within memory institutions were made in-house. Conformity to recognised systems and standards was an important element of professionalism alongside the expertise that resided within the archivists whose specialist knowledge helped to define the institution's unique contribution to the cultural heritage landscape.

As those bodies that fund such institutions have turned towards the benefits of the data revolution, decisions about day-to-day practice have been taken out of archivists' hands. Where memory institutions had operated with a relative autonomy that accompanied (and was driven by) their *authority* in their specialist area of knowledge – applying principles that were specific to and tailor-made for, for example, an archive on the site of a former concentration camp – compatibility of processes and systems for knowledge sharing is, in the knowledge economy, emerging as the most crucial of priorities. This competition of compulsions towards the general and the bespoke is taking place in a context of comparative frugality when considered alongside some of the more profitable applications of big data in government, bio-engineering, and, more generally, business. Sweeping tides of societal-level change and the neo-liberal imperative have reshuffled institutions' priorities, necessitating alignment with external processes, particularly as the alternative is to slip into irrelevance or obscurity. This 'destiny' has paved the way for infrastructure projects' influence on hitherto idiosyncratic institutional practices encouraging standardisation across the sector. There are different views on the desirability and degrees of idiosyncrasy. For Olson et al., cultural heritage practitioners' representation of the historical record requires them to be "'neutral' intermediaries between users and information" (Olson et al. 2001, p. 640). For Bowker and Star, using the value-laden tools of the archivists' trade requires ethical judgements as "[e]ach standard and each category valorises some point of view and silences another", making their decision-making power "not bad, but dangerous" (Bowker and Star 1999, pp. 5–6). Such 'danger' is ongoing, as the preservation and performance of cultural heritage is a never-ending process with no pretensions of arriving at an end product in which truth is settled and knowledge finalised (Crouch 2010). This is why memory institutions, as dynamic processes, cannot be imagined without carefully crafted narratives that position and re-position knowledge.

For philosopher Han, narration as a meaning-making process is diametrically opposed to addition, characteristic of "dataism" (Han 2017, p. 59). As a cultural move towards simplistic – 'more is better' – data festishisation, dataism is, in Han's reading, synonymous with "digital Dadaism", given that dataism, like Dadaism, "takes leave of meaningful contexts" (59), or, better said, context as such. Knowledge and memory, by contrast, do not lend themselves to addition; their transformative power resides in their layered sedimentations. Han suggests that correlation, one of the main 'wins' of big data analytics, represents a relation of probability, rather than necessity. Correlation is different from causation, "distinguished by necessity" (68), which is different from reciprocity where "A and B condition each other mutually" (68). The ability to link diverse contexts in meaningful, mutually conditioning ways is a prerequisite for rich knowledge. Traditionally, archivists have provided a web of such rich and meaningful connections.

In moving away from conventional archival practices, there is an essential paradigm shift: technology bypasses the overview of the traditional gatekeepers of knowledge, introducing a moment of societal disorientation, with individuals and institutions flooded with information (Berry 2011). Often compared to oil as well as gold (European Commission; Yi et al. 2014; Schafer and van Es 2017), the data revolution has precipitated a rush to capitalise on the flow of data by researchers eager to extract the value from the deluge while navigating the supposedly unique ethics of a digital field. But for all that has been said about the novel ethical challenges, many examples have parallels with ethical quandaries that have dragged on for some time in traditional Social Science and Humanities research. Recounting how researchers sub-contracted by Facebook did not consider their analysis of Facebook users' data to involve human subjects, van Schie, Westra, and Schäfer lament the ambiguity of informed consent and the barriers to contacting participants whose data is 'freely available' on social media platforms (van Schie, Westra, and Schäfer 2017, pp. 187–188).

Datified research practices are facilitated through the use of descriptive metadata, appropriate preservation systems, informed institutional practice, and information architecture for sharing across institutions. This structure is used by funding bodies like the European Commission to identify the most ambitious research projects. Funding calls offer large grants to researchers who can corral the most unlikely research interests into data-rich areas, "consigning research questions for which it is difficult to generate big data to a funding desert and a marginal position" (Kitchin 2014, p. 28). Within this model, the hallmark of epistemic authority lies with a data set's five-star (re-)usability rating,[1] the top level of Berners-Lee's Open Data Plan (Berners-Lee 2012) which can only be achieved by containing some of that knowledge complexity in a black box (Latour 1999). Such flattening of nuance is described as the defining characteristic of data engineering, leading to what McPherson calls a "lenticular view of knowledge", whose logic is that of "the fragment or the chunk, a way of seeing the world as discrete modules or nodes" (McPherson 2012, p. 140). The 2018 Knowledge Complexity study conducted by Edmond et al. investigated current practice in European archival institutions in order to understand the kind of research methods that are supported and to ask what the shift towards big data as the gold standard of knowledge production means for the future use of memory institutions and the historical record's complex knowledge (Edmond et al. 2018). The following discussion draws on the study's interview research with archivists and related cultural heritage practitioners.

Making the historical record: from hierarchy to data mine

Cultural heritage practitioners are generally seen as the guardians of the historical record. A major task in gatekeeping archival data is the creation of metadata describing knowledge sources, such as how a particular source came into being, where, and when; who created or modified it; how it came to that particular institution; where it has been used thus far and to what purpose. Such metadata – and, increasingly, archival data themselves – are becoming digitally standardised to enable machine reading and computational engagement with knowledge that was previously only accessible through a process of personal contact and close reading of related sources. Before archive catalogues were remotely accessible, visiting an archive in person to establish whether it might contain relevant knowledge by consulting its finding aid – a document of its inventory and descriptions of its holdings as well as, importantly, their particular structure, which would not necessarily relate to how similar collections at other institutions were documented – was the necessary first step for a researcher embarking on a new study. The use of a hierarchical structure to locate and contextualise sources has been an essential tenet of archival practice, with the making of the historical record in this image central to the archivist's expertise and authority. Constituting context requires cultural heritage practitioners to craft a narrative that makes sense of the prior journey and potential trajectory of cultural heritage knowledge, without over-steering away from more ambitious destinations. Duff, an information scholar, and her co-author Harris, archivist of the Nelson Mandela papers, describe context as, "in principle, infinite" (Duff and Harris 2002, p. 276). The archivist's task is therefore to create a meaningful context of nested sub-hierarchies or sub-contexts. Reciprocally, this means that, for archival workers, the archive is a situational and embodied praxis (Palladini and Pustianaz 2017, p. 12) generating a form of 'distilled' knowledge, given that the situated human body-mind is itself an archiving medium (15–18).

For some time now, however, it has been seen as the archivists' responsibility to adapt cultural heritage practices to the computational turn. More than twenty years ago, Hedstrom urged archival workers to "teach the users of electronic archives how to be discriminating and sceptical consumers of digital information" (Hedstrom 1998, p. 15). Until the majority of society was as "comfortable" and familiar with the digital form as with conventional documentation, she argued, archivists had a responsibility to help users "approach digital evidence with a questioning mind about how it was generated, why it was preserved, and how it might be interpreted" (15). That prophesied time of digital comfort has surely arrived and, I would argue, strengthened the need for such assistance, rather than rendering it obsolete as the level of familiarity with the digital threatens any headway that might have been made in the promotion of scepticism.

Archivists' role in promoting the use of holdings begins with what we may call their 'thick' description (Geertz 1973); a process recognised as being shaped by their educational and personal backgrounds, institutional cultures, and the power dynamics that govern the construction of meaning in disciplinary knowledge more broadly (Duff and Harris 2002). The Knowledge Complexity study found that the description of cultural heritage was loaded with artefacts of its journey to the user, which become *inscribed* in this metadata and are inseparable from the knowledge itself. The description was also transparent about what was deemed not to *belong*, and why, creating a dialogue between the resource, cultural heritage practitioners, and researchers – a dialogue that is a cornerstone of the research process and not a step that might be circumvented. For a researcher seeking to make (novel) use of a resource, appreciation of its full potential comes from developing an understanding of how the source came to form part of that particular archive, what it includes as well as excludes, rather than seeking to extricate holdings from the archivists' descriptions. Where institutions catered to other types of user, they made different decisions about how best to represent their holdings, as exemplified by archives that provided data about victims of the holocaust to their descendants as well as researchers. Practitioners therefore sought to maintain their freedom to use their discretion when deciding what form of description would be most useful for their users. In the knowledge economy, which seeks to produce value by capturing "within a generalized social activity, the innovative elements that produce value"

(Negri and Vercellone 2008, p. 44), knowledge is made increasingly interchangeable, as can be seen from the emphasis on transferable, rather than discipline-specific skills in Higher Education, foregrounding the exchange value of knowledge, rather than its specificity.

The Knowledge Complexity study also revealed a clear sense of what a valid engagement with an archive is, a drive to uphold the rigour of academic research, a qualified desire to expand use of their resources, and an expectation that users' skills in navigating the archive would need to be complemented by archivists' expertise. One archivist explained how she approached a new addition to the archive by looking through it "for all the names of cities, countries, regions" included in the source, which, evidently, "takes quite a lot of time", but provides in-depth knowledge of the subject matter and "helps us very much when we have to answer requests" (Horsley 2018a, np.). This example suggests that some aspects of description are routine (the sort of content a computer could conceivably produce), but that it is the archivist's *process* of familiarisation with the source leading to its description that embeds in her the knowledge that allows her to retrieve it in an interconnected form. Furthermore, an overwhelming amount of data does not become formally recorded; instead, metadata is stored as embodied knowledge in cultural heritage practitioners themselves. Invoking the Middle Ages monastic practice of copying the Scriptures, philosopher Levin suggests that the purpose of such a practice was not only dissemination, but also the impregnation of the scribe's body, or, the creation of deep, embodied knowledge (Levin 1985, p. 66). While archivists are neither monks nor scribes, they are mediators of memory and knowledge; they *assign* value to records at every stage in the records continuum (Blouin 1999); negotiate "shifting cultural notions of value" (Blouin and Rosenberg 2011, p. 153); mediate between dormant and active memory; and guard the use and misuse of cultural heritage despite the fact that the "power" (even if only in the form of discretion) they hold over "societal memory" is masked behind a "public image of [...] self-effacement" (Nesmith 2002, p. 32). Archivists mediate the archive as a social, cultural, and epistemic process. As there are invariably multiple views on cultural heritage, every archive is both a place of contestation and of "'dreams' of re-enactment for both the user and the archivist (curator), who together always are engaged either passively or actively in the process of refiguration that is never ending" (Moss 2008, p. 83). For Derrida, an archivist not only forms part of the politics of memory but "must practice a politics of memory and, simultaneously [...] a critique of the politics of memory" (Derrida and Stiegler 2002, p. 63).

The sorts of *uses* that were facilitated at the archives we focused on in the Knowledge Complexity study were determined at the many levels at which decisions were taken. Potential connections could be aborted where an item was loaded with meanings considered too profound to justify a more simplistic description demonstrating what they had in common with other items of a similar form. As there is "no representation without intention and interpretation" (Olson 1994, p. 197), the act of describing materials is in *reflexive dialogue* with cultural heritage practitioners' other archival tasks, such as classification, cataloguing, and comparison,

136 Nicola Horsley

as well as with their perception of their role within the memory institution and its mission. Documenting the context of knowledge, not only in terms of *what* it shows but "where it comes from, how it came to us, and how it came into existence" was agreed to be a vital function of the role of archives in supporting the appropriate use of their holdings, especially as, without such perspective, a singular document can be "misleading" (Horsley 2018a, np.). Many archivists also expressed caution, even where researchers were very "methodical", about the "quick wins" of the keyword search: "you miss things, because you don't look for other sources, which can be important. You have to get to know your material"; using digital tools only can impair "the feeling" for "the context" as well as "the methodology of searching" (Horsley 2018b, np.). One archivist, reflecting on the challenges of adapting to digital systems and research methods, lamented that a great deal of cultural knowledge at a national library went undiscovered. He argued that fostering a sense of how an isolated text relates to the collections in total is more important today than ever,

> because in the past people sort of knew there would just be thousands of boxes of stuff and they had an understanding if they only look into two that there still more than 900 that they haven't looked at. They don't necessarily have that same understanding by landing on a page that has some content.
> *(Horsley 2018c, np.)*

Duff and Harris emphasise the importance of the describer's continual process of working with context, "locating it, constructing it, figuring and refiguring it" as archivists select not only certain facts but entire "layers of knowledge for inclusion" (Duff and Harris 2002, p. 276). For example, in a family record, the father's high-ranking job might be foregrounded in the document as it was of importance at the time the data was recorded but a cursory note of the mother's charity work might be of interest to a researcher studying the origins of the charity or the period's gender and class attitudes to work. Duff and Harris see this process of not merely listing but *analysis* as work that can be done and understood by machines, however, they assert that the "primary medium" of such work is "narrative" (276), as, we might add, narration reflects use value while addition operates in a different realm, that of exchange value.

The turn to the logic of the key word search is a sea change for archival practice, as archivists' knowledge of the deep connections of hierarchical context must either endure while no longer reflected in the representation of knowledge or researchers' methods, or become entirely redundant. If the context of holdings becomes hidden when users drill down in this way, archivists' crafted narratives, which attempt to give items "a shape, a pattern, a closure – to end their inevitable openness, close off their referents" (276), will lie dormant. This may result in a lack of understanding of potential uses for items or, in the logic of openness, it may pave the way for new connections to innumerable unexplored referents. The benefits of discoverability and independence that researchers might enjoy as a result of digital dissemination are incontestable. However, the future use of complex, nuanced knowledge in research may be precarious, as complete digitisation of archives was widely regarded as impossible. For smaller institutions that had not previously enjoyed exposure to a wide audience, digitisation had expanded the proportion of material used but there are unforeseen consequences. The archival profession is among those whose expert work is being profoundly transformed by technology as users become accustomed to discovering data that *satisfices* rather than satisfies their research questions, offering a resolution to a similar, less complex query instead of a further step towards knowledge creation. Satisficing is a characteristic of the "bounded rationality" of digital systems defined by "limitations, contradiction and paradox" rather than "freedom" or "coherence" where "sacrifice becomes inevitable" because satisfying all, often contradictory criteria, "is impossible" (McKenzie 2001, p. 116).

In the ongoing process of research, it is to be expected that those satisficing answers will, in turn, generate future research questions creating a shift in research trajectories. Encouraging researchers to incorporate digital expediency at some level of their process reduced inefficient use of cultural heritage practitioners' time in a manner comparable to customer service roles that increasingly take care of enquiries that cannot be resolved by customers' interaction with virtual communication tools. Some archivists were apprehensive, however, that this utility could mask problems of discoverability where context was not clear. At a national library, for example, context was seen as even more important when researchers get used to finding holdings by drilling down directly from metadata because metadata was not available for all items. The head of the department overseeing the library's research was "certainly not confident" that the full wealth of the institution's knowledge could be found using its digital systems; together with only a very small percentage of its collections having been digitised and an even smaller percentage available online, there was concern that digital discoverability "skews the view of what we have" (Horsley 2018c, np.), resulting in a shrunken perception of available knowledge. Looking to the future, the interviewed archivists predicted uses of data linking that were cause for concern: "artificial intelligence has the potential to draw new conclusions", particularly from unstructured data, which had, until recently, "resisted the broader analysis" creating a "significant danger" that the inferences of machine processing that are the modus operandi of Google and Facebook could expose identifying data about individuals (Horsley 2018d, np.), thus compromising the role of the gatekeeper of material that is vulnerable to misuse.

Common knowledge

The practices of archivists have developed in tandem with the practices of researchers. It has been argued, however, that when it comes to recognising the imprint that interpretation leaves on knowledge, archival practice has not reached the same maturity of reflexivity characteristic of research practices. Cook and Schwartz identified a tendency towards technical explanations of archivists' role in knowledge creation, with little attention given to the complex knowledge that gives meaning to those technical record-keeping requirements, standards, templates, and architectures. By focusing "almost exclusively on the mechanics of archival processes, is not there reflected a desire to be the white-coated 'scientific' clinician, unsoiled by the messy interpretation that is always endemic to performance?" (Cook and Schwartz 2002, p. 175). Contrary to Cook and Schwartz's white-coated clinicians, our study's participants did not seek to separate themselves from their materials in order to maintain an illusion of unbiased 'science'. In describing their practice, rather than being preoccupied with the contamination of the 'essence of collections', they were more concerned with the cross-pollination of perspectives that would engender researchers' fruitful engagement with complexity. Fundamentally, cultural heritage practice is an ongoing dialogue that favours the latter.

While the structure of human knowledge is associative and relies on implicit, tacit knowledge and the ability to understand metaphors, machine learning relies on probability to make decisions based on associations that were made in the data used to train the machine, even if, like Alpha Go, it uses that data to depart from predictability. In 2015, Alpha Go famously defeated Sedol, the world Go champion, by relying on "many layers of neurons, each arranged in overlapping tiles, to construct increasingly abstract, localized representations" of huge quantities of images, which it then repeatedly parsed in the search for unusual, 'left field' images to surprise its opponent (Silver et al. 2016, p. 484). In memory institutions, however, novel connections are yet non-existent in machine learning, at least not in the sense of unique contributions to knowledge or 'Eureka' moments. If a machine points a researcher in a particular direction, it is because that path is already trodden, according to the type of knowledge the machine has been fed. There is an inherent responsibility to apply a sufficiently critical research methodology when working with data from any source so that not only the provenance of data but also the *twists and turns* of their journey to the user are understood, and forces acting to interpret their meaning are not black-boxed beyond the researcher's understanding (Latour 1987). The introduction of new technologies of knowledge could be seen to represent a moment of *breach and repair* in cultural heritage practice, whereby practitioners' reactions to the disruption of their practice offer the opportunity to glimpse the norms of archival thinking, in terms of how knowledge is arranged (hierarchically) and described (according to methodical standards), that may have been invisible until they were disrupted (Goffman 1967).

The Knowledge Complexity project found evidence of cultural clashes between archival thinking and computational thinking but, as Star suggests in reference to "the myth of two cultures", those who "work on machines vs those who study or work with people" (Star 1990, p. 84), cultural heritage practitioners' accounts tended to be more nuanced, with disruption described as "evolution" (Horsley 2018e, np.) in line with their expansive mission of "the enrichment of knowledge" (Horsley 2018f, np.). Archivists were keen to reap the benefits of an "outside opinion", seen as useful when positioning their institutions within the constellation of the sector (Horsley 2018e, np.). Their enthusiasm for archival resources fuelled their commitment to sharing their "hidden treasures" (Horsley 2018g, np.), but also "common knowledge", in the sense that such knowledge should be a commons. This vision was buoyed in what one archivist described as the "ego-less" institution, whose founding tenets were "openness and sharing" (Horsley 2018h, np.), and the democratic spirit of connecting to "different worlds" through infrastructures, which, it was hoped, may lead to more *comparative studies* based on cultural heritage materials that would not have been discovered in parallel previously (Horsley 2018a, np.).

Intellectual autonomy

Within the archival context, intellectual autonomy for researchers might be understood as operating as freedom *to* know about and be inspired by the work of others rather than freedom *from* those existing connections. For archivists, the intellectual autonomy they exercise in their professional capacity confers an authority that should aid the research process. Ethicist Roberts and philosopher Wood describe how virtuous intellectual autonomy, far from declaring independence from other influences, relies on the contributions of thought and technologies external to the individual researcher, whilst retaining the value of self-direction (Roberts and Wood 2007, pp. 259–260). The removal of the archivist's voice in this process is detrimental to researchers' engagement with sources. Adapting Latour and Callon's approach to 'following' scientists and engineers, it is instructive to look for instances where the interests of cultural heritage institutions are translated into technical problems to which data specialists can then apply technical solutions. Such a process of translation from the discourse of one world to another has been described by numerous scholars who assert that scientists define disciplinary boundaries and then translate interests between *social worlds* (Foucault 1969; Clarke and Fujimura 1992; Latour 1999). Archivists have related their experiences of both achieving some success in opening black boxes that separated them from technical colleagues and being positioned as passive recipients of a technical solution that was outside their realm of discourse. This division manifested as a challenge of communication whereby archival needs were not understood in their own terms. Even where there may have been a shared vision, there was consensus that the onus was on cultural heritage practitioners to learn the language of the technical (Horsley 2018e, np.).

Embracing big data approaches is a way to provide an alternative to other service providers in an increasingly accelerated knowledge economy. The changing use of archives disrupts some of the fundamental tenets of cultural heritage practice, both through Google's presence as a rival source of knowledge and in the ubiquity of search engine use infiltrating archival research methods. Practitioners' support for integrating search engines into the research process is partly motivated by a concern that the satisficing return of a Google result might attain a hegemonic position that ultimately will marginalise the role of the archive in knowledge creation as such.

As well as limitations to what data can be made searchable and machine readable, there is principled resistance to fully aligning with a new paradigm of data-driven research.

It was generally felt that the influence of Google went beyond the user-friendly interface of the search box and that the culture of search engine use was more like using a self-driving car, which requires the user to give in to the logic of the machine – and whoever programmed it. Looking to the near future, research methods are likely to become further removed from the researcher's hand as automated tools, machine learning, and AI play an increased role. At a national library there was an awareness of what such a future might hold as technologies that appear *neutral* "skew the perception of what knowledge is and introduce all sorts of bias into it", as, despite a perception of gaining vantage of the whole picture, researchers might see less than before "because they're only being shown the things that the algorithm believes they want to see" (Horsley 2018c, np.). Wherever an institution had progressed the sharing of only a portion of their holdings, there was a fear that the prominence of that knowledge cast a shadow over the rest. The path from analogue to digital to online was by no means assured for all holdings, as resources were finite and there was no justifying the disproportionate effort needed to accommodate the incorporation of the most complex knowledge. Eliminating hiddenness or occlusion is not, therefore, a rising tide lifting all boats; rather, it risks entrenching divisions that marginalise the most different institutional practices, users, and material. At times, the technologies adopted were also not fit for purpose, as evidenced by archivists unable to find data using their institution's own search engines (Horsley 2018c, np.). There are many risks inherent in changing practice; as cultural heritage practitioners step away from the *materiality* of collections, knowledge complexity could become under-exposed or enable undesirable data linking. The struggle between archival thinking and computational thinking and the conceit of routinisation raises questions about who will control cultural heritage knowledge in the future.

Conclusions

Where technologies are a black box, replacing one goal with another that more closely fits the solution offered derails arguments that such a method is not the best choice. Ruppert, among other researchers, argues that Humanities and Social Science researchers must meaningfully engage with and 'socialise' big data approaches because otherwise, they "will become ever-more alienated from the creative power of software analytics in *formatting* their working practices" (Ruppert 2013, p. 3; emphasis original; Ruppert et al. 2015). The historical record, on which collective memory is based, is a process, not a product. The dialogue between academic values, including intellectual autonomy, and the technologies that might serve them, should be ongoing. Opening and simplifying access to knowledge to the extent of imitating the functionality of Google presents its own dangers of obfuscation. The fluid nature of the historical record dictates that certain knowledge will be more prominent or more excluded at any given instance of its consultation. Every such instance, whether a seemingly passive fact-finding exercise, or analytical interpretation for research purposes, is an *activation* and a *re-contextualisation* of knowledge and memory.

The Knowledge Complexity study's findings demonstrate how strongly societal-level knowledge trends cross into the academic research domain. While routinised techniques are still less prominent than the application of individual cultural heritage practitioners' specialist skills, the conceit of routinisation affects practices that are non-routinisable by displacing them in favour of routinised ones, which necessarily offer different outcomes (Susskind and Susskind 2015). While appearing not to cause significant disruption, this brand of routinisation represents a subversion of the aims and identity of the profession it replaces. Hiddenness, dormancy, and occlusion are part of the making of the historical record. Appraisal, negotiation, inscription, and reconfiguration of meanings and values in cultural heritage are in never-ending dialogue with the past, the present, and the future. Practitioners in archival institutions make crucially important contributions to this process. Some knowledge has already escaped the fate of all the "lost data" hidden or destroyed according to law or left languishing in the "grey area" (Edmond et al. 2018, p. 20). However, the future of rigorous historical research depends on opening black boxes offering smooth directions to quick wins. Only when researchers are empowered to apply their intellectually autonomous imaginations to the complexity of the archive that, machines obfuscate, can the democratising potential of opening up access to cultural heritage and the making of memory be realised.

Note

1 From https://5stardata.info/en/ –

1 star: make your stuff available on the Web (whatever format) under an open licence
2 stars: make it available as structured data (e.g., Excel instead of image scan of a table)
3 stars: make it available in a non-proprietary open format (e.g., CSV instead of Excel)
4 stars: use URIs to denote things, so that people can point at your stuff
5 stars: link your data to other data to provide context.

References

Assmann A 2006, "Memory Individual and Collective", in Goodin RE and Tilly C (eds.), *The Oxford Handbook of Contextual Political Analysis*. Oxford; New York: Oxford University Press, pp. 210–224.

Berners-Lee T 2012, "5-star Open Data Plan". Available from: https://5stardata.info/en/ [accessed 2 September 2019].

Berry DM 2011, "The Computational Turn: Thinking about the Digital Humanities", *Culture Machine*, vol. 12, pp. 1–22.

Blouin F 1999, "Archivists, Mediation and Constructs of Social Memory", *Archival Issues*, no. 24, pp. 101–112.

Blouin F and Rosenberg W 2011, *Processing the Past: Contesting Authority in History and the Archives*. New York: Oxford University Press.

Bowker GC and Star SL 1999, *Sorting Things Out: Classification and its Consequences*. Cambridge, MA: The MIT Press.

Clarke A and Fujimura JH (eds.) 1992, *The Right Tools For the Job: At Work in Twentieth-Century Life Sciences*. Princeton, NJ: Princeton University Press.

Confino A 1997, "A Collective Memory and Cultural History: Problems of Method", *American Historical Review*, vol. 102, pp. 1386–1403.

Cook T and Schwartz JM 2002, "Archives, Records, and Power: From (Postmodern) Theory to (Archival) Performance", *Archival Science*, vol. 2, pp. 171–185.

Crouch D 2010, "The Perpetual Performance and Emergence of Heritage", in Watson, S and Waterton E (eds.), *Culture, Heritage and Representation*. London: Routledge.

Derrida J 1996, *Archive Fever*, trans. Prenowitz, E. Chicago, IL and London: University of Chicago Press.

Derrida, J 2010, *Copy, Archive, Signature: A Conversation on Photography*, trans. Fort J. Stanford, CA: Stanford University Press.

Derrida, J and Stiegler B 2002, *Echographies of Television: Filmed Interviews*, trans. Bajorek J. Cambridge: Polity Press.

Duff WM and Harris V 2002, "Stories and Names: Archival Description as Narrating Records and Constructing Meanings", *Archival Science*, vol. 2, pp. 263–285.

Edmond J et al. 2018, "KPLEX – Final Report on the Exploitation, Translation and Reuse Potential for Project Results". Available from: https://kplex-project.eu/ [accessed 20 November 2019].

Foucault M 1969, *The Archaeology of Knowledge*, trans. Smith, AMS. London and New York: Routledge.

Geertz C 1973, *The Interpretation of Cultures*. New York: Basic Books.

Goffman E 1967, *On Face-Work: An Analysis of Ritual Elements in Social Interaction*. New York: Doubleday.

Han BC 2017, *Psychopolitics: Neoliberalism and New Technologies of Power*, trans. Butler E. London and New York: Verso.

Harris V 2002 "The Archival Sliver: Power, Memory, and Archives in South Africa", *Archival Science*, vol. 2, pp. 63–86.

Hedstrom M 1998, "How Do Archivists Make Electronic Archives Usable and Accessible?", *Archives and Manuscripts*, vol. 26, pp. 6–22.

Horsley N 2018a, "Interview with Participant 1. Knowledge Complexity Data Set". Available from: https://easy.dans.knaw.nl/ui/datasets/id/easy-dataset:114127/tab/2 [accessed 2 September 2019].

Horsley N 2018b, "Interview with Participant 7. Knowledge Complexity Data Set". Available from: https://easy.dans.knaw.nl/ui/datasets/id/easy-dataset:114127/tab/2 [accessed 2 September 2019].

Horsley N 2018c, "Interview with Participant 10. Knowledge Complexity Data Set". Available from: https://easy.dans.knaw.nl/ui/datasets/id/easy-dataset:114127/tab/2 [accessed 2 September 2019].

Horsley N 2018d, "Interview with Participant 5. Knowledge Complexity Data Set". Available from: https://easy.dans.knaw.nl/ui/datasets/id/easy-dataset:114127/tab/2 [accessed 4 September 2019].

Horsley N 2018e, "Interview with Participant 3. Knowledge Complexity Data Set". Available from: https://easy.dans.knaw.nl/ui/datasets/id/easy-dataset:114127/tab/2 [accessed 4 September 2019].

Horsley N 2018f, "Interview with Participant 8. Knowledge Complexity Data Set". Available from: https://easy.dans.knaw.nl/ui/datasets/id/easy-dataset:114127/tab/2 [accessed 2 September 2019].

Horsley N 2018g, "Interview with Participant 2. Knowledge Complexity Data Set". Available from: https://easy.dans.knaw.nl/ui/datasets/id/easy-dataset:114127/tab/2 [accessed 2 September 2019].

Horsley N 2018h, "Interview with Participant 6. Knowledge Complexity Data Set". Available from: https://easy.dans.knaw.nl/ui/datasets/id/easy-dataset:114127/tab/2 [accessed 2 September 2019].

Kitchin R 2014, *The Big Data Revolution*. London: SAGE.

Latour B 1987, *Science in Action: How to Follow Scientists and Engineers Through Society*. Cambridge, MA: Harvard University Press.

Latour B 1999, *Pandora's Hope: Essays on the Reality of Science Studies*. Cambridge, MA: Harvard University Press.

Levin DM 1985, *The Body's Recollection of Being*. Boston, MA: Routledge & Kegan Paul.

Manovich L 2011, "Trending: The Promises and the Challenges of Big Social Data", in Gold MK (ed.), *Debates in the Digital Humanities*. Minneapolis, MN: University of Minnesota Press, pp. 460–475.

Manovich L 2014, "The Exceptional and the Everyday: 144 Hours in Kiev", IEEE International Conference on Big Data, Washington, DC.

McKenzie J 2001, *Perform or Else: From Discipline to Performance*. London and New York: Routledge.

McPherson T 2012, "Why are the Digital Humanities so White? or Thinking the Histories of Race and Computation", in Gold MK (ed.), *Debates in the Digital Humanities*. Minneapolis, MN: University of Minnesota Press, pp. 139–160.

Moss M 2008, "Opening Pandora's Box: What is an Archive in the Digital Environment?", in Craven L (ed.), *What are Archives? Cultural and Theoretical Perspectives: A Reader*. Aldershot; Burlington, VT: Ashgate, pp. 1–87.

Negri A and Vercellone C 2008, "The Capital–Labor Relationship in Cognitive Capitalism", *Multitudes*, vol. 32, no. 1, pp. 39–50. Available from: https://doi.org. 10.3917/mult.032.0039 [accessed 5 September 2019].

Nesmith T 2002, "Seeing Archives: Postmodernism and the Changing Intellectual Place of Archives", *American Archivist*, vol. 65, pp. 24–41.

Olson DR 1994, *The World on Paper*. Cambridge: Cambridge University Press.

Olson HA et al. 2001, "The Power to Name: Representation in Library Catalogs", *Signs: Journal of Women in Culture and Society*, vol. 26, pp. 639–668.

Palladini J and Pustianaz M (eds.) 2017, *Lexicon for an Affective Archive*. Chicago, IL: University of Chicago Press.

Radley A 1990, "Artefacts, Memory and a Sense of the Past", in Middleton D and Edwards D (eds.), *Collective Remembering*. London; Newbury Park, CA: Sage, pp. 46–59.

Roberts RC and Wood WJ 2007, *Intellectual Virtues: An Essay in Regulative Epistemology*. Oxford: University of Oxford Press.

Ruppert E 2013, "Rethinking Empirical Social Sciences", *Dialogues in Human Geography*, vol. 3, no. 3, pp. 268–273.

Ruppert E et al. 2015, "Socialising Big Data: From Concept to Practice", CRESC Working Paper Series Working Paper No. 138.

Schafer MT and van Es K 2017, *The Datafied Society: Studying Culture through Data*. Amsterdam: Amsterdam University Press.

Silver D et al. 2016, "Mastering the Game of Go with Deep Neural Networks and Tree Search", *Nature*, vol. 529, no. 7587, pp. 484–489.

Star SL 1990, "Power, Technology and the Phenomenology of Conventions: On Being Allergic to Onions", *The Sociological Review*, vol. 38, no. 1, pp. 26–56.

Susskind R and Susskind D 2015, *The Future of the Professions: How Technology will Transform the Work of Human Experts*. Oxford: Oxford University Press.

van Dijck J 2014, "Datafication, Dataism and Dataveillance: Big Data between Scientific Paradigm and Ideology", *Surveillance & Society*, vol. 12, no. 2, pp. 197–208.

van Schie G, Westra I and Schäfer MT 2017, "Get Your Hands Dirty", in Schafer MT and van Es K (eds.), *The Datafied Society*. Amsterdam: Amsterdam University Press.

Yi X et al. 2014, "Building a Network Highway for Big Data: Architecture and Challenges", *IEEE Network*, vol. 28, no. 4, pp. 5–13.

9

BEHERE: PROSTHETIC MEMORY IN THE AGE OF DIGITAL FROTTAGE

Natasha Lushetich and Masaki Fujihata

In *The Practice of Everyday Life* de Certeau suggests that memory is "a sort of anti-museum" (de Certeau 1988, p. 108). Memory is not "localizable"; it cannot be reduced to a place, object, or practice; rather, objects have "hollow places in which a past sleeps, as in the everyday acts of walking, eating, going to bed, in which ancient revolutions slumber" (108). For many critics, data, like all information, is additive, rather than narrative. On this view, narrativity is intimately related to contemplation and knowledge, which is seen as heterogeneous, deeply transformative, and temporally intense (Dean 2013; Han 2016, p. 17; 2017). Additivity, by contrast, is reduced to information. It is seen as homogeneous and temporally flat (Han 2016, p. 17). And yet, additivity cannot refer to repetition *without* difference alone, not only because information is "difference that makes a difference" (Bateson 1972, p. 582), but because scale, measurement, proportion, and their pertaining mathematical operations are metaphysical categories that aid coexistence in and with the universe. In the most famous mathematical work of ancient China *Jiuzhang Suanshu* (Nine Chapters on the Art of Calculation), written around 200 BC and used for centuries throughout Asia, field measurements, volumes of shapes and solids in building design, linear equations, the ratios of unknown dimensions, and recommendations for good health arising from these calculations, all bring scale, proportion, frequency, density, and velocity to bear on the structure of physical and social reality (Schwartz 2008). Quantity is here inseparable from quality; extensive quantities, such as length, height, and volume are not categorically separate from intensive qualities like concentration, pressure, and density except, say, at 0 or 100 degrees Celsius where a quantity such as a gallon of water, turns not into a different quantity, but a different quality: ice or vapour. Rather, extensive quantities permeate intensive qualities through and through. Similarly, in the philosophy of

146 Natasha Lushetich and Masaki Fujihata

the Japanese philosopher Nishida, the 'metaphysical' is not separate from the physical; it is produced through a dynamic process of inter-expression. Nishida writes:

> Creation does not mean that being arises from nonbeing. Creating in that sense would be merely accidental and arbitrary. Nor does it signify that being merely arises from being either. Creation in that sense would merely be a necessary result, a form of causal determinism. Creation, real creativity, entails that the world [...] expresses itself within itself.
>
> *(Nishida 1992, p. 71)*

For Nishida, the "world" has "the logical form of a self-transforming matrix" (73) which "expresses itself within itself" through the "inter-expressive, mutual revealment of self and other" (49) where "other" refers to all existents and their co-dependent origination. It is in and through this structuring relation that "the concrete world" becomes "metaphysical" (Nishida 1970, p. 29).

Since the late 1980s, media artist Fujihata's work has been concerned with scale, shape, duration, spatial and temporal concentration and sedimentation, as well as with memory: the memory of the world, human memory, and the memory of media. His 1989 video *Parametrized Objects* manipulated the architectural parameters of solid structures, transforming them into immaterial objects. The 1990 *Forbidden Fruits* used a mathematical function called B-Spline to create curved 3D models that resembled water drops, peaches, and human torsos created without any reference to natural forms shaped by physical laws. A similar form of data relationality was explored in the 1994 *Impressing Velocity*. Here Fujihata climbed Mt. Fuji with his assistants carrying (what was then) a bulky and cumbersome Global Positioning System and a video camera to record the time, distance, altitude, and their constantly changing relationship to the human body (Kusahara 2017, p. 65). In the final exhibit, videos, diagrams, maps, and the computer-generated images obtained from the data showed the virtual shape of Mt. Fuji proprioceptically experienced by the climber's body in the process of climbing. Similarly, in the 2002–2012 series *Field Works*, Fujihata collected spatial and temporal data from various human activities in a natural environment, tracing the participants' embodied experience through the GPS system. In the 2012 iteration of the series – *Voices of Aliveness* – he reworked the obtained data as 3D images, human as well as location sounds, and presented them as an interactive installation with a stereoscopic projection. As even a cursory glance shows, all these projects are ephemeral "monuments of culture" (Fujihata and Sosnowska 2013, np.). However, they are also prescient *formal* investigations into the memory of geolocative, communication, and tracking devices without which today's datascape would be difficult to imagine. As media theorist Ernst notes, over the past few decades, geospatial memory has changed drastically; today, "tools" which are themselves "senders" produce geospatial information in the "the geographic" as well as electromagnetic "fields" weaving "time" and "space" into a "spatio–temporal data tissue" (Ernst 2018, np.).

Recorded sound, movement, action, and their respective velocities, form data tissue in which quantity and quality inter-express medially. A medium is not a container; it is a spatio–temporal milieu as well as a practice where objects, operations, and subjects converge. The highly problematic dualism of agent and patient that stems from the history of Western metaphysics denies things agency, attributing it, instead, to human subjects: programmers or designers. Contra this view, media theorist Vismann suggests that a gadget or medium's features cannot be *independent* of their conditions of production, material properties, even their spatial and temporal circumstances. Vismann draws our attention to what she terms "auto-praxis" (*Eigenpraxis*) of media and gadgets (Vismann 2013, p. 84) – their manner of unfolding, of processing data, or memory. But what precisely is medial memory? The short answer to this question is: the trace of the signal as well as noise, as when we are listening to a 1930s record and we hear what is recorded – a song or an instrumental composition, or the signal – and the crackling of the record, or noise (Ernst 2014). It is the signal–noise, quality–quantity nexus that reflects the auto-praxis of the medium. Consider, for example, Paik's 1965 *Zen for Film*, a clear 16 mm leader, devoid of any recorded material whatsoever. Approximately twenty minutes long, *Zen for Film* exposes the cinematic medium – the blank celluloid and the projection apparatus – to the cinematic gaze. In Paik's words, *Zen for Film* discloses "time without contents" (Paik quoted in Kaye 2007, p. 52) "posit[ing] a concrete present" in the "moving-image tale of the celluloid's journey through the transport mechanism of the projector" (Jenkins 1993, p. 137). This journey is "unique in each telling as *Zen for Film* maintain[s] on its celluloid surface" a *record* of all its viewings and screenings "in the form of accumulated scratches, dust, dirt, rips and splices" (137). The scratches, rips, and splices are both signal and noise, one of the intentions of *Zen for Film* being to highlight the operation of the cinematic apparatus in a way that shows the simultaneous past-ness and present-ness of film as a medium. Although vastly different from Paik's, Fujihata's work ponders the inter-expression of data, gadgets, people, and media. It ponders prosthetic memory. In human terms, prosthetic memory is a deeply felt memory of a past event through which a person or a group did not live but which has been relationally constructed by viewing films or other media, listening to audio recordings or reading books (Landsberg 2004). In medial terms, it is the memory embedded in a medium's "auto-praxis", its manner of processing time, space, energy, and matter.

In the most recent project *BeHere: The Past in the Present* (2018–), simultaneously an interactive augmented reality installation (where real-life objects are enhanced by 3D computer-generated objects) and a smartphone application, Fujihata draws on oceans of data – hundreds of thousands of photographs selected from the vast photo libraries across the Internet, taken mostly as street snapshots and uploaded by amateurs. With these processed or 'distilled' images, Fujihata reconstructed the relational microphysics of the 1940–1970 Hong Kong re-staging micro-events of the Wan Chai district, filming them with the aid of photogrammetry, and subsequently rendering them as 3D model data. Often used to model engineering structures, forensic scenes, or, more generally, to photograph the topology of objects, photogrammetry captures a site or a scene with dozens of cameras in a 360 degrees view. In *BeHere*, 70 synchronised cameras were used to photograph re-enacted scenes of everyday life. The obtained images were processed as 3D models, so that the final *BeHere* application, downloadable to viewers'

FIGURE 9.1 Masaki Fujihata, *BeHere*, Wan Chai, Hong Kong, 2018.
Source: Photo: Shuichi Fukuzawa. © Shuichi Fukuzawa. Courtesy of Shuichi Fukuzawa

mobile devices, consisted of movable, manipulable virtual sculptures made of time. These temporal sculptures were virtually placed in ten Wan Chai locations, from the Blue House cluster, and the old Wan Chai post office to Dominion Garden. Viewers could visit spots listed in the application's menu, and access – even recompose – the 3D scenes in real time. Perhaps most surprisingly, and certainly most delightfully, they could also step into the picture (time-travel style) and insert themselves in the past–present continuum of a physical–virtual reality.

Important to mention at this point is perhaps that, in *BeHere*, the vast snapshot archives were not searched with the aim of finding some sort of bygone Wan Chai essence or stereotype. Rather, the purpose was to find that which lies behind, beneath, or at the edges of the perceptible, yet is neither 'background' nor 'foreground' but, rather, the inter-expression of quality and quantity. In the pages that follow, we focus on the ways in which re-actualised, augmented photographs of a bygone era, transplanted into the present moment, co-create and amplify prosthetic memory. Virtuality, in one of its early, and perhaps most famous definitions, is the "ability to work from a conceptual model", rather than actual experience, but "act as if the actual experience had occurred" (Peirce 1960, p. 261). As Peirce suggests, a fox or a wolf can find a trail on an unfamiliar territory, and this process *actualises* the virtual (261). In human lives, the reverse occurs when another human being dies. Death virtualises the actual. The dead relative, partner, friend, or neighbour continues to exist in human memory as well as in various media: photographs, stories, or complex databases. In the current cultural perception, data processing is often mistakenly conflated with statistics. It is suggested that in "calculating 'average values'" data remains "blind to the event" while it is not "what is statistically likely, but what is unlikely – the singular, the event – [that] will shape history" (Han 2017, p. 76). While we do not disagree with Han – events, rather than statistics or 'average values' have always shaped and will continue to shape history – we are suggesting that image-software-facilitated sifting through hundreds of

BeHere: Prosthetic memory **149**

thousands of photographs reveals something far more mysterious than the (statistical) average. It reveals to the human eye imperceptible *meta-event*: the structuring, process, and movement of inter-expression. In the social realm, this equals what philosopher Nancy has called the *clinamen*, that unidentifiable inclination to and towards another, or others (Nancy 1991, p. 3), a form of relationality that cannot be reduced to a common denominator or a cohesive force. In *BeHere*, this elusive differential relation is discernible in three realms: in the latent, or semi-visible image which emerges from what we call 'digital frottage'; in the prosthetic, remediated co-presence of the people depicted in the images, in the actors bringing the depicted micro-relationalities to life, and viewer/interactants witnessing the event; and finally, in the affective anarchive, which is both an archive and not an archive, and, as such, inter-expressive, rather than cohesive. In articulating these relations we also hope to articulate the interpenetration of micro- and meta-events, of over-arching, phenomenal, and micro-temporal scales that are the "tissue" (Ernst 2018) of prosthetic memory.

The latent image

Photographs have historically been used as models of veracity, to support different forms of knowledge production such as legal, scientific, or technical knowledge. In contrast to these factual images, forms of visual depiction that encourage the ripening of the semi-visible image in the observer have been associated with drawing and painting: pointillism, *sfumato*, or one-line drawing. In these techniques, as in many others, the image is *extracted* from the invisible or the semi-visible and completed *in* and *by* the observer. Human processors, or artists, have traditionally been seen as the only 'agents' capable of extracting the latent image, largely due to their ability to capture the memory of the world by simultaneously capturing its *process* of sedimentation and human perception of that process. Photography, by contrast, has been relegated to showing the so-called 'objective reality'. We would like to suggest that the latent image, a record of the world as process, cannot be attributed to 'human processors' alone, but forms part of an algorithmic constellation. Today, images "have become a medium for conveying algorithm"; consequently, the role of the artist has "shifted from image production to algorithmic production" (Fujihata in Fujihata and Duguet 2016, pp. 002–016). But let us, before going any further, first explain what we mean by 'algorithm'.

Just like a medium is not a container, an algorithm is not an abstract mathematical idea imposed on concrete data. It is an emergent phenomenon, an active co-creator of prosthetic memory and the memory of the world. Since time immemorial, diverse civilisations have marked territories – rocks, soil, trees, or human bodies – through techniques of spatial and temporal abstraction such as encircling, incising, carving, and scarifying. In this context, algorithms were codified rituals. In the Middle Ages, they were heterogeneous methods used for predictive operations. Today, they are computerised procedures. In all these cases, algorithms are "emergent diagrams contingent on repetition and the processual organisation of time, space, objects, and actions" (Lushetich 2020, np.). In the current datified landscape, space, time, and interaction have become algorithmic procedures (Fujihata in Fujihata and Duguet 2016, pp. 002–016), interpenetrated by diagrammatic processes or digital *frottage*. An often-used Surrealist technique discovered by painter Ernst in 1925, frottage is "obtained by rubbing charcoal or pigment on a paper" placed "over some rough surface" (Ernst quoted in Frey 1936, p. 15). The paper, which can be placed over many different objects and surfaces and rubbed many times in succession, reveals the objects' semi-visible texture while simultaneously exposing the working of material memory, the fact that the world's processes – wind, rain, dust, dirt, pollen, mucus, among many others – sediment in the object, often in a relief form. As neurologist Damasio suggests, human memory is multiplicitous; the memory we have of a thing or a person is not stored in a 'frozen' form but, rather, as a set of "dispositions" or "codings for reactivation" that inter-express with circumstantial existents every time a particular memory is recalled (Damasio in Damasio and Mulder 2003, p. 153). Damasio seems to be echoing Vismann as well as Bergson here. For philosopher Bergson, both human memory and the memory of the world bring the relaying of impressions – such as a paper placed over a number of different surfaces and drawn upon in succession – into dialogue with contagion. In frottage, the paper documents the various interactions; it calls forth the trace of past actions and interactions. In overlaying inter-expressions of diverse material sedimentations through the contagion of particular points, parts or reliefs, it activates mnemonic fulcrums. Similarly, human perception, which consists of "an incalculable multitude of memory fragments" (Bergson 1939, p. 39), imprints "on the body a certain attitude in which memories will insert themselves", which is why "the present perception" always seeks "the recollection of the anterior perception, to which it bears semblance" (112). Incoming perceptions are imprinted on the body by calling to memory, which answers by providing the closest match but "[b]ehind these images identical to the object", there are always others that "resemble the object; it is just that their kinship to the object is different or more distant" (112–113).

What this means is that the working of human memory, like the working of material memory – of which fossils are a good example – is like frottage, that is: *transversal*. All life forms are enmeshed in other life forms. The difference between one form and another – plant, rock, animal, human, machine – is never absolute. What we call the 'world' is a movement that brings together different mnemonic processes creating a continuity of spatial and temporal layers. At the tectonic level, and at the finite, human (or animal) level, there is biological and material synchrony because the fabric of becoming is woven of the imperceptible *traces* of past events, things, and beings. For Bergson, memory and matter form a continuum across rocks, plants, animals, human consciousness, and unconsciousness; indeed, the entire universe is made of image assemblages (Bergson 1939, p. 24). Bergson, like Damasio after him, is careful not to use the trope of a frozen image, despite the fact that he was writing "in the midst of the popularization of photography driven in part by Kodak's 1888 release of its first Brownie box camera" (MacKenzie and Munster 2019, p. 4). Writing in 2019, media theorists MacKenzie and Munster shift Bergson's notion of image assemblages to the context of contemporary computation, where image assemblages are "entities in a computational relationality" forming part of data sets modulated across contemporary data practices (5). Image aggregates here "constitute the (non-human) activities of perception as a mode of cutting into/selecting out of the entire flux of image-ensemble-world" (13). This correlation between human and machine systems – based on Bergson's conflation of memory, action and perception – is not new. Wiener, too, thought that "viewing complex actions out of accumulated systematic behavior of networked neurons puts the emphasis on the *process*, or algorithmic pattern that facilitate[s] processing" which is "productive in itself" (Halpern 2015, p. 56). Today, image-processing software like Hadoop or Spark, sifting through vast image collections, performs digital frottage. Like analogue frottage, digital frottage acts transversally through "multiple points" of "other images" (Bergson 1939, p. 38). The present-day processing of images, which, according to Vismann, is never merely additive but involves a co-action of the medium, is algorithmic in the sense that it is diagrammatic; it has an aggregating or assembling function.

In *BeHere*, the images obtained through data processing and digital frottage as new configurations of machinically (rather than humanly) perceived existents, shed light on that which eludes the (naked) human eye: the micro-movement of easing into a body posture adopted in waiting, a gesture used to signal that one is about to say something, the gentle wind in the hair of the *al fresco* diners, a strangely off-balance chair, a particular way of sitting, walking, or talking as well as what is usually referred to as noise: an overexposed, underexposed, or blurred (part of a) photograph. None of these movements, attitudes, objects, or blurs appear in a *particular* image, or in two, three, or five images, nor do they show an average or a stereotype, much like a paper placed over multiple surfaces and rubbed in succession does not show the statistical average, but a contagion of *specific* points or reliefs that cue attentional fulcrums: the merging of the semi-visible and the intuited. In *BeHere*, the images of bygone Wan Chai emerged from a transversal inter-expression of the signal (the captured scenes) and noise (the over-exposed, underexposed, or blurred parts of photographs) that emphasise random pictorial elements while making others fade or disappear). These transversal images, which resemble the Bergsonian 'grooves' into which memories insert themselves, or Damasio's "reactivation codes", were further 'frottaged' with an entirely different medium: the human narrative. Fujihata engaged in extensive interviews with the elderly local residents and used their divergent micro-memories of how and where something used to be done to re-create 'ordinary' scenes of bygone Wan Chai. Yet another layer of mediation – actors – was used to enact fragments of everyday actions like eating, writing, calculating, weaving baskets, chatting, or waving to a neighbour. These micro-scenes were recorded with the aid of photogrammetry and placed in an augmented reality environment where viewers could interact with the twice-remediated scenes from the past.

Prosthetic co-presence

As anyone who has ever lost a dear person knows, people who pass away do not disappear for as long as they are anchored in the living (human) or medial memory.

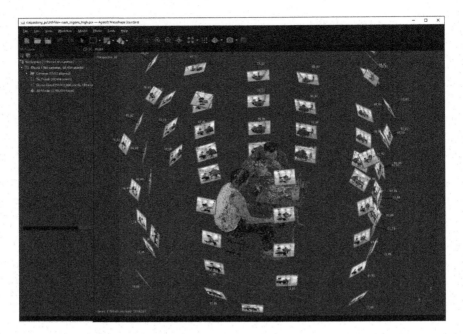

FIGURE 9.2 Masaki Fujihata, *BeHere* photogrammetry, screen capture, Hong Kong 2018.

Source: © Masaki Fujihata

But how do we remember the deeply ingrained, non-person-specific sociality, ways of being imperceptibly embedded in life media – walking, sleeping, or eating – that underlying, yet invisible, relationality? In a recent discussion of different cultural practices and their influence on memory, Wang suggests that Europeans and Euro Americans have a more developed episodic memory – being elected the class president, for example – due to the individualistic cultural orientation, while Asians and Asian Americans have a more developed relational memory, the ability to remember aspects of life with no person-specific content, such as catching a train with a group of people every week (Wang 2009). Although there are subtle cultural differences at work in the way we do many things in life, there is also a more fundamental, inter-expressive sociality at work in all human relations. When we come into this world, as helpless infants, we are dependent on our parents or carers for survival. Our cognitive faculties are underdeveloped and we have no experience or habits to fall back on. We learn to speak our parents or carers' language/s and adopt their expressions, gestures or attitudes; we are formed by and through their habits. As humans, we are profoundly iterative beings: formed by others, who were, in turn, formed by others. Anthropologist Mauss called micro-ordinary actions like walking, sitting, or swimming "body techniques"; in his later work, he made explicit connections between these "body techniques" and the disseminating power of media like film and television (Mauss 1973, p. 72). Mauss's

BeHere: Prosthetic memory **153**

point was that the behaviour of fellow humans, their embodied manner of being, 'sediments' in our senses of sight, hearing, touch, movement, or balance. This sedimentation of behaviour, the invisible, intangible 'background' of being, is precisely what *BeHere* brings to light through micro-actions, rather than individualised stories about how person X did Y.

For Nishida, the social world, like the physical world, unfolds as inter-expression. "The I understands the thou by expressing the thou" because "the other is in the self and the self in the other" (Nishida 1966, p. 163). The self being in the other while, at the same time, being in its own self, while the other remains 'other', also means that the self is constituted in its communication with the world, which, like the encounter of multiple transversal images in digital frottage, is also contagion. In other words, the self and other are also "expressive" of "the I-and-Thou relationship" (163), a bi-conditional articulation where the self is identical *and* alter, singular *and* social. In *The Fundamental Problems of Philosophy*, Nishida asks: "[w]hat is the personal?" (Nishida 1970, p. 8), and suggests the following answer:

> the exterior becomes interior in the self-determination of the personal self. For example, without a desire for water there is no self, and without the self there is no desire for water [...] When the self obeys desire the self is lost. Desire is born to die and dies to be reborn. Such a thing is [...] a determination of the indeterminate. Likewise, personality cannot be unique. Personality can only be conceived in relation to other personalities, in the sense of seeing the "Thou" in the depths of the "I" and the "I" in the depths of the "Thou".
>
> *(8–9)*

What we usually refer to as the individual self is a transition, not only in terms of its relationship to the 'Thou' but, equally importantly, to its own self. The "'I' of the present regards the 'I' of yesterday and the 'I' of tomorrow as a 'Thou'" (10–11); these other 'Is' are 'others' just like any other 'other'.

In *BeHere*, anyone with a mobile device can experience the recreated micro-events from the past – events that may have taken place on the very spot they are presently occupying. The 3D images can also be shared with others. A present-day inhabitant or visitor, expressive of present-day sociality, can enter into a relationship inter-expressive of the Nishidian otherness through (social) choreography, by, for example, coordinating their pose to complement or contrast that of the 3D figures, or by adopting particular mimetic gestures such as pointing at something, holding their handbag in a particular way, looking in a certain direction or changing the context of the 3D figures and placing them elsewhere: on a terrace, in a park, or on a motorway. Moreover, by inserting themselves in the image, viewers also create an instant self–other past–present-ness in their own life, articulating the "I-and-Thou" relationship in three senses of the word: in the sense of prosthetic co-presence with the never-encountered inhabitants of Wan Chai; in the sense of past-ness and thus also otherness of their own self; and, by articulating the iterative nature of the singular–plural becoming – the inclination to, from, or towards another, or the *clinamen* (Nancy 1991).

Augmented reality anchors the simultaneous unfolding of different temporalities by relying on real time technology. For many critics, manipulating virtual content in real time flattens the temporal multidimensionality required by any complex organism as part of its integrative function of memory, or alternatively, chaotically mixes antagonistic temporalities, such as creative and routine time, internal and external rhythms (Alhadeff-Jones 2016). However, these critiques, which stigmatise the performativity of real time as reductive, because immediate, and, therefore, temporally and experientially 'thin', are based on two reductive notions. The first is that time, as a unified whole, is divisible into compartmentalised subcategories; the second that there is a separation between interiority and exteriority, the close and the distant, where time is seen as a synthesising function of space and knowledge. *BeHere* utilises real time technology to expose the Möbius strip-like relationship to what is usually referred to as 'interiority' and 'exteriority'. The project creates what is best described as a 'temporal swelling' as well as experiential 'ecstasy' if we understand the word *ek-stasis*, not in the emotional sense, but in its original meaning, to stand beside 'one's usual being'. The swelling of time experienced by the viewer/interactant can be compared to the Portuguese notion *saudade*, which refers to a simultaneous feeling of joy and pain, caused by a form of pre-booked nostalgia, where, upon seeing a beautiful sight or a dear person, the experiencer is catapulted from the present moment to a future moment from which they look back on the present moment, perceive it as a past moment, and are overcome by a form of corporal ecstasy, that is, essentially, a finite being's relationship to its finitude.

In a less pronouncedly emotional register, *BeHere* expands the past-in-the-present-in-the-future-in-the-past relation by placing a past event in a real-time augmented reality where the event can be altered, and used to socially choreograph the existing interaction, thus amplifying both the present reception of the past, and the future reception of the present, given that posed photographs (the interactant adopting a pose and inserting the image into the past event), unlike snapshots, always look to the future. This temporal swelling brings to the fore the usually imperceptible temporal background, which consists of two different yet mutually affecting species of time: phenomenal time and the specious present. Phenomenal time is the time apprehended experientially by the human being, in the context of its own existence, marked by our invariable finitude within which we regard our past as our factuality and our future as our possibility. The specious present is the temporal spread of the now moment, which, to use Varela's definition, consists of a continuous temporal streaming of retention – or that which has just past – and protention or that which is about to happen (Varela 1999). Not dissimilarly to feedback and feedforward, retention causes a 'slippage', or a progressive slowing down; protention, on the other hand, produces affective colouring, caused by this 'slippage'.

The combination of the two magnifies the object of our contemplation, causing a temporal swelling. In *BeHere*, the temporary sensation of standing beside one's usual being comes from inserting oneself into a re-enactment of a past event and

BeHere: Prosthetic memory **155**

the immersion in the magnified micro-temporal now moment, or the transversal 'mixing' of the specious present and its larger-scale perception of phenomenal time, which, in this case, refers to the simultaneity or collision of the experiencer's past and future and the effect the mixing of the specious present and the phenomenal time has on the configuration of the interactant. What this particular feature of *BeHere* articulates is the simultaneously synchronous and dyachronous nature of all human existence. We are always both here and elsewhere, both continuous and discontinuous, both actual and virtual. In Nishida's theory of temporality, continuous time, flowing from the past to the future is 'located' in discontinuity; every new moment is different from the previous precisely because it is discontinuous. Each 'present' is severed from the 'past present' by a non-present, which means that continuous time disappears and is determined again in the next present. In this sense, discontinuity is the *basho* of continuity; *basho* means "that in which" and is permanently engaged in a dialectical relationship with "that which" or the content of *basho* (Nishida 1970, pp. 6–7).

Another important layer of prosthetic presence in *BeHere* is the use of actors to re-enact the next-to-imperceptible micro-scenes of everyday life. This particular form of prosthetic and amplified presence is simultaneously signal and noise. Actors' presence has traditionally been aligned with the Benjaminian concept of auratic presence. Benjamin defines "aura" as "the unique phenomenon of a distance however close it may be" (Benjamin 1999, p. 222), a phenomenon that brings together the immediacy of presentation in the here and now, and the intuition of past and distant processes. In an ephemeral medium like performance, the actor's presence displays the accumulated repetition and retention of particular gestures, postural schemas, actions, and interactions, which manifest in the here and now, making visible a part of the cumulative-retentive process. We could call this part of the accumulated presence 'signal' – an actor rehearses to anchor the rehearsed gestures and actions to her body, body techniques, and behaviour. But there are also other forms of presence more akin to noise, where what is perceived as the actor's unique ability to command attention, is, in fact, a trace of a number of libidinal surrenders to the 'here and now', to the audience's attention and receptivity. In *BeHere*, actors (inter-)express the *clinamen* through the (intentional) process of anchoring rehearsed gestures to their body, body techniques, and behaviour. However, as actors, they are also amplified carriers of past relationalities, comparable to the auditory noise of a record, or the visual noise of Paik's *Zen for Film*. What we perceive as presence in actors who are used to being looked at, is a long series of actor–audience mediations, of libidinal surrenders and heightened receptivity. This difficult-to-tell-apart inter-expressive fusion of signal and noise is also amplified by *BeHere*'s anarchiving and anarchival tendencies.

The affective anarchive

There are, broadly speaking, two kinds of memory, although they are by no means separate: the explicitly articulated, shared, collective memory encapsulated in symbols, stories, and customs that "call to mind the collective nature of the activity of remembering" (Kuhn 1995, p. 6); and the inexplicit, unarticulated memory, or mnemonic noise. Explicit, collective memory is often invented or distorted; its purpose is to transmit information "deemed vital for the constitution and continuation of a specific group" (Assmann 2010, p. 43). However, members of a given group, neighbourhood, city, or region, neither remember the same things nor do they remember them in the same way. Collective memory is thus always already a process of ordering disorder, or crafting signal from noise. Building on Fujihata and Duguet's 2016 monograph *Anarchive*, which journeys through Fujihata's entire oeuvre in the form of a ring binder – the archetype of an archive file – yet has augmented features that enable the reader to access videos and 3D simulations on their iPads or iPhones while leafing through the physical book, *BeHere* articulates the impossibility of merely 'storing' data. Contrary to received belief, archives do not "store memory"; rather, they "offer the *possibility* to create memory" (Menne-Haritz 2001, p. 59; emphasis original) despite the fact that they also "perpetuate what a society has consciously selected and maintains as salient and vital for a common orientation and a shared remembering" in the visual, literary, auditory, and other cultural canons (Assmann 2006, p. 221).

An anarchive, by contrast, is both an archive and the archive's noise. As a mnemonic project, *BeHere* is an archive because it has all the characteristics of an archive: it inscribes spatially and creates meaning; it also has a mediating function (Assmann 2011). Spatial inscription refers to any system that takes "memory out of mental storage and fix[es] it independently of living bearers" (Assmann 2011, p. 328). In *BeHere*, the downloadable application inscribes remembering spatially in an augmented way, both virtually and physically, in the ten selected locations, as well as in the interactants' bodies, since remembering is an act of embodiment, too. We are in a constant exchange with our environment; as we settle in a new (actual or virtual) place, the place settles in us. Hence the paradox of place and habit: although we can experience 'place' everywhere, everywhere it recedes into the perceptual 'background', as we become engrossed in daily routines and micro-routines. *BeHere* brings this complex relation to the fore with the aid of machinic perception and medial memory. It presents the interactant with an "affective archive", an intimate process of embodied meaning making experienced virtually and within the interactant's lived environment, a process where the body becomes a medium of "distilled memories" and incorporated techniques (Palladini and Pustianaz 2017, pp. 12–13).

The mnemonic process unfolding in *BeHere* takes place simultaneously in the viewer/interactant, in their social partners, and in objects. Social partners – passers-by, friends, or acquaintances – communicate the social context of bygone Wan Chai by communicating the difference between the present-day passers-by and the re-enacted figures' actions and body techniques. Objects such as clothes, baskets, plates, glasses, and newspapers communicate the cultural 'texture' of a past era, too. In a mediatised culture, memory is linked to concrete physical places and objects. However, it is also linked to randomly accessible, generic electronic 'places' that are often short-lived. The average life of an url is 44 days; computers no longer read relatively recent (less than ten years old) inscription devices such as CD ROMs or even CDs. Digital information is far more prone to decay than paper, already a more fragile (because flammable) medium than the stone tablets it replaced.

In *BeHere*, this inherently indeterminate, both displacing/disorientating and re-orientating feature of digital media is presented in an anarchival form. An anarchive points both to alternative memories, or possibilities of interpretation, and to the digital media's fundamental instability. Predicated on "techno-mathematical substructures of algorithms" embedded in computers and their "dynamic Random Access Memory (DRAM)" (Ernst 2014, np.), the constant updating and migration of digital media have imposed a drastic "change from the ideal of archival eternity to permanent change" (np.). This is why the anarchival "corresponds to a functional core criterium of techno-mathematical communication theory: the signal-to-noise ratio" where "[a]rchival value loses its apparent semantic meaning in favour of statistical probabilities" and where the information source "selects a desired message out of a set of possible messages" (Weaver quoted in Ernst 2014). In fact, information as such applies not to the individual (semantically meaningful) message but to the "entire informational landscape", which, invariably, is temporary order "wrenched from disorder" (Ernst 2014, np.). *BeHere*'s particular form of archiving – recomposing, saving, editing, sharing – as well as its particular form of an-archiving – the iterative opening-up of new, augmented forms of co-presence, by, for example, inserting new figures into a scene, or displacing the existing ones, articulates the continuity of discontinuity of a collective, cultural, and artefactual kind.

While bringing the past into the present, the *BeHere* application both stabilises the trans-temporal past–present–future relationship and exposes its fragility. This paradoxical situation echoes Nishida's notion of time as both continuous and discontinuous. There has to be something continuous in time for change to be change. And yet, time *is* change. As change, it is discontinuous (Nishida 1970, p. 117). Likewise, memory, too, is both continuous and discontinuous. While human memory is predicated on repetition and re-performance, which separates signal from noise, adding precision to the signal, in medial memory, repetition erodes the signal and amplifies noise. The multiplicitous approach of *BeHere*, which relies on found images, human micro-narratives, performative re-enactments of micro-events, and a real-time augmented reality interface, affords the perception of the imperceptible or semi-perceptible, in the visual, temporal, social, and mnemotechnical realms. The continuous inter-expression of signal and noise here articulates the meta-event: the 'abyssal ground' that is always already "the finitude of singularities" (Nancy 1991, p. 26). The latent image, the twice-removed co-presence, and the disorientating–re-orientating anarchive all open onto the incomprehensibility of non-being – or death – of forgetting, human as well as material perishability. In the *BeHere* application, a mortal being encounters another mortal being via a twice re-mediated presence and this encounter takes place in (temporal) *ek-stasis*. Occurring in an indeterminate realm, the encounter cannot produce an enveloping insided-ness, community, or overarching unity, only a communication of finitude as exposed in the non-unified space – or rather, spacing – between the 'being', the 'in', and the 'common'.

158 Natasha Lushetich and Masaki Fujihata

References

Alhadeff-Jones M 2016, *Time and the Rhythms of Emancipatory Education: Rethinking the Temporal Complexity or Self and Society*. London and New York: Routledge.

Assmann A 2006, "Memory, Individual and Collective", in Goodin RE and Tilly C (eds.), *The Oxford Handbook of Contextual Political Analysis*. Oxford; New York: Oxford University Press, pp. 210–224.

Assmann A 2010, "Re-framing Memory: Between Individual and Collective Forms of Constructing the Past", in Tilmans K, Van Vree F and Winter J (eds.), *Performing the Past: Memory, History and Identity in Modern Europe*. Amsterdam: Amsterdam University Press, pp. 35–50.

Assmann A 2011, *Cultural Memory and Western Civilization: Functions, Media, Archives*. New York: Cambridge University Press.

Bateson G 1972, *Steps to an Ecology of Mind*. New York: Ballantine Books.

Benjamin W 1999, "The Work of Art in the Age of Mechanical Reproduction", in *Illuminations*, trans. Zohn H. London: Pimlico, pp. 211–244.

Bergson H 1939, *Matière et mémoire*. Paris: Les Presses Universitaires de France.

Damasio A and Mulder A 2003, "The Memory as Living Archive: Interview with Antonio Damasio", in Brouwer J, Mulder A, and Charlton S (eds.), *Information is Alive: Art and Theory on Archiving and Retrieving Data*. Rotterdam: V2_Publishing/NAI Publishers, pp. 153–182.

Dean J 2013, "Communicative Capitalism: This is What Democracy Looks Like", in Medak T and Milat P (eds.), *Idea of Radical Media*. Zagreb: Multimedijalni Institut, pp. 60–71.

de Certeau M 1988, *The Practice of Everyday Life*, trans. Rendall S. Berkeley, CA: University of California Press.

Ernst W 2014, "Between the Archive and the Anarchivable", *Mnemoscape*, No.1. Available from: www.mnemoscape.org/single-post/2014/09/04/Between-the-Archive-and-the-Anarchivable-by-Wolfgang-Ernst [accessed 6 December 2019].

Ernst W 2018, "Tracing Tempor(e)alities", *Media Theory – Special Issue: Geospatial Memory*, vol. 2, no. 1. Available from: http://mediatheoryjournal.org/wolfgang-ernst-tracing-temporealities/ [accessed 6 December 2019].

Frey JG 1936, "From Dada to Surrealism", *Parnassus*, vol. 8, no. 7, pp. 12–15.

Fujihata M and Duguet AM 2016, *Anarchive No. 6*. Paris: Éditions *Anarchive*.

Fujihata M and Sosnowska E 2013, "Interview with Masaki Fujihata", unpublished doctoral dissertation, quoted in Sosnowska E 2017, "Sensoryscapes Multisensory Media Art by Masaki Fujihata", in Kluszczyński RW (ed.), *Augmenting the World: Masaki Fujihata*. Gdańsk: LAZNIA Centre for Contemporary Art.

Halpern O 2015, *Beautiful Data: A History of Vision and Reason since 1945*. Durham, NC: Duke University Press.

Han BC 2016, *Le parfum du temps: Essai philosophique sur l'art de s'atttarder*. Paris: Edition Circé.

Han BC 2017, *Psychopolitics: Neoliberalism and New Technologies of Power*, trans. Butler E. London and New York: Verso.

Jenkins B 1993, "Fluxfilms in Three False Starts", in Armstrong E and Rothfuss J (eds.), *In the Spirit of Fluxus*. Minneapolis, MN: Walker Arts Center, pp. 122–139.

Kaye N 2007, *Multi-Media: Video – Installation – Performance*. London: Routledge.

Kuhn A 1995, *Family Secrets: Acts of Memory and Imagination*. London: Verso.

Kusahara M 2017, "The Early Years of Fujihata's Art", in Kluszczyński RW (ed.), *Augmenting the World: MASAKI FUJIHATA and Hybrid Space-Time Art*. Gdansk: LAZNIA Centre for Contemporary Art, pp. 46–67.

Landsberg A 2004, *Prosthetic Memory: The Transformation of American Remembrance in the Age of Mass Culture*. New York: Columbia University Press.

Lushetich N 2020, "Algorithms and Medial Efficacy", *The Philosophical Salon*, 13 January 2020. Available from: https://thephilosophicalsalon.com/algorithms-and-medial-efficacy/ [accessed 17 January 2020].

MacKenzie A and Munster A 2019, "Platform Seeing: Image Ensembles and Their Invisualities", *Theory, Culture, Society*, vol. 36, no. 5, pp. 3–22.

Mauss M 1973, "Techniques of the Body", *Economy and Society*, vol. 2, no. 1, pp. 70–88.

Menne-Haritz A 2001, "Access: The Reformulation of an Archival Paradigm", *Archival Science*, vol. 1, pp. 57–82.

Nancy JL 1991, *The Inoperative Community*, trans. Connor P. Minneapolis, MN and London: University of Minnesota Press.

Nishida K 1966, *Intelligibility and the Philosophy of Nothingness*, trans. Schinzinger R. Honolulu: East-West Center Press.

Nishida K 1970, *Fundamental Problems of Philosophy*, trans. Dilworth DA. Tokyo: Peter Brogren the Voyager's Press.

Nishida K 1992, *Inquiry into the Good*, trans. Abe M and Ives C. New Haven, CT and London: Yale University Press.

Palladini F and Pustianaz M 2017, *Lexicon for an Affective Archive*. Berlin: Intellect. Ltd.

Peirce CS 1960, *Collected Papers, Vol. 6. Pragmatism and Scientific Metaphysics*. Cambridge, MA: Belknap Press of Harvard University Press.

Schwartz R 2008, "A Classic from China: The Nine Chapters", *The Right Angle*, vol. 16, no. 2, pp. 8–12.

Varela FJ 1999, "The Specious Present: A Neurophenomenology of Time Consciousness", in Petitot J et al. (eds.), *Writing Science. Naturalizing Phenomenology: Issue in Contemporary Phenomenology and Cognitive Science*. Stanford, CA: Stanford University Press, pp. 266–314.

Vismann C 2013, "Cultural Techniques and Sovereignty", trans. Iurascu I, *Theory, Culture & Society*, vol. 30, no. 6, pp. 83–93.

Wang Q 2009, "Are Asians Forgetful? Perception, Retention, and Recall in Episodic Remembering", *Cognition*, vol. 111, pp. 123–131.

PART IV
Patterning people

10

SURFACES AND DEPTHS

An aesthetics of big data

Dominic Smith

In *The Fourth Revolution*, Floridi suggests that the "real epistemological problem with big data is small patterns" (Floridi 2014, p. 16). The reason for this is that "so many data can now be generated and processed so quickly, so cheaply, and on virtually anything" (16). For Floridi, it follows from this that the pressure "on the data *nouveau riche*, such as Facebook and Walmart, Amazon or Google", as well as on "the data old money, such as genetics or medicine, experimental physics or neuroscience", "is to be able to spot where the new patterns with real added-value lie in their immense databases [...] This is a problem of brainpower rather than computational power" (16). This suggestion is both insightful and important. As this chapter will argue, however, its purview on big data as an "epistemological problem" is insufficient. Let me start with some big data on images online: there are currently over 10 billion searchable images on Google Images (Siegler 2010); 95 million images are shared daily on Instagram (Lister 2019); there are over 240 billion images on Facebook (George 2014); over 1.8 billion digital images are uploaded to the Internet daily (Eveleth 2015); "[t]weets with images receive 18% more click throughs, 89% more likes, and 150% more retweets" than those without (Smith 2020). These data were produced by five separate searches in 90 seconds on a standard big name search engine. They were conducted in the standard way, keying in natural language terms. All are out of date by up to 10 years, and all are from advertisement-driven sources ranging from clickbait to journalism. They are all drawn from the first page of search results, and I didn't clear my cookies. My search terms were: *How many images on Google Images/Instagram/Facebook/Twitter/the Internet?*

My rule for finding out all of the above was intentionally anecdotal and haphazard. But it was not inconsistent with a general situation where "size is the first, and at times, the only dimension that leaps out at the mention of big data" (Gandomi and Haider 2014, p. 137). Why this contrived performance? To focus on just some of the ways that a problem like 'big data' gets mediated for the 'everyday' or 'average' user of the Internet. That is, for the user whose everyday experience of data is mediated by all manner of ambient conditions ranging from the 'brand power' of big name search engines, platforms, and hardware, to anecdote, chance, convenience, cookies, natural language, and, at the most metaphysical level, time itself.

How should we mediate big data in this simultaneously mundane but headily complex context, where it is not merely an epistemological problem for the '*nouveau riche*' or 'old money' mentioned by Floridi in the quote above, but where it also implies a cluster of ontological, economic, sociological, political, and logical problems for what Dean has called the "rest of us" – that is, "those of us whose work, lives, and futures are expropriated, monetized, and speculated on for the financial enjoyment of the few" (Dean 2012, p. 69)? Overwhelmingly, the patterns of behaviour and existence of the 'rest of us' constitute the human-generated data that then get leveraged by the data '*nouveau riche*' and old money alike. The 'rest of us' do this, moreover, as a mass of what Deleuze calls "*dividuals*" – beings interpellated to no longer think of themselves as autonomous 'individuals' in the sense of classical liberal philosophy (Deleuze 1995, p. 182).[1] The aim for this chapter is to use a very particular type of image to sound out these issues: oceanic ones. This means the investigation will be *partial* and *iterative*: partial in the sense of 'incomplete', and iterative in the sense of generating difference through repetition in an attempt to problematise the relationships obtaining between 'parts' and 'wholes'. What is perhaps most important to emphasise here, however, is that this will primarily be an *aesthetic* investigation: that is, one concerned with how we can *envision, feel* and *imagine* our way around a problem like 'big data'.

The argument of the chapter is that the 'real problem' of big data, *pace* Floridi, is as *aesthetic as it is epistemological*, and, by extension, that an aesthetic investigation of the problem can be an important overture into its ontological, economic, sociological, political, and logical dimensions. Notwithstanding the hype around 'big data', nor a perceived 'leapfrogging' of academic channels that has taken the problem directly from industry to more 'popular outlets' (Gandomi and Haider 2014, p. 137), the premise of this chapter is that we do not really know how to feel about big data as a problem, nor how to imagine it as a new medium while the aesthetic preconditions for such knowledge remain underexplored. These preconditions concern how we *make sense* of data: both in terms of how we produce it (as partly the by-product of our lived and felt behaviours), and in terms of how we perceive it (for instance: as so much 'content' for data centres that are at once increasingly ubiquitous yet remote, 'black boxed', and 'invisual' in their modes of data analysis, with all manner of implied shifts across our concepts of tangibility, space, temporality, and visibility (MacKenzie and Munster 2019).

The first section explains my choice of image. The second section considers a problem concerning *the superficiality of apparent depths*: for all their epistemic depth and sophistication, contemporary data analytic methods are often aesthetically shallow. The section that follows considers an inverse problem of the *depths of apparent superficiality*. The contention here is that one way to enrich how we feel, sense, and imagine our way around a problem like that of big data is to understand the images that typically mediate our experience of it, not as superficial *clichés* or 'mere metaphors', but as potentially instructive media in their own right, with distinct genealogies and iconographies, capable of acting as new critical and creative matrices.[2] The final section concludes with an argument for an 'oceanic' aesthetics capable of sounding surfaces *and* depths of the problem, and briefly differentiates the approach of this chapter from other approaches to big data aesthetics.

Inverting the algorithm

Suppose I invert the variables of the simple algorithm with which I began. I am now no longer searching for big data on images, but for *images of big data*. And suppose I tweak my method by spreading the search across different interfaces, platforms, and hardware. I have wiped the cookies from five different browsers, and am using five different IPs, five different ICTs, and five different networks. Here is what my image searches for 'Big Data' consistently throw up: lots of images of 1s and 0s; many Prezi and PowerPoint slides; images of the world; hands englobing the world; word clouds including terms such as 'potential', 'petabyte', 'zettabyte', 'sets'; colour palettes mostly comprising futuristic blues and whites … There are many representations of geometric nodes and lines and points arranged in hub-and-spoke and point-to-point networks. What feature just as frequently, however, are *waves and undulations*, sometimes in the abstract (sine waves), and sometimes in a more literal sense (cartoons of tidal waves set to inundate).

My aim for this chapter is to explore the aesthetics of this last type of 'oceanic' image. There are, I think, three main factors worth mentioning here that recommend this. First, the act of inverting the variables of my original algorithm is meant to shift from an epistemic order (statistics on data) to an aesthetic one (how data is typically perceived) while emphasising a shared background logical structure. Second, a focus on images in general is warranted in the context of big data by the fact that they, along with audio, video, clickstream, and sensor data, make up a large part of the 'unstructured data' that comprise an estimated 80 to 95 per cent of all big data, in contrast to an estimated 5 per cent that is structured as "tabular data found in spreadsheets or relational databases" (Gandomi and Haider 2014, p. 138; Kitchin 2014, p. 77). By some estimates, unstructured data is growing at 15 times the rate of structured data (Kitchin 2014, p. 6). Third, a focus on 'oceanic' images in particular is warranted by something that distinguishes this type from many of the others just described. While the others tend towards what could be called '*clichés* of the digital' (1s and 0s, nodes, networks), the oceanic ones, although in many ways just as clichéd, pertain to a different imaginary, with a different history: they are what could be called '*clichés* of the analogue'.

The superficiality of apparent depths

The first point just raised implies a paradox: "structured data" form the major focus of the predictive data analytics that are typically associated with big data, but only a

166 Dominic Smith

small part of all big data (Gandomi and Haider 2014, p. 138; Kitchin 2014, p. 77). So long as data analysis methodologies remain focused on structured data, then, there is a sense in which they are destined to remain on a superficial level, no matter how 'deep' or sophisticated these analyses become. Big data is often conceived in terms of three Vs: volume, variety, and velocity (Laney 2001). 'Volume' refers to 'magnitude of data' conceived in Terabytes (1,000 GB) or Petabytes (1,000 TB). As discussed above, size and volume are typically the first dimensions that "leap out at the mention of big data" (Gandomi and Haider 2014, p. 137). 'Variety' is the key characteristic for distinguishing between "structured" and "unstructured" data. It refers to the "structural heterogeneity in a dataset" (Gandomi and Haider 2014, p. 138). In a passage worth citing at length, Kitchin describes the heterogeneity between "structured", "semi-structured", and "unstructured" data:

> *Structured data* are those that can be easily organised, stored and transferred in a defined data model, such as numbers/text set out in a table or relational database that have a consistent format (e.g. name, date of birth, address, gender, etc.) Such data can be processed, searched, queried, combined, and analysed relatively straightforwardly using calculus and algorithms, and can be visualised using various forms of graphs and maps, and easily processed by computers. *Semi-structured* data are loosely structured data that have no predefined data model/schema and thus cannot be held in a relational database. Their structure is irregular, implicit, flexible and often nested hierarchically, but they have a reasonably consistent set of fields and the data are tagged … *[U]nstructured data* do not have a defined model or common identifiable structure. Each individual element, such as narrative text or photo, may have a specific structure or format, but not all data within a dataset share the same structure. As such, while they can often be searched and queried, they are not easily combined or computationally analysed.
>
> *(Kitchin 2014, pp. 5–6; emphasis original)*

The paradox I raised above appears, *prima facie*, not to take account of the dynamics of a contemporary situation where data analysis methodologies are making increased inroads into unstructured data through advances in machine learning and data mining.[3] This is because it appears to presuppose a difference in kind between structured and unstructured data when, as Kitchin's above account implies, the difference is more one of degree: if one wants to analyse unstructured data or render them more conventionally intelligible or perceptible, one strives to convert them into structured data, through classification and categorisation, and this is possible because there exists a sliding-scale between unstructured and structured data, through semi-structured data. There is, however, a reason why the paradox stands: the kind of conversion just discussed glosses over a difference between epistemic and aesthetic registers. As Kitchin's sliding scale implies, one can perfectly well seek to convert unstructured data into quantified structured data with the right data analytic tools, and to produce new information and knowledge thereby. My

Surfaces and depths **167**

point, however, is that structured and unstructured are aesthetically different qualities, requiring not conversion but aesthetic enquiry on their own terms (Massumi 2002, pp. 133–143).

The stakes of this issue become clearer if we move to consider the third feature that is usually held to define big data: velocity. This refers to "the rate at which data are generated and the speed at which [they] should be acted upon" (Gandomi and Haider 2014, p. 138). As described by Kitchin, velocity is the feature that contributes most to "set[ting] big data apart and mak[ing] them a disruptive innovation [...] that radically changes the nature of data and what can be done with them" (Kitchin 2014, p. 68). Let's take it for granted that data analytics will meet this novel situation by converting an increasing velocity of unstructured data into structured data, and that, aided by advances in machine learning and data mining, they will be increasingly successful in doing so.[4] In what ways might this still remain on the surface of big data as an aesthetic problem concerning sense, feeling, and imagination?

Consider this passage from Kitchin, where he elaborates on velocity:

> A fundamental difference between small and big data is the dynamic nature of data generation. Small data usually consist of studies that are freeze-framed at a particular time and space. Even in longitudinal studies, the data are captured at discrete times … For example, censuses are generally conducted every five or ten years. In contrast, big data are generated on a much more continuous basis, in many cases in real-time or near to real-time. Rather than *a sporadic trickle* of data, laboriously harvested or processed, data are *flowing at speed*.
>
> *(Kitchin 2014, p. 76; emphasis mine)*

'Small data' are produced according to traditional research methodologies such as censuses, surveys, and interviews. They are limited in "scope, temporality and size" and are typically costly to obtain (Miller 2010; Kitchin 2014, p. 27). Big data are (or aim to be) *exhaustive* in scope (capturing entire populations or systems), more *fine-grained* in data resolution and detail (for instance: they aim to link data points to real-world entities through concrete relations of indexicality that go beyond the symbolic or iconic measures of traditional data sets), *relational* in nature (containing common fields enabling the conjoining of different data sets), and *highly flexible* (high in extensionality and easily scalable to incorporate new data points) (Kitchin 2014, pp. 67–79). Big data are also more typically the product of unconsciously proffered 'data exhaust' than the kinds of volunteered data that constitute traditional small data sets (68, 87–93).

Kitchin's point, developed in his book, is that there have been fundamental ontological and epistemological shifts from small data to big data across the 2000s and 2010s, to the point where, until the advent of 'big data', "all data were, in effect, small data and therefore did not require labelling as such" (27). My point is that there have been concurrent (better: 'confluent') aesthetic shifts. In contrast to the other shifts just discussed, which are rightly perceived as 'deep', these latter may seem superficial, like so many 'small patterns' on the surface of a problem. My claim,

168 Dominic Smith

however, is that they are just as fundamental, and that considerations of big data will remain superficial so long as they do not take account of the dynamics of sense, feeling, and imagination implied. Reconsider the quote just cited from Kitchin. How does it work on an aesthetic level? At the beginning, small data are coupled to a filmic/photographic register ("freeze-framed at a particular time and space"). By the end, we have shifted completely: to a liquid register of "trickles" and "flows".

This aesthetic is not restricted to Kitchin's approach. It is, in fact, an instructive microcosm of a recurrent 'oceanic' aesthetic hidden in plain sight and iterated across discussions on big data. Whether at the level of specialised work in data management (Laney 2001), the ethics of computation (Floridi 2013, pp. 2–3), or popular bestsellers on the nature of the contemporary Internet (Harari 2015, pp. 448–449; Zuboff 2019, pp. 255, 307), we are *drenched* in a register of 'trickles', 'ebbs and flows', 'undercurrents', 'torrents', 'floods', 'deluges', 'immersion', 'inundations', 'peaks and troughs', 'data dives', 'drowning in data', and 'oceans of data'. Indeed, one might note that this register was practically written into the discourse around big data as a potentiality from the start, by the 'liquid' character of at least two of the three Vs discussed above (volume and velocity).[5] It might readily be countered that this aesthetic is composed entirely of 'mere metaphors' and *clichés*. This is to presuppose that it is informationally redundant, and, *a fortiori*, that it can perhaps be overlooked in favour of deep data-driven dives into the epistemic and ontological implications of big data. The contention I have sought to unfold in this section is that this cannot be the case.

Consider one last iteration of the passage from Kitchin. Specifically, consider what occurs in the interval between the filmic and liquid registers: we shift quickly through registers of hunting and imprisonment ('capture'), agriculture ('harvesting'), and industry ('processing'). These function in some ways like the speeding up of a film – as if they were so many cutaway juxtapositions designed to reinforce a sense of *mise en scène*. What is perhaps most significant about the passage, however, is the qualitative leap at the end: at the beginning and in the middle, we are concerned with human-scale activities that have to do with control of an environment (filming, capturing, harvesting, processing); by the end, a trickle has become a flow, giving a sense of a larger 'oceanic' environment in the process of exceeding and decentring the human. Even supposing that all the registers in Kitchin's passage are clichéd, what happens at the end is qualitatively discontinuous with what comes before in aesthetic terms, and cannot be written off as mere redundancy or 'noise'. Instead, it is almost as if a reel of celluloid film has sped up and burn out, plunging us into a qualitatively different situation: from imaginative immersion in a screen that projects our received sense of control, to immersion in a swelling sea.

The depths of apparent superficiality

What if the currents of superficiality run much deeper throughout this chapter than I have just made it appear? I have been interested from the start in such things as first-person phenomenological reports, 'everyday' experience, and searches on big name search engines. And what could be more superficial for approaching a problem as rarefied and 'deep' as that of big data than the image of an ocean, with all its hackneyed romantic connotations? Rather than writing this apparent superficiality off, I want to use this section to explore the possibility that it might harbour under-acknowledged depths. The aim in this sense is not merely to acknowledge the phenomenological and aesthetic dimensions of big data; it is to treat the kinds of metaphors and *clichés* discussed at the end of the previous section as much more than 'mere' metaphors and *clichés*. They will instead be treated as the linked surface phenomena of a deep 'paradigm' or 'grammar' that mediates how we feel, sense, and imagine our way around big data as an emergent problem (Wittgenstein 2009; Bloomenberg 2010). This is not to claim that this paradigm is an eternal archetype in some Platonic or Jungian sense, or that it is the only possible one.[6] The claim is simply that an oceanic paradigm is pervasive in the mediation of big data as an aesthetic problem at this historical juncture, and that, rather than discounting this as surface spume, it may warrant investigation.

Consider two sets of 'oceanic' images from the visual arts: *Arkhipelagos (Navigating the Tides of Time)*, a 2013 black and white video triptych on a 20-minute loop by the Finnish duo IC-98, and Vija Celmins' series of untitled sea drawings, conducted from the late 1960s (Rippner and Celmins 2002, pp. 9–25). I have chosen to discuss these images here because of apparent *superficial similarities* between them considered as separate series (both involve monochromatic images of ocean surfaces), and because of apparent *deep differences* between both of them and the kinds of 'oceanic' images mentioned at the beginning of this chapter. The choice not to produce images from either series here, moreover, is intentional. I am concerned with how imagination sounds the lineaments of *the absent and unrepresented*.[7] The foreground of *Arkhipelagos* depicts a sea of lugubriously shifting waves that never fully crest or break. This is offset by images of rafts in the background that appear out of kilter with the movement of the waves, and that never fully hove into view. In contrast, the images that compose Celmins' series are snapshots that freeze the incessant 'becoming' of a sea into instants. What is perhaps most aesthetically engaging, however, is the disjunct between the images that compose this series and Celmins' process of rendering them: photographs are taken instantaneously and can represent a moment in the actual becoming of a sea; but Celmins' images, notoriously, are not photographs; they are hand-drawn products of minutely attentive draughtswomanship, and because they are dilated in time in this way, they depict a sea that is as much imaginary as 'actual'.

Now consider two further features of Celmins' series that stand in specific contrast to those of *Arkhipelagos*: Celmins' use of the void white spaces of her paper, and the sense of perspective offered to the viewer. The waves of Celmins' series are anything but 'tidal' or 'tsunamic', but her manipulation of void space does at least give some sense of waves breaking. This sense is, in spite of the explicit sense of movement in *Arkhipelagos*, something almost entirely stripped from its waves. Second, the images in Celmins' series position their viewers above the waters, as if one were hovering like an angel (or a seagull). This generates a sense of surveying something over which one could conceivably exercise control. In unsettling contrast, *Arkhipelagos* places its viewer *beneath* its waves, but not *under* them, as if rooted in the perpetual trough of some metaphysical *uber-wave*, of which all the others would be epiphenomena. In what ways is this more than superficial *ekphrasis*, conducted between two series of images that remain randomly chosen and partial? First, because it taps into the reservoirs of a confluent 'oceanic' paradigm running between the images. Second, because, when set against a problematic like that of big data, it provides allegorical points of analogy and disanalogy for sounding and refining our understanding, in terms of precisely the kinds of issues just discussed: *movement and velocity, presence and absence*, and *perspective.*

Consider that Celmins' images form a 'freeze-frame' of the kind mentioned in the quote from Kitchin I cited at the end of the second section. They do this, moreover, by arresting the vectors of waves that are as 'actual' as 'imaginary'. In this sense, Celmins' images can be read as potent allegories of the notorious epistemological problem of 'spurious correlation', which affects small and big data sets alike, but which becomes vexed in the case of big data sets. This problem occurs when correlations are mistakenly inferred between uncorrelated variables, and becomes vexed in the case of big data because of the difficulty of exercising adequate epistemic controls due to the massive size of the data sets (Gandomi and Haider 2014, p. 143). Stare at the images of Celmins' series for only a short time, and it becomes difficult *not* to hallucinate movement into these images of seas that are as imagined as actual, as abstract as 'concrete'. It is therefore not too much of a stretch of the imagination to say that Celmins' series allegorises and refines our understanding of some of the key epistemic issues involved in big data (for instance: imaginary objects, true and false representation, and issues of false correlation between/extrapolations beyond elements of the 'given').[8]

Second, note that both *Arkhipelagos* and Celmins' series can, at a particular level of abstraction, themselves be conceived as 'small data sets': just as *Arkhipelagos* consists of a series of *frames-as-data points* correlated by the temporal norms of filmic media and the aesthetic norms of IC-98's practice, Celmins' series consists of a series of *drawn images-as-data points*, correlated by the norms of her practice of rendering. Viewed at this level of abstraction, *Arkhipelagos* and Celmins' series emerge as similar data sets: arrest the movement of any particular frame from *Arkhipelagos*, and something superficially akin to an image from Celmins' series will result. What gets elided, however, is an important qualitative distinction between the pair that only emerges when they are viewed at the level of abstraction of *artworks* emerging on different media, under the influence of different aesthetic traditions: link and speed up the drawings of Celmins' series into a film, and what will result will be much more jarring than the lugubrious yet quasi-naturalistic rhythms of the waves in *Arkhipelagos*. Expressed at the 'data set' level of abstraction invoked above, the reason for this is that, unlike in the case of *Arkhipelagos*, there are too many omissions and discontinuities in the data set of images to meet the criterion of selection for a data set that is a film (typically: 24 continuously related frames per second).

What this ignores, however, is that these omissions play a constitutive role in the aesthetic of Celmins' series: despite the hyper photorealism of her drawings, any sense of movement in the series is engendered not by the aspiration to be 'filmic', but, paradoxically, by discontinuity and a pervasive aesthetic of 'frozenness' across a sea that is as real as it is imaginary. What's more, Celmins' series is open-ended: the set is added to often after an interval of many years (Rippner and Celmins 2002). What this allegorises, I submit, are further features that are crucial to a more refined understanding of big data (for instance: how data sets are ontologically constituted just as much by 'presences' as 'absences', and how superficially similar data sets can produce radically different results depending on the levels of the abstraction/methodologies/time frames according to which they are mediated). Third, it should be emphasised that none of these aesthetic considerations occur in a vacuum. They emerge instead in terms of aesthetic perspectives that have histories. Specifically, these oceanic images are linked to what I called 'clichés of the analogue' at the end of the first section. As discussed, what initially struck me about the oceanic images rendered by my image search was how they differed from 'clichés of the digital'. Simply put: they were *explicit analogues of* an 'elemental' or 'natural' world, whereas the other images (1s and 0s, nodes, networks) were only implicitly analogous in this way; instead, their function seemed overwhelmingly to be concerned with bringing a new 'digital' world into being.

But a further sense of the analogue is relevant here. In the technical sense, the analogue is, as Massumi puts it:

> a continuously variable impulse or momentum that can cross from one qualitatively different medium into another. Like electricity into sound waves. Or heat into pain. Or light waves into vision. Or vision into imagination. Or noise in the ear into music in the heart ... Variable continuity across the qualitatively different: continuity of transformation.
>
> *(Massumi 2002, p. 135; emphasis original)*

We can add 'data into oceans' to this list. As demonstrated in immediate terms by my image search for 'big data', and in more mediate terms by the soundings taken of the literature on this topic, 'a continuously variable impulse or momentum' exists in the contemporary imaginary which suggests 'oceans' as an appropriate medium or paradigm into which 'data' might be qualitatively transformed. This impulse is continuous with more than is typically acknowledged. In the visual arts, literature, poetry, and religious iconography, sea tropes frequently suggest melancholy, mourning, voyage, adventure, and transition (think, for instance, of Woolf's *The Waves*, Seascapes by Friedrich or Turner, or the myth surrounding Cnut's attempts to stem the tide as an allegory of the limits of earthly power (Bachelard 2015); in modern philosophical aesthetics, oceanic imagery is continuous with a sense of the sublime that goes back at least as far as Burke, and that was refined by Kant in terms of the "dynamical sublime" (Kant 1987, pp. 119–123); by extension, 'big data' finds itself linked to a concept of a "technological sublime" that predates it (Nye 1996).

172　Dominic Smith

This kind of historically situated qualitative transformation and perspective is not something to be lamented, as if it constituted a distortion or loss of message. Instead, it can be drawn upon to amplify, distil and refine our understanding of the complexities surrounding a problem like big data in important ways, through processes of allegorisation, analogy, and disanalogy. What results from these processes need not be an elitist or exclusive aesthetics; rather, it can speak to the 'rest of us' by tapping the deep reservoirs of a shared imaginary. As demonstrated by the superficial (but typical) search conducted at the start of this chapter, problems like big data are frequently mediated today in ways that leave us feeling as though we are 'drowning' in turbid data. How might an undercurrent of aesthetic reflection help us to swim?

Surfaces and depths: an aesthetic of big data

I like to use the example of the roar or noise of the sea that strikes us when we are on the shore. To hear this noise as we do, we must hear the parts which make up this whole, that is the noise of each wave, although each of these little noises makes itself known only when combined confusedly with all the others, and would not be noticed if the wave which made it were by itself. We must be affected slightly by the motion of this wave, and have some perception of each of these noises, however small they may be; otherwise there would be no perception of a hundred thousand waves, since a hundred thousand nothings cannot make something.

(Leibniz 1996 [1765], p. 54)

In *The Data Revolution*, Kitchin reproduces a well-known "knowledge pyramid" (Adler 1986; McCandless 2009; Kitchin 2014, p. 6). At the base, we find *the world* (an environment rich in potential data), which then gets represented through actually recorded *data* (abstracted elements of the world), then formed into *information* (linked/correlated data), which, in turn, gets refined into *knowledge* (organised information). At the tip, we find *wisdom*, construed as 'applied knowledge' (Kitchin 2014:10). The contention developed in the present chapter might be expressed like this: *it would be aesthetically wise to reconsider this pyramid as a wave.*

Specifically, I have in mind a wave of the kind mentioned by Leibniz in the quote above. These waves are aesthetically *expressive*, not simply epistemically representative: in contrast to the 'knowledge pyramid', which is meant to function as an *analogue of* our contemporary epistemic situation, Leibniz's waves are expressive of the sort of continuous qualitative variation that makes up the very being of the analogue. Specifically, his example is expressive of relations of *folding, enveloping, implication* and *complication*: each wave, while ephemeral, unstable and fleeting, is a qualitatively defined part of a complex sea; and these parts function not through relations of aggregation (they are not 'blocks'), but through expressive relations of synthesis and qualitative transformation (waves do not sink to the bottom of the sea in the way that the blocks of a pyramid would; they crest and break, each expressing part of the roar, noise and weight of the entire liquid body, 'however small they may be'). We know a great deal about how Leibniz's advances in mathematics and logic were inspirational for contemporary computing (Wiener 1968; Pekhaus 2018). The suggestion here is simply that it is worth considering these advances in continuity with the striking aesthetic expressed above. Such an aesthetic cannot be written off as 'superficial noise'. On the contrary, it should be perceived in exactly the way Leibniz suggests: as a qualitatively significant variation on themes that are expressed elsewhere across his philosophy and that of others.[9]

In attempting to sound this wave, I started from a simple algorithm, the terms of which were inverted or involuted. The aim here was to at once separate and logically relate epistemic and aesthetic registers. Next, I attempted to unfold some of the consequences of the involution: the aesthetic superficiality of apparent epistemic depths was explored, then the potential epistemic depths of aesthetic superficiality. Where we have ended up is with the glimmer of a structure that would be less *monolithic*, less beholding to an architecture of '*blocks*', '*points*' or '*units*' (that is: less 'digital') and more *expressive* of the fragile, dynamic, and interrelated nature of our data, information, knowledge, and wisdom.[10] Or perhaps this is just wilful and superficial romanticism … After all, haven't I overlooked something very obvious about big data aesthetics that was expressed in all those Prezi and PowerPoint slides thrown up by my image search at the beginning of this chapter? Namely, the fact that data visualisation is a well-established field, shot through with established diagrammatic types: from histograms and scatter plots to flow charts. On the one hand, there is a temptation to be polemical in response: contemporary data visualisation models can often be instrumentalised as part of a data rhetoric that bewilders and belittles, leaving us 'all at sea' (Galloway 2015, pp. 78–100). A more constructive response would simply be this: as is recognised in the literature, such established models do not stand to lose anything from immersion in different aesthetic and iconographic genealogies which, in many cases, precede and condition them (Kirk 2019). But perhaps there is a more suggestive and tendentious point still: what if the kinds of absent series from IC-98 and Celmins discussed above turned out to be just as good (and in some circumstances considerably better) for 'data visualisation' than received diagrammatic types? And what if this was not in spite of the felt and forced absences and obscurities they imply, but because of them?

Reconsider the passage from Floridi cited at the beginning of this chapter. Nothing he writes there is incorrect. On the contrary, it is insightful and important. The contention is simply that it is insufficient: big data is not merely an 'epistemological' problem of how to turn data into information/knowledge/wisdom; it is not merely a problem for the *nouveau riche* or old money; and it is not merely a problem of 'brainpower' or 'computational power'. Beneath this already complex and eddying surface, big data is also an embodied and environmental problem of feeling, affect and imagination for the 'rest of us'. What may be required to plunge through this surface is not just more explanation or simplification in terms of received diagrammatic types; instead, a more baroque epistemology coupled to a more oceanic aesthetics may be required – one of surfaces *and* depths, capable not

174 Dominic Smith

just of simplifying complexity, but of finding new ways to dramatically explicate, complicate, and implicate us in it.[11]

Notes

1 Floridi has instructively written on this tension in terms of 'human interfaces' (2019a; see also Floridi 2013, pp. 210–227).
2 I have in mind Deleuze's sense of the problem or 'Idea' here, not as an abstract 'element of knowledge', but as an affective provocation to learning. (See Deleuze 2004a, p. 241, especially on the example of 'learning to swim'.)
3 Developments in facial recognition and generative modelling in physics and astronomy experiments are examples of this. The latter experiments often generate terabytes of data daily, the majority of which are unstructured. Generative modelling has been viewed as a 'third way' for structuring the data, between the traditional human-centred approaches of observation and simulation:

> The best-known generative modeling systems are "generative adversarial networks" (GANs). After adequate exposure to training data, a GAN can repair images that have damaged or missing pixels, or they can make blurry photographs sharp. They learn to infer the missing information by means of a competition (hence the term "adversarial"): One part of the network, known as the generator, generates fake data, while a second part, the discriminator, tries to distinguish fake data from real data.
>
> *(Falk 2019)*

4 Such extrapolations are allowable based on developments in some of the key enablers of big data. Specifically: computational power, data storage, machine learning, and neural networks (Floridi 2014, pp. 6–19; 2019b, pp. 207–213; Kitchin 2014, pp. 80–99).
5 On the day I started writing the second section, I was co-opted to attend training for 'SEAtS', a proprietary platform licensed to Universities. It uses exhaust and volunteered data from smartphones to monitor student attendance (SEAtS 2020). What is it about the oceanic imaginary surrounding data that convinced the platform's marketing team they should insist on such a tortured acronym?
6 Other possible paradigms include weather systems and 'clouds' (see Bridle 2019, pp. 20–26), 'signal and noise', or the registers of 'rhizomes' or 'networks' (although see Galloway 2014, on 'network pessimism').
7 If images of either series are desired, search online, and note both differences and similarities involved in this process and the kind of searches conducted at the start of this chapter.
8 Etymologically, data are, to emphasise, literally 'that which is given' in Latin (Kitchin 2014, p. 2). This is transmitted well in the French term for data (*les données*).
9 A key source for exploring this would be Bachelard, who was as influential in epistemology and philosophy of science as philosophical aesthetics (see especially 2015). Another would be Deleuze. Aside from the fact that he wrote a book dedicated to the importance of '*le pli*' ('folding'), on Leibniz, Deleuze develops the links between this 'trait' (2014, p. 1) and notions of implication, explication, and complication throughout his work (see 2004a and 2004b especially). Oceanic imagery also plays a related important role throughout Deleuze's work (for instance: Deleuze invokes an image of 'two drops of water' on the first page of *Difference and Repetition* (2004a, p. 1), and that of '... a single and same Ocean for all the drops' on the last (2004a, p. 378), and discussions of 'surfaces' and 'depths' feature throughout *The Logic of Sense* (2004b)). Tangentially, a focus on these aspects of

Deleuze's work may have the capacity to take us beyond a focus on the 'rhizome', which has arguably become overdetermined in Deleuze scholarship.

10 This point is consistent with MacKenzie and Munster's related claim that

> engagement with the technical architectures of ISPs [Image Signal Processors], GPUs and deep learning models offers a way to disinvest some of the numerical sublime that inflects responses to image aggregates, or indeed any "big" data.
>
> *(2019, p. 18)*

Whereas the kind of 'big data on images' cited at the beginning of the present chapter exemplifies the 'mathematical sublime', the oceanic images pursued throughout resonate with what Kant calls the 'dynamical sublime'. I agree with MacKenzie and Munster's claim that we should 'disinvest' from the mathematical sublime, and have attempted to unfold a *cliché* of the dynamical sublime as one way of doing this.

11 See endnote 9 above.

References

Adler M 1986, *A Guidebook to Learning: For a Lifelong Pursuit of Wisdom*. London: Macmillan.

Bachelard G 2015, *L'Eau et les Rêves: essai sur l'imagination de la matiere*, Paris: Librairie José Corti.

Bloomenberg H 2010, *Paradigms for a Metaphorology*, trans. Savage R. Ithaca, NY: Cornell University Press.

Bridle J 2019, *New Dark Age: Technology and the End of the Future*. London: Verso.

Dean J 2012, *The Communist Horizon*. London: Verso.

Deleuze G 1995, "Postscript on Control Societies", in *Negotiations: 1972–1990*, trans. Joughin M. New York: Columbia University Press, pp. 177–182.

Deleuze G 2004a, *Difference and Repetition*, trans. Patton P. London: Continuum.

Deleuze G 2004b, *The Logic of Sense*, Stivale C and Boundas C (eds.), trans. Lester M. London: Continuum.

Deleuze G 2014, *Le Pli: Leibniz et le baroque*. Paris: Editions de Minuit.

Eveleth R 2015, "How Many Photographs of You are Out There in the World?", *The Atlantic*. Available from: www.theatlantic.com/technology/archive/2015/11/how-many-photographs-of-you-are-out-there-in-the-world/413389/ [accessed 16 January 2020].

Falk D 2019, "How Artificial Intelligence is Changing Science", *Quanta Magazine*, 11 March. Available from: www.quantamagazine.org/how-artificial-intelligence-is-changing-science-20190311/ [accessed 16 January 2020].

Floridi L 2013, *The Ethics of Information*. Oxford: Oxford University Press.

Floridi L 2014, *The Fourth Revolution: How the Infosphere is Reshaping Human Reality*. Oxford: Oxford University Press.

Floridi L 2019a, "Marketing as Control of Human Interfaces and Its Political Exploitation", *Philosophy and Technology*, vol. 32, pp. 379–388. Available from: doi:10.1007/s13347-019-00374-7.

Floridi L 2019b, *The Logic of Information: A Theory of Philosophy as Conceptual Design*. Oxford: Oxford University Press.

Galloway A 2014, "Network Pessimism". Available from: http://cultureandcommunication.org/galloway/network-pessimism [accessed 16 January 2020].

Galloway A 2015, *The Interface Effect*. Cambridge: Polity.

Gandomi A and Haider M 2014, "Beyond the Hype: Big data Concepts, Methods, and Analytics", *International Journal of Information Management*, vol. 35, no. 2, pp. 137–144. Available from: https://doi.org/10.1016/j.ijinfomgt.2014.10.007 [accessed 16 January 2020].

176 Dominic Smith

George 2014, "How Many Photos have we Uploaded on Facebook? How About 240 Billion. Or 217 Each". Available from: https://mybilliondollarapp.com/how-many-photos-on-facebook-how-about-240-billion/ [accessed 16 January 2020].

Harari YN 2015, *Homo Deus: A Brief History of Tomorrow*. London: Vintage.

IC-98. 2013, *Arkhipelagos (Navigating the Tides of Time)*. Available from: https://vimeo.com/65639595 [accessed 16 January 2020].

Kant I 1987, *The Critique of Judgement*, trans. Pluhar WS. Cambridge: Hackett.

Kirk A 2019, *Data Visualisation: A Handbook for Data-Driven Design*. London: Sage.

Kitchin R 2014, *The Data Revolution: Big Data, Open Data, Data Infrastructures & Their Consequences*. London: Sage.

Laney D 2001, "3-D Data Management: Controlling Data Volume, Velocity and Variety. Application Delivery Strategies by META Group Inc". Available from: http://blogs.gartner.com/doug-laney/files/2012/01/ad949-3D-Data-Management-Controlling-Data-Volume-Velocity-and-Variety.pdf [accessed 16 January 2020].

Leibniz GWF 1996 [1765], *New Essays on Human Understanding*, trans. Remnant P and Bennett J. Cambridge: Cambridge University Press.

Lister M 2019, "33 Mind-Boggling Instagram Stats & Facts for 2018". Available from: www.wordstream.com/blog/ws/2017/04/20/instagram-statistics [accessed 16 January 2020].

MacKenzie A and Munster A 2019, "Platform Seeing: Image Ensembles and Their Invisualities", *Theory, Culture & Society*, vol. 36, no. 5, pp. 3–22. Available from: https://doi.org/10.1177/0263276419847508 [accessed 4 August 2020].

Massumi B 2002, *Parables for the Virtual: Movement, Affect, Sensation*. London: Duke University Press.

McCandless D 2009, "Data, Information, Knowledge, Wisdom". Available from: https://informationisbeautiful.net/2010/data-information-knowledge-wisdom/ [accessed 16 January 2020].

Miller P 2010, "Linked Data and Government", *ePSIplatform Topic Report no.7*. Available from: www.europeandataportal.eu/sites/default/files/2010_linked_data_and_government.pdf [accessed 16 January 2020].

Nye DE 1996, *American Technological Sublime*. Cambridge, MA: MIT Press.

Rippner S and Celmins V 2002, *The Prints of Vija Celmins*. New York: The Metropolitan Museum of Art.

SEAtS. 2020, "SEAtS Software: The Student Success Platform". Available from: www.seatssoftware.com/ [accessed 16 January 2020].

Siegler MG 2010, "Google Image Search: Over 10 Billion Images, 1 Billion Pageviews a Day", *Tech Crunch*. Available from: https://techcrunch.com/2010/07/20/google-image-search/?guccounter=1 [accessed 16 January 2020].

Smith K 2020, "60 Incredible and Interesting Twitter Stats and Statistics", *Brandwatch*. Available from: www.brandwatch.com/blog/twitter-stats-and-statistics/ [accessed 16 January 2020].

Wiener N 1968, *The Human Use of Human Beings*. London: Sphere Books.

Wittgenstein L 2009, *Philosophical Investigations*, trans. Anscombe GEM and Rhees R. Oxford: Wiley-Blackwell.

Zuboff S 2019, *The Age of Surveillance Capitalism: The Fight for the Future at the New Frontier of Power*. London: Profile Books.

11

POV-DATA-DOUBLES, THE DIVIDUAL, AND THE DRIVE TO VISIBILITY

Mitra Azar

Introduction

Big data is an ensemble of complex molar data sets, digitally extracted from the world with a view to value production, chiefly through targeted data collection and predictive analytics. But how precisely is this molar mass of data funnelled towards the molecular shaping of the user's digital and affective milieus? For Deleuze, aggregates of matter with physical mass, solidity, and circumference are molar. They are structured, 'earthly' modes of being. A landscape is molar, as are mountains, riverbeds and buildings. The molar pertains to matter, mass, solidity, stability, and cohesion (Deleuze 1993, p. 6). The molecular, on the other hand, refers to the dynamic interpenetration of chemical processes, to the movement of fire, water, and wind, and their "complex interactions" (9). The molecular is situated between aggregates of mass and duration. In a famous example of a teaspoon of sugar dissolving in a glass of water, Deleuze suggests that the ionisation of sugar molecules epitomises "pure ceaseless becoming" (Deleuze 1986, p. 10). In *The Fold*, he stresses the microscopic, sub-scale working of the molecular, which "pulverize[s] the world" (Deleuze 1993, p. 87). The molar and the molecular are, of course, not mutually exclusive; the molar "processes" molecular components, and vice versa (Deleuze 1992, p. 34). For example, the molarity of the cinematic apparatus is interpenetrated by the molecularity of the cinematic image defined by Deleuze as "dividual": "[t]he cinematographic image is always dividual"; the reason for this is that the molarity of the screen as the "frame of frames" cannot be "divided into parts without *qualitatively* changing each time" (Deleuze 1986, pp. 14–15; emphasis mine). Both the molecular and the dividual are here "intensive multiplicities composed of particles that do not divide without changing in nature" (Deleuze 1992, p. 34). This has important political implications. In *A Thousand Plateaus,* Deleuze and Guattari use molar and molecular to differentiate between divergent political operations: the molar governmental superstructure, with its regulated and visible *modi operandi*, and the molecular "micropolitics" of perception, affect, even errant conversation, which have an oblique, diffuse, next-to-imperceptible way of unfolding (Deleuze and Guattari 1987, p. 220). Another way of putting it would be: molar power moulds the individual from the outside, as in the disciplinary society described by Foucault, structured around physical enclosures – the school, the factory, the hospital, the prison – in which the individual is an integral unit (Foucault 1978). Molecular power, on the other hand, controls and modulates the dividual's multiple, recombinant, yet unique combinations of non-integer fractions: "[e]nclosures are [...] distinct castings, but controls are a modulation, like a self-deforming cast that will continuously change from one moment to the other" (Deleuze 1992, p. 4). Deleuze uses the expression 'dividual' in a different context in "Postscript on the Societies of Control", where he defines the transformation of processes of individuation from Foucault's disciplinary society to what he calls the society of control: "the numerical language of control is made of codes that mark access to information, or reject it [...] Individuals have become dividuals [...] samples, data, markets or 'banks'" (5). In its more contemporary theorisation, the term 'dividual' suggests "cuts and divisions" as well as "qualitatively diverse, variously paced, but analogous processes of participation" which bring along an "ambiguous expression of affect that cannot be called individual" (Ott 2018, p. 35), extending into new, digital "orders of space and time" and affording new forms of "plasticity and mutability" (6).

In this chapter, my suggestion is that the techno-embodied orientation of the contemporary subject is defined by the constant oscillation between, and the interpenetration of, the molar and the molecular. I argue that this form of techno-embodied orientation can best be understood through the cinematic notion of Point of View (Branigan 1984). In cinema theory and practice, the (subjective) Point of View (or POV) is an aesthetic format; the expression refers to a camera movement that introduces a vicarious feeling of embodiment into the cinematic image by reproducing the movement of the actor's body. The viewer here sees what the actor sees, as if occupying the same physical spot and angle. A cinematic POV is simultaneously molar – it is part of the cinematic apparatus, the screen, where the image manifests for the audience – and molecular – the camera movements mimic or double the micro-movements of the actor's body. My argument is that a new form of cinematic POV emerges in algorithmic form, moulded and simultaneously modulated by big data, designed to articulate the liminality and interpenetration of the molar and the molecular. More specifically, the contemporary subject's techno-embodied orientation (their POV), emerges from the interaction of the user's bodily situated-ness and their multiple online platform activities scattered across a variety of technological devices and networks, giving shape to new forms of distributed agency. I argue that the funnelling of data analytics in real time – which manifests as what is usually referred to as user-tailored content and digital routes that emerge from the traces of their previous activities and interaction – mimics or *doubles* their embodied POV creating a fully datafied, discrete version of it, which I call the POV-data-double. I use the expression 'double' as the body of the (actual, embodied) subject is here temporarily removed from their POV-data-double – a trace of their past and present movements through the digital landscape – only to be reassembled at a later stage through the content created at the level of the interface by the very process of data doubling. Zuboff, in her work on surveillance capitalism, terms the continuous stockpiling of behavioural data – from physical movement in space detected by geolocative systems to the frequency and duration of (any form of digital) contact, browsing and shopping habits, preferences and choices – "the behavioural surplus" (Zuboff 2019, p. 13). This behavioural surplus produces the emergence of a mirror image in the form of a shadow text: unlike the (obligatory digital) self-authored text that explains who one is and what one does, the shadow text is the text written by non-human others. It is a text the user is, by definition, unaware of, a form of forensic and datafied reconstruction of their behaviour, which, for Zuboff, is a means to profit, creating "new *behavioral futures markets* in which users are the *human natural* source" (13; emphasis original). While I share Zuboff's concern about computational technologies which increasingly predict the user's inner desires, feelings, and motivations by virtue of "weaving themselves into the fabric of everyday life until they are indistinguishable from it" (Weiser quoted in Zuboff 2019, p. 16), my emphasis is on the *mechanics* of this process, which takes place in and through a molar–molecular doubling. The interpenetration of the molar and the molecular can be grasped through the algorithmic variation on the cinematic POV – a perceptual re-embodiment of the camera's machinic, actor-replacing point of view. In the algorithmic environment, the invisible POV-data-double *mirrors* the user's daily online and offline behaviour, shaping, with the aid of predictive analytics, their feelings and intentions – by, for example, directing them coercively towards unintended or useless purchases, or suggesting activities, groups, and contacts that shape their social milieu and influence behaviour, and, in this way, further propel molecular dividuations within a seemingly molar structure of big data. In the first stages of algorithmic processing, the sea of big data is raw, unstructured, one could even say disorientated; the data has no goal. It has not been formatted to target something or someone. The process of meaning making which turns an unstructured mass of data into specific and usable information – specific and usable for a particular purpose – consists of creating patterns, parameters, and directions that are simultaneously quantitative, qualitative, spatial as well as temporal. There is, therefore, always a specific–generic, micro–macro, molecular–molar relationship at play in the numerous and complex processes that give big data an orientation, turning an apparently confused mass of data into *somebody's* data sets, that further shape or guide this particular person's practices or ideas. These processes are not public; neither are they visible in the conventional anthropomorphic sense of the word. The user is oblivious to the processes that lead to the composition of their invisible POV-data-double, which manifests at the level of the interface in the form of a supposedly objective online content offered to the data-double's techno-embodied counterpart. In the pages that follow, I examine the aesthetic structure behind the processing of the user's (small) big data, the generation of their unique dividual algorithmic ghost – or POV-data-double – and its political implications.

From the cinematic POV to POV-data-double: metainterface and big data invisualities

There is a curious paradox at work in the current "regime of visibility" dominated by visual media: the demand to visualise "processes and practices that do not belong to the realm of the visual or aren't even visible as such" (van Winkel 2005, p. 1). Despite the fact that images are omnipresent and unavoidable in the digital era, as a "social force they are less powerful than the imperative to visualize", itself a product of the obligatory economic principle of permanent growth (1). This is why van Winkel suggests that there are simply "too few images. The dynamics of contemporary culture are determined by visual shortage rather than visual surfeit. The demand for images – not just 'complex' or 'interesting' images, but any images – by far outstrips supply" (1). The drive to visibility has created a pressure to make everything visible. Van Winkel terms non-visual materials that the drive to visibility *forces* into visibility "missing visuals" (1). The hypertrophic production of images is, in this interpretation, not an excess, but, rather, a symptom of the impossibility to curb, stop, or satisfy the drive. No matter how big, complex, or detailed big data is, it is never enough as it is always possible to generate new data and make more comprehensive data sets. Within this framework, big data is situated in the space between the missing visuals and the drive to visibility. It is a form of *practical operationalisation* of the drive to visibility that funnels data towards the economically and culturally dictated, yet, ultimately, impossible production of the "missing visuals". This can be compared to MacKenzie and Munster's notion of invisuality which the authors explain in the following way:

> contemporary image ensembles are not simply quantitatively beyond our imagining but qualitatively not of the order of representation. Their operativity cannot be seen by an observing "subject" but rather is enacted via observation events distributed throughout and across devices, hardware, human agents and artificial networked architectures such as deep learning networks.
>
> *(MacKenzie and Munster 2019, p. 3)*

Departing from Bergson's notion of the universe as "an aggregate of images" (Bergson quoted in MacKenzie and Munster 2019, p. 5), MacKenzie and Munster theorise image aggregates as a manifestation of the world's plasticity and flux, yet also as "entities in a computational relationality", which includes artificial intelligence architectures (5). The artificial-intelligence-generated image aggregates "constitute the (nonhuman) activities of perception as a mode of cutting into/selecting out of the entire flux of image-ensemble-world" (5). MacKenzie and Munster use the expression "platform seeing" to refer to a form of seeing that captures images "not simply quantified, but labelled, formatted and made 'platform-ready'" (3).

In this computational *milieu*, the drive to visibility makes use of cloud-stored invisualities to produce POV-data-doubles. POV-data-doubles are, in turn, designed to produce (a form of) missing visuals that appear at the level of the interface. In other words, big data operationally 'drives' the invisuality of platform seeing towards the missing visuals, which are both the engine and the horizon of the drive to visibility. The hyper-proliferation of big data's invisualities aimed at the production and/or circulation of (new) data and thus also new (missing) visuals, is what the drive to visibility seeks to produce. The production of ever-new visuals is an attempt to bestow visibility on the missing visuals by passing through the constitution of a POV-data-double, designed to harness and orientate the production of the missing visuals at a molecular level. From raw data assemblages, big data is funnelled into data sets that furnish the materials (images and information) for the constitution of the POV-data-double, which emerges from the extraction of the user's geolocation, frequency of (a specific kind of) communication, network, spread, average themes, and topics. In this way, the POV-data-double becomes a data matrix for the (molecularly tailored) production of the (missing) visuals that are *attached* to the user's techno-embodied POV and form part of a techno-perceptive visuality, despite their fragmented and, effectively, dividual nature. The production of the POV-data-double and the missing visuals has a precedent though; it resembles the functioning of the cinematographic POV. When looking at a cinematic POV – a fast-paced sequence of jumping out of an airplane, for example – the viewer gets the kinaesthetic, haptic, and propriocentric impression that they are *re-embodying the actor's POV*, that they are seeing what the actor is seeing, moving together with the actor's body, jumping out of an airplane, and with the moving image itself. Similar to the seamless overlaying of the camera and the body in a cinematic POV, big data analytics overlays the POV-data-double and the user's embodied POV.

This process unfolds in two stages: at the invisual level of MacKenzie and Munster's Bergson-inspired notion of image/data aggregates, and at the level of the aggregates' funnelling towards visibility, that is, towards the visualisation of van Winkel's forever-out-of-reach-remaining missing visuals. Both stages are predicated on what Andersen and Pold call the metainterface, a paradigm that turns ideology into a cloud of diffuse, networked services constantly extracting and processing data. Because of its (continually growing) size, variety, complexity, and velocity, big data has effectively turned the interface – a computer screen, for example – into a metainterface, into "a situation where the computer's interface seemingly both becomes omnipresent and invisible" and is "at once embedded in everyday objects and characterized by hidden exchanges of information between objects" (Andersen and Pold 2018, p. 5). Moving beyond human-computer interaction, the metainterface is the sum total of the Internet of Things, wearable technology, cloud computing, and a variety of smart environments – cars, homes, buildings, and cities. The metainterface reorganises the relationship between signs and signals embedding ideology in code, thus continuing the prime function of ideology, which is to influence behaviour. In a city, any residential building is potentially an Airbnb; "with Uber, any car can become a taxi and any person its driver. [...] Theoretically, anything can signify anything. All one needs to decode and access the city is the right interface" (83). Important to emphasise is that the metainterface is closely related to cloud computing, an interconnected, global phenomenon with a standardising infrastructure hidden from view which 'feeds' the insatiable hunger of the drive for a constant production and circulation of data and images, a bulimic attempt to make everything visible. The metainterface is the technological infrastructure of big data's platform seeing and invisualities, while the 'traditional' interface (such as a mobile phone screen) is experientially marked as the surface for the possible appearance of the missing visuals. Within this structure, the task of big data is to generate POV-data-doubles, algorithmic shadows of the user's techno-embodied POV in order to capture the user from within, so to speak, as in a POV cinematographic shot, by overlaying the machinic and the embodied. In the process of filming, this overlaying is achieved by temporarily removing the physical body of the actor and putting the camera in its place. Similarly, in the digital world, the user's body is temporarily removed from the data matrix, given that data harvesting algorithms turn embodied individuals into a variable composition of their fragmented micro-movements, combined with billions of other micro-movements on a platform or within a network. In both cases, the cinematic and the digital, the temporary removal (dispersal or abstraction) of the embodied subject, gives rise to forms of machinic re-embodiment: on film, the camera offers the replaced actor's body to the audience for physical re-embodiment; in the data matrix, the data extracted from the interface is offered at the level of the metainterface, the sum and agglomeration of all one's interfaces, in the form of a POV-data-double. This invisible POV-data-double operates as an algorithmic dividual whirlpool, directing the circulation of data and images back to the user device's interfaces – which capture data and images, that, inevitably, will be captured again and again, and turned into new big data invisualities, foregrounding new dividual facets to be targeted in the data matrix. A good example of the POV-data-double and the operationalisation of the drive to visibility is Tinder, the geosocial networking and online dating application, which combines the erotic drive with the drive to visibility. Tinder allows users to anonymously view other members' profiles; if they 'like' their photos and biographies, they are matched with members with similar tastes and can exchange messages (in other words, become visible to each other). In order to match compatible users, Tinder relies on the Elo scoring system, an algorithm invented for the purpose of grading chess players via a micro-system that monitors their moves as well as the average times it took to make a specific move, their succession, direction and cohesion, predicting the outcome of the chess match. In a zero–sum game – a game where what is gained by one player is lost by the other – the system appraises the players' skills differentially so that the difference in the rating is used to forecast the outcome of a specific match, which further contributes to the players' overall rating (Elo 1978). Tinder utilises this set of equations to parse and combine 'players' on their app, based on their micro-moves and their geolocative temporalities, turning Elo's rating into a "desirability rating" (Carr 2016). "People who are on a same [ranking] of giving and receiving when it comes to right ('like') and left ('pass') swipes, are understood by Tinder's algorithms to be equally often desired by other users" (Rolle 2019, np.). According to Tinder's chief scientist Liu, the complex algorithmic architecture that produces personalised recommendations relies on the information gathered from swiping (a verb used to define the action of liking or disliking a profile), such as quantity, speed, tempo and repetition; the TinVec neural network further maps these swipes into vectors so that "similar vectors are mapped into nearby points" (Liu 2017, np.). What is interesting in TinVec's neural architectures is that they operate like a *collaborative filter*, mapping the users' mutual compatibility without working on the particular user as individual, or working on them directly. Rather, TinVec harnesses the data stream coming from the users' log-in platform, their Facebook, Instagram, or Spotify accounts, their mobile phone, tablet or computer, their geolocation, the pattern of their 'scattered-ness' across multiple devices and networks and interactions. A POV-data-double thus emerges from a complex algorithmic structure digesting a huge number of data-points, actions and reactions and using them to create algorithmic shadows, tailored to produce personalised predictions, which, in turn, crave more data, or, in van Winkel parlance, the materialisation of the missing visuals, in a temporally micro-structured way. A case in point is the 'Super Likeable' function of Tinder, which allows users to 'swipe' an extra Super Like from the chosen cluster of profiles, algorithmically selected on the basis of the swiper's ever-evolving POV-data-double, or the 'Top Picks' function, which proposes a special profile a day – a profile that is, in algo-rithmic terms, the most desirable for the particular 'swiper'. Both Super-Likeable and Top Picks wed the erotic drive to the crave for the missing visuals and the drive to visuality, perpetuating data production and funnelling it in a micro-temporal, palpably affect-influencing way, which is what makes Tinder highly addictive. Users believe that the next swipe will be the right one, and if not the next one, then the one after, and so on *ad infinitum*, which generates steady activity, produces more and more data, modulates affect and creates further dividuations – or arborisations of affect – although this is by no means specific to Tinder, or to other dating applications, but includes all forms of online communication and interaction. Let us take a closer look at the similarities and differences between cinematic and datified dividuations in order to elaborate the political implications of van Winkel's drive to visuality, and MacKenzie and Munster's platform seeing.

The dividual between molar and molecular: from cinema to the metainterface

The term dividual, as defined in Deleuze's above-mentioned "Post-Scriptum", refers to the fragmentation of the contemporary subject in the face of digital tech-nology. In *Cinema I*, it refers to the dividual nature of cinema. For Deleuze, the cinematic images are time itself, and, as such, invariably dividual; they change quali-tatively from frame to frame, and from cut to cut, continually emerging from the middle image – the image the spectator perceives as the moving image – but which is, in fact, a series of 24 discrete frames, that we perceive to be the moving image. Significantly, movement and qualitative change are, for Deleuze, the dividual prop-erty of all forms of affect, in tune with affect's heterogeneousness, modulation, non-locality, yet singularity and cohesion. This form of dividuality is different in quality from the dividuality articulated in "Post-Script". Presciently, Deleuze theorised computational technologies as increasingly moving towards capturing the dividual, and not the *individual*, which is why computational technologies reproduce the analogue dividual by reproducing the modularity and heterogeneousness characteristic of the dividual nature of affect. Affect is of crucial importance here; as Ott notes, "affect is impersonal [...] distinct from every individuated state of things; it is nonetheless singular and can enter into singular combinations or conjunctions with other affects" (Ott 2018, p. 35). The analogue dividual is a multitude of continuously unfolding affective states; the digital dividual is an attempt to capture this affective dimension *as it unfolds*. The role of affect within organic, cinematic and algorithmic POVs cannot be overemphasised. In a cinematic POV, the audience feels as if they were inside the screen, inside the cinematic machine breaking through the so-called fourth wall, which, in early theatre performance and film, separates the actors from the spectators. Algorithmic technologies, by contrast, produce the overlaying of the human and the machine "by inserting the machine into the human, and not vice-versa" as is the case with film (Azar 2019, p. 163). They do so by "accessing the affective gap the POV emerges from", which occurs, first, by breaking through the screen of the body, and second, by extracting data below the threshold of human perception and exposing humans to a "quantified version of their very affective fabric" which, in its datafied form, "contributes to the constitution of new forms of human-machinic *Umwelten* with complex political implications" (163). The most obvious of these implications is perhaps the exploitation of the unconscious dimension of human malleability.

Given this state of affairs, the question of determining the relationship between the metainterface, the analogue individual, and affect is of crucial importance. The dividual, affective, unstable, transitory parts of what we usually refer to as the 'individual' are the metainterface's raw material. In a recent paper, D'Amato traces the influence of Simondon on Deleuze's concept of individuation, suggesting that

> users individuate by interacting through and with a digital milieu, their online actions feed the individuation of the dividual, and this process constitutes the basis on which the digital milieu through which users individuate gets modified by suggestion algorithms, influencing, in turn, their individuation.
>
> *(D'Amato 2019, p. 5)*

Although this description seems to resonate with the *operational structure* of the metainterface described above, the idea of the dividual capable of individuating is problematic to say the least. The inability of the dividual to individuate is key to understanding the failure of the metainterface to generate the 'right', and thus no longer 'missing' visuals. Contrary to intuition, this drive-based inability, which does not refer to flat failure but to a paradoxical form of 'constantly succeeding at the micro level, yet always failing at the macro level' is key to the perpetuation of the metainterface and its continuous production and circulation of data and images.

Furthermore, the impossibility of the dividual to individuate marks the distinction between the process of individuation at work in a cinematographic POV shot and the process of dividuation that takes place at the level of the metainterface, where the algorithmic shadow cannot aid the user's individuation in an agency-eliminating process that can only be described as (digital) dividuation. Deleuze suggests that this is the case in the molecular functioning of the society of control "which in no way attests to individuation" but "substitutes for the individual or numerical body the code of a 'dividual' material to be controlled" (Deleuze 1992, p. 5). Otherwise put, dividuation, as Ott, too, argues, is both the process and "human entity that is even more complex than that posited in Simondon's conception of individuation" which "calls for specific forms of observation that accentuate the micro- and macro-structural heterogeneity of their interrelationship" (Ott 2018, p. 7). This constant and complex molecular modulation makes it necessary to take a closer look at the role of situated-ness and algorithmic within-ness in POV-data-doubles.

In MacKenzie and Munster's "platform seeing", the dividual nature of POV-data-doubles creates a form of intimacy and within-ness with the user and their missing visuals, exposing the user to the multiplicity of their various dividual parts via the vicarious projection of tailored data emerging from these parts. The data are designed to produce the user's re-embodiment on the plane of the interface, and in this way, attempt to modify their behaviour. At first glance, the cycle of removal and subsequent re-immersion of the body in cinema and data tailoring practices works similarly: the aim of both apparatuses is the seamless overlaying of machine and body, camera and actor, data and user. However, it is also different: the molarity and mass-orientated projective apparatus of the cinematic cycle is different from the atomic molecularity of big data's algorithmic processes. The integration of the audience or user into the technological apparatus tends towards the molar in the cinema and towards the molecular in the metainterface. Despite this, the cinematic POV sits at the threshold of the transformation of the technological apparatus from a molar to a molecular modus operandi, to the point that it is possible to trace molarity and molecularity in the history of cinematic visuality. The cinematographic POV is located in the indeterminate zone between the molar and the molecular; molar because the camera doesn't track the actor's actual movements, nor does it reproduce them but merely imitates them; molecular, because the movement of the camera modulates the actor's movements durationally, *as if* becoming these very movements. Consequently, the spectator can modulate their own projected body and movement along the lines suggested by the molecular movement of the camera, instead of aligning them with the molar and static projecting apparatus. If the projecting apparatus constitutes the molar tendency of cinema as a system of cultural production situated within the disciplinary regime of modernity outlined by Foucault and referenced by Deleuze (Deleuze 1992, p. 1), the cinematographic POV opens film to the molecular. If, in its molecular facet, the cinematographic POV prefigures the functioning of platform seeing and metainterface, the (dis)integration of the user into the data matrix functions differently, and at different scales. On one hand, molecular modulation replaces molar moulding: the POV-data-double is defined by a constant state of modulation in relation to the data extracted from its multiple dividual and modular combinations. On the other hand, the projective faculty does not emanate from the user's consciousness (or the audience's), nor does it emanate from the projective apparatus. Rather, it emanates from their algorithmic double, which projects, at the level of the interface(s), the missing visuals the user is destined to fall into, and thus, invariably, also, re-embody. This process occurs molecularly and dividually because parts of the user's algorithmic shadow are foregrounded and recombined with other parts in an effort to generate multiple algorithmic models emerging from the same POV-data-double for the production of a targeted variety of missing visuals. This is how the dividual nature of the POV-data-double attempts to capture the (in)dividual, at a level of imbrication or within-ness more precise than the within-ness of the cinematic POV, which eventually triggers a re-embodiment of the user in the image, and their re-orientation.

The POV-data-double and the statistical cinema

The process of formation and re-orientation of different types of POV-data-doubles is implied in Pasquinelli's notion of the statistical cinema (2019), a type of cinema produced by machine learning and the processes of classification, information diffraction, distortion, and regression towards the mean, characterised by algorithmic projection at the level of the metainterface. For Pasquinelli, "the analogy of optical media illuminates the features of AI better than the analogy of the human brain [...] with statistical models performing a corrective role similar to that of lenses in optical media" (Pasquinelli 2019, p. 12). The formation of algorithmic data-doubles, accompanied by their tailored sets of missing visuals, allows us to understand Pasquinelli's anatomy of machine learning as statistical cinema: a continuous production and projection of both algorithmic and techno-embodied POVs onto the interface and metainterface. Furthermore, by addressing the process of ongoing 'dissonance' between the various human and algorithmic steps – which form the very basis of POV-data-doubles' constitution – Pasquinelli's critique of AI systems enables us to understand why the missing visuals eventually fail to instigate new processes of individuation that may return agency to the user and allow them to recompose their digital dividual parts. Statistical cinema operates through data compression resulting in "obfuscation that is irreversible" (12), necessitating a "reduction of the labels and categories that are initially present in the training dataset [...] in a technique called dimensionality reduction" (12). Inevitably, the missing visuals emerging from this process cannot produce new forms of individuation, as they are themselves not new. In fact, they produce normalisation or the "equalisation of anomalies to an average norm" (12). Pasquinelli uses the notion of the algorithmic POV to explain the projective working of the seamless overlaying of the body and the machine typical of the cinematic POV. It is precisely the overlaying of the techno-embodied data-double and the missing visuals that produces the sensation of within-ness characteristic of the cinematic POV, despite the logical regression that defines the statistical cinema's projections.

This within-ness is not rhetorical. It indicates the (ideological) belief that to capture the individual from within means to fragment and discretise it, dividuate its parts and organs, in search of its analogue dividual components. In fact, a dividual is both analogue and digital as both realms are characterised by processes of modulation between planes located at different scales and embedded in qualitatively and quantitatively different techno-phenomenological milieus, as defined by the nature of the POVs: a threshold of the transformation of one plane or scale into another. Digital dividuals are the invisual form that data and images take. As such, they can be assembled at different human and algorithmic scales in the form of algorithmic orientations, and, subsequently, POV-data-doubles, turned into missing visuals at the level of the interface where the cycle of data extraction begins all over again. In so doing, the digital dividual modularily captures the analogue dividual supposedly extracted by the dismembering of the individual orientation of the user across a number of devices, interfaces, and networks. The dividual nature of the POV-data-double emerging from this process is characterised by the sort of modulation that operates "like a sieve whose mesh varies from one point to another" (Deleuze 1986, p. 179). Consequently, the data and the images the user perceives on the interface are projected from within the algorithmic ghost, produced by the metainterface to *dividually* complement the user's techno-embodied POV. This complementing does not occur at a perceptive and cognitive level accessible to human beings. It is constituted by and through the modular assemblage of dividual fragments extracted from the user. The interface receives data and images tailored around the POV-data-double. Once these images appear at the level of the interface in the tentative form of the missing visuals, they begin to operate as baits for re-orienteering the user's techno-embodied POV. The overlaying of the user's techno-embodied POV and POV-data-double occurs through data and images that, although themselves not embodied, push towards a re-embodiment of the POV-data-double, with the aim of producing a feeling of within-ness in the user. This feeling of within-ness, in turn, amplifies the feeling of embodiment in the user, particularly when it occurs at the level of the metainterface, complemented by the shrinking of the distance between the body and the interface (one's mobile phone). Yet, this overlaying is never complete; the POV-data-double is not a faithful mirror of the user's techno-embodied POV, no matter how complex and rich the data sets emerging from the POV-data-double. Ultimately, big data and its funnelling operations fail. The projection of the POV-data-double on the user's interface (which functions as a screen and absorbs it), generates mirroring effects constituting digital echo-chambers, milieus where previous actions, choices, tastes of beliefs are fed back into the user's interface to re-design (or, rather, confirm) their techno-embodied position in the world. This is why, in reality, these images cannot be the missing visuals – if, by the missing visuals we understand the sort of visuals capable of freeing the user from the vicious circle of digital dividuation and putting them back into the open processes of individuation, or, rather, trans-individuation (Stiegler 1998). That said, the various big data operations – collecting, sifting, matching, funnelling, and profiling – sustain the drive to visibility by changing their orientation towards hypermediacy. Hypermediacy is one of the main features of the metainterface, characterised by the extraction of (big) data through a modular process of correlating everything to everything else. The result of the drive to visibility is (the drive to) hypermediacy, the horizon of which is transparency. Transparency, in this sense, is the seamless overlaying of body and machine; the hidden horizon shared by the cinematographic POV and the POV-data-double. But where do these drive-based failures leave us? What are their political implications, or implications for collective life? Let me try and sketch the relationship between big data, POV-data-doubles and the missing visuals through a 2018 artistic project entitled project DoppelGANger.agency.[1]

Coda: DoppelGANger.agency

Critically engaging with the implications of AI-powered facial recognition technology, POV-data-doubles, and the missing visuals, the art project DoppelGANger.agency approaches the ambiguous role of the human face, situated at the threshold between the molar and the molecular. Unique and singular, and yet evilly datafied by the metainterface and numerous data infrastructures that 'drive' the collection of biometric and affective data in spheres of life as diverse as border control, health administration, humanitarian aid, penal and justice systems, and financial security, the face has become one of the most relevant yet controversial bio-techno-political battlefields of the current epoch (Azar 2018a). "If face-tracking technologies are based on the idea that one's face is unique and not replicable", entertaining face-tweaking apps available on the market seem to suggest the precise opposite: that the uniqueness of face is "hackable" (31). Today, the face is the site where contradictory regimes of truth coexist and feed each other in a form that "keeps an appearance of immediacy while hiding layers of algorithmic complexity" (31). Recently, Generative Adversarial Networks (or GANs), a type of neural network-driven AI, have managed to process autonomously huge databases of real human faces and to generate hyper-realistic faces that do not belong to any living human being in the data set. These AI human faces are both faces of missing humans (humans who do not exist in the actual world) and faces of algorithmically generated ghosts. DoppelGANger.agency uses the AI-generated faces as street posters for missing humans. On the one hand, the face is a synecdoche for an embodied POV. The posters are an attempt to give these faces a (human) body. On the other hand, these faces are a visual metaphor for the POV-data-double. They turn the ghostly consistency of data processing and the invisibility of our algorithmic shadows into an algorithmic, yet *affectively* 'real' face. These DoppelGANgers are a form of missing visuals emerging from the real human faces the GANs in question were trained on. But can such combinatorics assuage the drive to visibility? Can they raise awareness of the steadily proliferating molecular panopticons, or POV-opticons? (Azar 2018b) The DoppelGANger agency claims that these algorithmic faces could "provide new ways to protect privacy" in the form of a "blockchain of faces" that will allow people to, once again, regain "full anonymity with the help of unique proxy faces" (Azar 2018c).The agency also designs algorithmic masks to allow protesters around the world to evade face recognition technologies by 'dividuating' algorithmic faces, extracting single facial features and printing them on wearable fabrics so as to enable protesters to dodge common mask bans.Yet, on a Reddit group dedicated to the billposting of DoppelGANger faces, potential users were sceptical about the good intentions of the start-up, linking even mock transparency to persecution and dividual algorithmic production to the underlying 'truth', actual-world existent or individual: "It creeps me out [...] like I wouldn't want to be 'found' matching one of those faces [...] then what? They'll come and get me?" (DoppelGANger.agency 2018, np). Although, undoubtedly, people with different perceptual and cognitive habits will interpret the activist-artistic intentions behind this project differently, it is important to understand the gap that exists between our operative notions of embodiment, uniqueness and replicability, not as a worn-out human–machine polarity but as a key element for reinventing visibility based on the drive to visibility, algorithmic POVs, and the missing visuals, in a gesture of radical techno-politics capable of re-articulating the cultural, social, and aesthetic implications of this gap.

Note

1 See: http://doppelganger.agency/.

References

Andersen C and Pold S 2018, *The Metainterface*. Cambridge, MA: MIT Press.
Azar M 2018a, "Algorithmic Facial Image: Regimes of Truth and Datafication", *APRJA – Research Values*, vol. 7, no. 1, pp. 26–35. Available from: https://aprja.net//issue/view/8309/828 [accessed 4 August 2020].
Azar M 2018b, "From Panopticon to POV-opticon: Drive to Visibility and Games of Truth", Proceedings from POM Beirut, May. Available from: http://dx.doi.org/10.14236/ewic/POM19.18 [accessed 4 August 2020].
Azar M 2018c, DoppelGANger.agency. Available from: http://doppelganger.agency/ [accessed 4 August 2020].
Azar M 2019, "POV-matter, Cinematic POV and Algorithmic POV between Affects and Umwelten", *APRJA*, vol. 8, no. 1, pp. 157–168. Available from: https://aprja.net//issue/view/8133/866 [accessed 4 August 2020].
Branigan E 1984, *Point of View in the Cinema*. Berlin: Mouton de Gruyter.
Carr A 2016, "I Found Out My Secret Internal Tinder Rating and Now I Wish I Hadn't", Fastcompany.com, January 11. Available from: www.fastcompany.com/3054871/whats-your-tinder-score-inside-the-apps-internal-ranking-system [accessed 29 December 2019].
D'Amato P 2019, "Simondon and the Technologies of Control: On the Individuation of the Dividual", in *Culture, Theory and Critique*, vol. 60, pp. 300–314.
Deleuze G 1986, *Cinéma 1. The Movement-Image*, trans. Tomlinson H and Habberjam B. Minneapolis, MN: University of Minnesota Press.
Deleuze G 1992, "Postscripts on the Societies of Control", *October*, vol. 59, pp. 3–7.

Deleuze G 1993, *The Fold: Leibniz and Baroque*, trans. Conley T. Minneapolis, MN: University of Minnesota Press.

Deleuze G and Guattari F 1987, *A Thousand Plateaus. Capitalism and Schizophrenia II*, trans. Massumi B. Minneapolis, MN: University of Minnesota Press.

DoppelGANger.agency 2018. Available from: http://doppelganger.agency/ [accessed 23 December 2019].

Elo A 1978, *The Rating of Chessplayers, Past and Present*. New York: Arco.

Foucault M 1978, *Discipline and Punish: The Birth of Prison*. New York: Pantheon.

Liu S 2017, *Personalized User Recommendations at Tinder: The TinVec Approach*. Keynote at ML Conference, San Francisco. Available from: www.slideshare.net/SessionsEvents/dr-steve-liu-chief-scientist-tinder-at-mlconf-sf-2017 [accessed 23 December 2019].

MacKenzie A and Munster A 2019, "Platform Seeing: Image Ensembles and Their Invisualities", *Theory, Culture & Society*, vol. 36, no. 5, pp. 3–22.

Ott M 2018, *Dividuations*. Cham: Palgrave Macmillan.

Pasquinelli M 2019, "How a Machine Learns and Fails – A Grammar of Error for Artificial Intelligence", *Spheres – Journal for Digital Cultures*, #5 Spectres of AI, November. Available from: https://spheres-journal.org/contribution/how-a-machine-learns-and-fails-a-grammar-of-error-for-artificial-intelligence/ [accessed 29 December 2019].

Rolle M 2019, "The Biases We Feed to Tinder Algorithms. How a Machine-learning Algorithm Holds up a Mirror to Society", *Diggitmagazine.com*, February 25. Available from: www.diggitmagazine.com/articles/biases-we-feed-tinder-algorithms [accessed 29 December 2019].

Stiegler, B 1998. *Technics and Time I-II-III*. Stanford, CA: Stanford University Press.

van Winkel C 2005, *The Regime of Visibility*. Rotterdam: NAi.

Zuboff S 2019, "Surveillance Capitalism and the Challenge of Collective Action", *New Labor Forum*, vol. 28, no. 1, pp. 10–29.

12

READING BIG DATA AS THE HETEROGENEOUS SUBJECT

Simon Biggs

Our (human) perception is that big data originates at, or is concerned with, the cosmic scale, beyond the sensorium of the individual human being. We associate big data with sophisticated visualisation and mapping techniques in disciplines like astronomy (modelling the formation of galaxies); epidemiology (mapping disease across global populations); and meteorology (forecasting the state of atmospheric physics and chemistry). Big data's unimaginably large data sets evoke the trepidation of the sublime as the cosmic infinite (Burke 2015 [1757]). For centuries, art has evoked scale, both cosmic and microscopic as we find in the romantic figure-in-a-landscape paintings of Friedrich's *Wanderer above the sea of fog* (Friedrich 1818), Gursky's photographic work *Amazon* (Gursky 2016), or Lozano-Hemmer's microscopic *Pulse Index*, a series of screens endlessly replicating digital visualisations (Lozano-Hemmer 2010). These works cue a powerful sense of infinity without recourse to the algorithmic methods currently associated with big data. Fundamentally, big data is a method of organisation and presentation, a representational trope which renders legible, to machines, large sets of information, while simultaneously conditioning the 'givens' it mediates: knowledge, perception, imagination, and human subjects. In this chapter, I analyse the relationship between the infra-ordinary (Perec 1974 [1973]), big data and the related social ontology of the 'black-box' in order to develop the concept of iridescence, to query subjectivity as a big-data-mediated multiplicitous and discontinuous construct, as present in my works *Dark Matter* (2017) and *Heteropticon* (2019). In this context I also consider Deleuze's proposition that the sublime reflects cosmic perception beyond human memory (Deleuze 1994).

The infra-ordinary

Although most often associated with cosmic scale, big data can be found in ordinary quotidian contexts; in what French twentieth-century author Perec referred to

192 Simon Biggs

as the infra-ordinary. Rather than considering big data as the evocation of the cosmic sublime – the collection of all the world's actions stored as recordings or machinic memories – we might consider how it is contingent upon, and reveals, the everyday and trivial and how it offers insights into the dense ambient noise that is our daily lives. We should not assume that the mediation of our world, through big data capture, analytics, preservation, and recycling – creating an eternal presence for everything that has ever existed – is an innately sublime state. The manner in which embedded and pervasive surveillance technologies operate in urban space is an example of big data as a mediator of physical and social space. For Perec, the habitual, everyday rhythm of the infra-ordinary renders us unaware of the potentialities of things around us; headline-grabbing events distract us from the details that really matter:

> The daily newspapers talk of everything except the daily [...] What's really going on, what we're experiencing, the rest, all the rest, where is it? How should we take account of, question, describe what happens every day and recurs everyday: the banal, the obvious, the common, the infra-ordinary, the background noise, the habitual? But that's just it, we're habituated to it. We don't question it [...] This is no longer even conditioning, it's anaesthesia. We sleep through our lives in a dreamless sleep. But where is our life? Where is our body? Where is our space?
>
> *(Perec 1974 [1973], pp. 205–207)*

Perec raises the possibility, perhaps counter-intuitively, as to whether the reading processes associated with big data, such as machine-based pattern recognition, which invariably entails information diffraction and synthesis, might help us gain insights into the infra-ordinary; to lift the anaesthetic veil of the everyday and allow a more vivid engagement with the iridescent ambient 'noise' that was his concern. Perec directs our attention to our body as an object in space to be drawn out of the noise, read, and questioned. Here I focus on the *multiplicitous positions* from which data can be viewed or read, and the infinite fracturing of the viewer, or reader, this implies. The strategies of distant reading, employing the techniques of statisticians in analysing big data, including frequency graphs, maps and charts, allow us to augment our reading of a text and see "swarms of hybrids and oddities" for which the usual taxonomies "offer very little help. It's fascinating, to feel so lost in a universe one didn't even know existed" (Moretti 2013, p. 181). Distant reading evokes the dense and dynamic character of big data, cultural or otherwise, swarming and hybridising as we watch. Distant reading is to conventional literary theory what the sequencing of DNA is to Linnaean taxonomy[1] (a powerful top-down method for sorting living things into groups, such as plant species, based on similarity of appearance or behaviour) in that it reveals ontological connections that disrupt established classifications. Distant reading is the human equivalent of machine reading, where computers are trained to process natural language and discover relations and connections between textual elements, which allow for a form of pattern recognition and thus machine

Big data: The heterogeneous subject **193**

'understanding'. This approach relies to a significant extent on black-boxing, the encapsulation of processes as cipher, symbol, or some other abstraction, that allows a logical scaffolding of otherwise overly complex information to "focus on inputs and outputs and not on its internal complexity" (Latour 1999, p. 304). In machine learning and large neural networks, as employed in Deep Learning, black-boxing refers to the way information encapsulation, compression, and cleansing (erasing superfluous information) creates irreversible obfuscation. While relaying data, layers of neurons erase superfluous data from the previous layer gradually omitting an increasing number of links, which obfuscates the logic of the sequence, generating opaqueness.

Cultural black-boxes

Big data exists at the core of our culture, operationally mediating our interactions with corporations, the state, and each other; social media algorithms deliver news targeted to our preferences; facial recognition systems monitor our public spaces. Big data forms part of the knowledge economy that underpins our collective being (Zuboff 2019), emerging, at this scale of complex interaction, as units or entities of information and knowledge of which we are profoundly ignorant (Wiener 1961, p. xi). This knowledge "we don't know we know", is our collective sub-conscious at work (Žižek 2005). In this sense, there is little that is novel in how big data mediates society. Our social apparatus has, very possibly since its origins, been built as a series of black-boxes that model the operation of power in culture. Although Joly has disabused the notion that Bourdieu's concept of habitus might be considered a form of 'black-box' (Joly 2018), habitus nevertheless offers a frame-work for understanding how the black-box might operate as:

> systems of durable, transposable dispositions, structured structures predisposed to function as *structuring structures*, that is, as principles which generate and organize practices and representations that can be objectively adapted to their outcomes without presupposing a conscious aiming at ends or an express mastery of the operations necessary in order to attain them.
>
> *(Bourdieu 1990, p. 53; emphasis mine)*

Our daily life is pervaded by black-boxes; if we were to spend time deconstructing the conventions that determine our contemporary quotidian – our traffic man-agement systems, for example – we would have little time to do anything else. Reverse engineering the black-boxes that constitute our culture is an epic task, the dimensional equivalent of big data. But isn't such reverse engineering, the task of the artist? For McLuhan, the artist can counter these (invariably black-boxed) technological effects as they are the "expert aware of the changes in sense percep-tion" (McLuhan 1964, p. 33). Wasn't this the aim of Perec's novels or the literary works of his Oulipo compatriots Calvino and Queneau? The authors associated with Oulipo (*Ouvroir de literature potentielle – Workshop of potential literature*), founded

194 Simon Biggs

by Queneau and Le Lionnais in 1960, experimented with methodologies aimed at revealing the quotidian black-boxes of daily life. The group sought to de-sublimate our preconceptions through the use of arbitrary but strictly logical, even mathematical, rule-based writing techniques to question the ontology of their own creations and reveal how black-boxing operates to *constrain* imagination. More recently, the above-mentioned photographic constructions of Gursky, evoking bland repetition whilst capturing vivid detail, thus echoing Perec's notion of the infra-ordinary, probe our ignorance of that which we know, including our guilty collective secrets. Here, light operates to render objects and the space they inhabit transparent, presenting to the viewer a state of permanent visibility that facilitates the function of the panopticon (Foucault 1977) sublimated in our culture. As a model mechanism for the black-box, a super-ego regulator at the heart of our culture and our collective being, the panopticon operates in plain sight, brilliantly and pervasively lit, in a collective blind-spot.

Butterflies

Iridescence is a property of many phenomena, often found in nature, such as in butterfly wings, jewel beetles or bird feathers. In the case of static iridescent objects or surfaces this quality is only perceivable if one assumes, through continuous movement, multiple points of view. The butterfly's wings are iridescent because they consist of multiple surfaces that reflect light as well as colour, at different wavelengths depending on viewing angle. Structured as a "lattice of scales that cover both sides of the wing substrate", butterfly wings create the variations in colour that lead to iridescence "by the interaction of light with the scales' optical materials" (Giraldo and Stavenga 2016, pp. 381–388). It is in shifting between variable loci of perception that the spectral range of colours of a bird's feather, or a butterfly's wing, becomes visible, revealing the object's iridescence. In the case of a static object, iridescence reveals, to the observing subject, the object's existence in time–space as a series of simultaneous instances of the object that echoes the apparent discontinuity of the iridescent subject. This easily observable multiperspectivalism cues a heightened sense of reality, where our own difference, in time and space, reveals the many aspects of an object that otherwise appears homogeneous and static. Similarly, the multiplicitous and heterogeneous properties we associate with big data – a microscopic slice of life captured by many different systems – vocal recognition recording, geolocative presence, commercial transactions, and social-media interactions – can inform the ontology and perception of the observing subject; a form of heteropticon, which is a complement to the concept of the panopticon, an eye composed of numerous states and instances that permits an iridescent engagement with things – an eye of difference.

The antithesis of the panopticon can be found in Foucault's notion of heterotopia, a conception of spaces and places characterised by their otherness, where multiple worlds exist interstitially in what appears to be a single world (Foucault 1998). Foucault contests the concept of linear time and homogeneous

Big data: The heterogeneous subject **195**

space through notions of utopia, an unreal space, and heterotopia, which refers to a simultaneously mythical and real space. For Foucault, all cultures are heterotopic in that they are based on crisis and deviation, such as sacred and forbidden places and places for 'non-conforming deviants': psychiatric hospitals or prisons. In addition to being culturally constituted, heterotopias bring together contradictory sites such as sacred gardens represented as microcosms of the world in the patterns of a Persian rug. They cleave traditional time, bringing together spaces that represent a quasi-eternity, like museums, or are profoundly ephemeral, like fairgrounds. Finally, heterotopias are not accessible to all; one enters a heterotopic space either because one is forced to, like a prison, or through rituals associated with purification, like saunas or hammams. Heterotopias exist as liminal conditions.

As in Gursky's photographic works, the panopticon renders everything equally visible, transparent, or equivalent. In contrast, heterotopic sites are characterised by their ambiguity, where the subject can remain hidden, at least in part, in a liminal in-between space. An example might be a masked orgy, where the anonymity shared between subjects fosters transgressive relations distinct to those typically found in heteronormative, or homonormative, domesticity. The notion of the heteropticon is similar to heterotopia, albeit not entirely; the heteropticon is not a space composed as difference but, rather, the perception of space and the subject, from many simultaneous points of view. If the panopticon is a single all-seeing lens, at the centre of a social collective, then the heteropticon can be conceived of as a potentially infinite number of eyes, distributed through a space, generating a discontinuous and multifaceted vision of that which it beholds. Heteroptic sight is iridescent in nature.

In a number of artworks, developed over the past decades, I have explored how both complex and simple things might be viewed from simultaneous multiple points of view. Projects such as *Babel* (2001) employed multiple point-of-view renderings of three-dimensional data sets to create complex heterogeneous readings. In *Babel*, a web-browser that can operate within web-browsers, a set of volumetric Dewey Decimal maps are generated by multiple people browsing the system simultaneously on the Internet, allowing them to navigate the World Wide Web by using the Dewey Decimal Breakdown system. Not unlike a Linnaean taxonomy, the Dewey Decimal system is a hierarchical but infinitely divisible method for categorising things by subject or topic, specifically books in libraries. A Dewey Decimal map is a graphical visualisation of the system as a data matrix. This visualisation of the web in *Babel* is presented as complex arrays of three-dimensional layers or matrices of Dewey Decimal numbers, where each user of the site generates their own volumetric array as a number range that is rendered in a unique colour. In addition, all the users of the system can see what the other users are seeing, from their various perspectives, thus enabling a shared visualisation which results in a shifting layering of the varyingly coloured Dewey Decimal arrays that create an iridescent effect, not unlike a butterfly's wing. *Babel* functions by acquiring the real-time mouse-locations of multiple networked online web-browsing users to generate a multi-perspectival view of a number of Dewey Decimal number ranges. The software does this for all users of the interface simultaneously: the database can be seen, by each user, from all the users' points of view. Individual users can select a specific Dewey Decimal number, from any of the layered visualisations, by clicking on it. This causes their web-browser to open a new window and to load the webpage found at the address, which resolves following the Dewey Breakdown. For example, 700: Fine Art; 750: Painting and paintings; 751: Painting techniques, procedures, apparatus, equipment, materials, or forms, 751.7: Specific forms; 751.73: Murals and frescoes. As the work encompasses the full range of Dewey Decimal values, a user might find themselves opening a webpage that is associated, by its meta-data, with any topic classified within the Dewey Decimal system. If the user happens to be an expert user of Dewey Decimal (perhaps a librarian or scholar) then they might anticipate the topic of the webpage they are about to alight upon. However, whilst the *Babel* interface allows the user to navigate the web it does so in what is a visually confusing manner. A dense array of Dewey Decimal numbers offers little information to guide us in our engagement with the ever-expanding range of websites that might be navigated to. As more users simultaneously engage with the *Babel* website, the proliferation of distinctly colour-coded number arrays creates a kaleidoscopic effect that makes it difficult to determine not only what website a number might refer to but the numbers themselves. The screen becomes a chaotic display of shimmering fields, as the overlaying grids of numbers generate tertiary moiré effects, as can be seen from Figure 12.1.

FIGURE 12.1 Simon Biggs, *Babel*, screen still, production documentation, London, 2001.

Source: Photo: Simon Biggs. © Simon Biggs

Big data: The heterogeneous subject   197

I have further explored the potential of artworks to evoke multiple points of view, defined as multiple hybrid subjects, or collaborative readers, in projects such as *Dark Matter* and *Heteropticon*. *Dark Matter* (2017) is a fully immersive, physically interactive video projection environment that explores the possibility of perceiving the body as an absence, inferred from the physical and cultural information around it (something we don't know we know). When there are multiple viewers within a single virtual three-dimensional scene (as in an augmented reality projection system), a problem emerges concerning how to define the point of view that is required to generate the visualisation. Should the location be that of a 'lead' viewer, offering that person a satisfying first-person experience of physical immersion but providing others a secondary observational (third-person) experience of the scene, where they have no agency (or control) in respect of how the scene is viewed? This seems an unsatisfactory solution, as it privileges one viewer to the detriment of the others. Alternatively, the solution might be to generate an averaged point of view by determining a point in space equidistant between the positions of all the viewers in the space, offering no single viewer a privileged first-person view but allowing all the viewers to have a sense of how their position and angle of view contributes to the visualisation. However, whilst offering everyone some sense of interactive immersion, this solution leaves everyone in a less than satisfactory situation in gaining a fuller sense of agency. A third alternative is to generate a visualisation of the scene from all the points of view representing the physical locations of the viewers, which allows all the viewers to have a full sense of immersion and their agency within it, even their smallest movements affecting the scene before them. However, this solution means that everyone can see what everyone else can see, leading to a potentially chaotic experience (as in the work *Babel*). Whether this might be considered a negative or positive outcome depends on your intentions. Another possible strategy is to treat the positions of viewers in a virtual 3D space as dynamic vectors that define not only a point of view but also an orientation, such that two or more viewers collectively and tacitly control the various parameters that define how a visualisation is generated from a dynamic point of view. This strategy, incorporating heteroptic visualisation strategies, is used in *Dark Matter* (see Figure 12.2).

Here, the point of view (the position from which the three-dimensional scene on the screen is rendered) is dynamic. When there is one viewer (interactor) within the work the scene is rendered from a point outside the interactive space. This point of view is static and produces a conventional outsider's viewpoint of the three-dimensional scenario (an idealised third-person point of view). However, when more than one interactor is in the interactive area of the installation, the position of the virtual camera that determines the point of view, is relocated to the head of the first interactor and its focal point becomes that of the second interactor. This visualisation technique produces a situation where "what is rendered in the surrounding three-dimensional projections is a function of a point of view determined by the position of the heads of two of the interactors" (Biggs 2018). Here the conventional unitary subject we associate with the concept of the reader is reconceived as that of the co-reader, whereby the engagement with an object by multiple subjects

FIGURE 12.2 Simon Biggs, *Dark Matter*, installation view, studio documentation, Cherryville, 2017.

Source: Photo: Simon Biggs. © Simon Biggs

requires that they operate as a heterogeneous super-subject. The outcome is a constantly variable engagement with a visual world comprised of thousands of text fragments that can be read in an innumerable variety of conjunctions, a recombinant poetic space of apparently infinite dimensions. The proposition of the work is that "reading can become a collaborative and multimodal process" (Biggs 2018), problematising both the reading subject, and the "read" or interpreted object, as plural and heterogeneous. *Heteropticon* (Biggs 2019) renders the viewer(s) as a heterogeneous subject of multi-dimensional self-contemplation. During the research project *Scale* (Biggs et al. 2009), a collaborative workshop involving a number of artists, dancers, choreographers, musicians, ergonomists, and computer scientists, I developed an imaging technique predicated on the concept of discontinuous and heterogeneous vision. This involved developing an algorithm that allowed real-time live video to be mapped onto stored human motion-capture data. A live video image of dancers was cut-up in real-time by the algorithm, into small rectangular image-maps which were then mapped to a motion-capture sequence of previously recorded dance movement. The position and size of the image-maps were determined by the three-dimensional locations of the individual motion-capture data points, each control-point's location being mapped to an equivalent position in the live video signal, the control-points z location being used to determine the scaling of the image-map acquired (for example: the closer the z position to the viewer/dancer the larger the image-map appeared). A live dancer could then dance

Big data: The heterogeneous subject **199**

in front of the video projection, composed of motion-capture data, just as a dancer dances in front of a mirror during rehearsals, and could see themselves visually mapped onto the motion data of the recorded dancer. So long as the live dancer's movements corresponded with those of the recorded dancer's data, the numerous tiny images of the live dancer would appear at the corresponding motion-capture coordinates in the projection, affirming the dancers' movement as congruent. This process produced an iridescent and fragmentary mirror reflection of the live dancer.

As an interactive artwork, *Heteropticon* employs an imaging technique that is an iteration of the technique developed during the Scale project. While the technique used in the *Scale* workshop involved mapping two-dimensional live video data to three-dimensional recorded motion-capture data, in *Heteropticon* the mapping process involves both live video and live motion-capture data. In the *Scale* project, the point of view from which the imagery was rendered was static. Like *Dark Matter, Heteropticon* employs a dynamic point of view in order to enhance the spatial perception of the layered imagery. However, in *Heteropticon* the viewpoint is not entirely defined by the interactors' physical position and activity but is rendered as a drift, or dérive. Guy Debord conceived dérive as "a technique of rapid passage through varied ambiences" involving "playful-constructive behavior and awareness of psychogeographical effects" different from the classic notions of "journey or stroll" (Debord 2006 [1956], p. 62). In *Heteropticon*, the relationship between observer and observed is reversed. The interactor sees themselves in a projected image that appears to be an electronic mirror. However, this is a distorted mirror, where the image reflected back to the observer is tessellated and fragmented in three-dimensional space, resembling the compound-eye vision of a fly. *Heteropticon* presents the observer, the 'reflected' viewer or subject, as an iridescent object, shifting through its heterogeneous instances as it is deconstructed in a virtual space viewed from multiple shared, subjective, but detached, points of view – a fractured and folded place of collective drift. The work offers viewers, as individuals and groups of interactors, insights into how they might become heterogeneous and iridescent. *Heteropticon* (Figure 12.3) functions by acquiring a live video image of the interactor(s), who are located in a dark space where only the central area is illuminated. At the same time, employing a Microsoft Kinect motion-tracking sensor, a three-dimensional model of the interactor's body is acquired by the computer system. This allows the software to determine the interactors' joint locations. A total of six interactors can be simultaneously tracked and visualised. These virtual three-dimensional joints are employed as 'attractors' for hundreds of invisible objects that occupy the three-dimensional volume of the projected image space. These objects exist within a physics engine, which calculates the collisions, forces, ricochets, and trajectories of the objects. The invisible objects are all trying to accumulate around the virtual joints of the interactor(s) and subsequently ricochet chaotically off one another and the interactors' joints within the projected space, creating a fluid flocking of three-dimensional coordinates dynamically related to, but not the same as, the coordinates of the joints of the interactor(s). In a sense, this is a fuzzy and de-familiarised, perhaps liminal, computational model of the

FIGURE 12.3 Simon Biggs, *Heteropticon*, screen still, production documentation, Cherryville, 2018.

Source: © Simon Biggs

interactor's body, invisible to the interactor. The three-dimensional coordinate of each of these invisible objects is converted to the corresponding two-dimensional coordinate the object occupies in the projected screen image, producing a simple two-dimensional x and y coordinate, used to determine the origin of a rectangle, 36 by 36 pixels in size, employed to define and capture a corresponding region of pixels around the same coordinate in the live video-feed of a digital video camera, located above the projection and focused on the centre of the installation space. This fragment of the video's memory map (image) is copied to memory, creating a small tile-like image of what is in front of the screen at that location. The small image fragment, similar to a small mirror, is mapped onto a similarly sized 3D rectangular plane that is then co-located with the three-dimensional coordinate of the object that provided the two-dimensional origin point for the acquisition of the video tile, a process that allows hundreds of two-dimensional video fragments to be mapped into a corresponding three-dimensional representational space, creating a fragmented mirror effect composed of innumerable elements. The effect is not unlike Paul Cézanne's treatment of form, space, and light in his later paintings of Mont Sainte-Victoire (Cézanne 1902–1906). To render a three-dimensional scene on a two-dimensional screen a 'virtual camera' is required, consisting of a mathematical model of the camera, including its location, orientation and field of view, that determines what the camera can see and what is rendered by the software to the screen. In *Heteropticon*, the camera exists in three states. Its first state is the default state; the camera located at an imaginary static location behind the projection screen, looking from the screen towards a point in the centre of the interactive space. When an interactor enters the installation the virtual camera is

Big data: The heterogeneous subject **201**

relocated to a second-state, a position that corresponds to the head position of the interactor in the virtual three-dimensional volume, projected into the virtual space in front of the screen and focused on the centre of the interactive space, where the interactor(s) are located. This creates a second-state camera, with parallax, a geometry allowing the interactor to observe their own reflected image on the screen. When the interactor moves around before the projection they can observe subtly amplified shifts in their angle of view, revealing the fragmented image of their body to be a three-dimensional construct composed of numerous small images of different body fragments, while the various components of the construct shift their relative positions as a function of their spatial distribution and the shifting point of view of the virtual camera.

When proposing the concept of dérive, Debord suggested that the activity was most effectively undertaken not by individuals but by small groups of people. In *Heteropticon*, this idea of enhanced multiple agency is deployed in the form of a collectively determined drifting camera. If there is one interactor in the installation, then the virtual camera remains co-located with their virtual head's coordinates in the three-dimensional space, thus allowing the system to render the image from the point of view of the interactor. However, when more interactors enter the space, the camera drifts to a coordinate located equidistant in a three-dimensional space between the interactors' virtual heads, with the camera oriented so it remains focused on the centre of the space, creating a point of view detached from the interactors, although affected by them all. If any interactors move, the location of the virtual camera also moves, drifting to an equidistant point between the locations of the interactors' virtual head joint locations. As the virtual camera is detached from any one interactor's point of view, drifting between them all, and focused on all the interactors, rendered on the screen as three-dimensionally fragmented constructs, what the interactors see, from a place other than that which they occupy, is their own bodies as tessellated and exploded structures floating in a dark undefined spatial volume that is the projected image upon the screen. They appear as iridescent others.

Iridescence

Cézanne, whose paintings have fragmented and iridescent properties that might be considered a precursor to, and inspiration for, a work such as *Heteropticon*, said "I am one with the canvas. We are an iridescent chaos. I come before my motif, I lose myself there ... we germinate" (Cézanne quoted in Bogue 2003, p. 164). Deleuze observed that "[i]n painting, Cézanne's landscapes of 'iridescent chaos' are percepts, Bacon's portraits of heads-becoming-animal are instances of affects" (164). Percepts and affects are considered as "pure being of sensation" (Deleuze 1994, p. 167) and Deleuze notes that "one is not in the world, one becomes with the world, one becomes by contemplating it. Everything is vision, becoming. One becomes universe. Becoming animal, vegetable, molecular, becoming zero" (169). Deleuze appears to be seeking to evoke a sublime state of consciousness attained through heightened awareness engendered by the experience of the work of art as "pure

202 Simon Biggs

sensation". As sensation, Bacon's portraits, can be read, like Cézanne's landscapes, as iridescent, demanding of the viewer that they adopt multiple points of view, just as the artist did in their creation. This might be apprehended as similar to the Oulipian reverse engineering of the unknown known. Deleuze and Guattari observed how the self may be 'dismantled' in order to become other and thus recognisable,

> To become imperceptible oneself, to have dismantled love in order to become capable of loving. To have dismantled one's self in order finally to be alone and meet the true double at the other end of the line. A clandestine passenger on a motionless voyage. To become like everybody else; but this, precisely, is a becoming only for one who knows how to be nobody, to no longer be anybody. To paint oneself gray on gray.
>
> *(Deleuze and Guattari 1987, p. 218)*

This scenario offers us the opportunity to consider how we might be capable, with our limited human senses and finite neural tissue, of engaging big data as sensation, apprehension, and appreciation. We know this intuitively, from when we look up into the sky at night to contemplate the cosmic bodies above our heads, even if we can't determine, from our own senses and intellectual capabilities, how those bodies might interact with one another in the future (as a machine might).

The machine, reading big data, has the unrelenting capacity to consider every detail equally and determine probable future emergent patterns, from prior existing patterns, of data (events) that have not yet occurred. People, on the other hand, can call upon their imagination to envisage possible futures in a less deterministic way. Deleuze has speculated on the relationship between memory and imaginary futures. As Ansell-Pearson notes, he considered Proust's *À la recherche du temps perdu* as being concerned less with memory and the past than the future:

> the "search" is not steered by the effort of recall or the exploration of memory, but by the desire for truth ... Memory intervenes in this search only as a means but not the most profound means, just as past time intervenes as a structure of time but not the most profound one ... The stress on the need to overcome memory, and an advocacy of the superiority of the future, are prevalent throughout the span of Deleuze's oeuvre.
>
> *(Ansell-Pearson 2010, p. 161)*

Of particular relevance to the discussion here is Deleuze's view that art is engaged with cosmic perception *beyond memory*, as "art resides" in an "enlarged perception" expanded "to the limits of the universe", which requires creating art in such a way that "perception breaks with the identity to which memory rivets it" (161). The implication here is that the human capacity to determine probable future events is enabled not by the ability to recognise patterns in large memorised data sets but in the enhanced perception of the moment, where imagination transcends memory. This would appear to be a very different process than that employed by large data sets. The determinism of machine forecasting is useful when the future is likely to be similar to the past. However, the future has a capacity to defy such prescribed expectations. Without cosmic accident the asteroid that wiped out the dinosaurs, leading to the rise of mammals, may never have occurred; humans may never have evolved to be a dominant species. Could an imaginary Jurassic machine-learning system, 100 million years past, no matter how large the sample data set, have been capable of forecasting the rise of mammals, the planetary dominance of a single primate species and the proposition of the Anthropocene? Machines, with their pattern-recognition-based data processing, do not deliver perfect predictions. Our weather forecasts are often incorrect, but they are statistically reliable (American Meteorological Society 2015).

Big data can be seen to evoke the infra-ordinary; where everything is of equal value or, more accurately, without value – just data (although data is never without value, being created at the juncture of socio-technical relations). The heteroptic eye, that envisions the world in a constant state of iridescence, as a reflection of its own iridescence, is the eye that sees the infra-ordinary. As previously noted, big data mediates not only the object under observation (information) but also the observing subject. Subsequently, that subject is objectified and divided, rendered iridescent. Foucault has identified this process in understanding how humans are made into subjects, suggesting that "I have studied the objectivizing of the subject in what I call 'dividing practices'. The subject is either divided inside himself or divided from others" (Foucault 1982, pp. 777–778). Foucault further notes that "the human subject is placed in relations of production and signification" (778), which, like the above-mentioned operations of big data – mining, looping, sharing, interpreting, recycling – mediate the subject, just as they mediate the object (for here everything is information). Through this process we observe ourselves, as the subject, being divided, our perception similarly exploded into a multi-perspectival perceptual apparatus, in an iridescent state. The *Heteropticon* project is an experiment that seeks to identify how we become divided, how we find ourselves becoming (or, to echo Cézanne, 'germinating') as quotidian other – not a specific other, in the form of another subject, but as a heterogeneous other, constructed in the form of a collective (distributed) subject.

This discussion has considered the modalities of how the observing subject might be re-presented to itself, reflected or mirrored as a heterogeneous object, within artworks that mediate that representation through data. In projects such as *Babel*, *Dark Matter*, and *Heteropticon*, the observing subject, whose active influence within the work defines them as an interactor, is reconfigured as heterogeneous. The image of the observing subject, in *Heteropticon*, appears as iridescent and motile. It is the product of a visual apparatus that sublimates inter-subjective difference in order to amplify internal difference. The subject, in its quotidian experience, is disrupted not in order to achieve a utopian condition (Lefebvre 1991 [1947]) but to reverse engineer the black-box, our unknown knowns, and reveal our infra-ordinary heterogeneous existence. In this sense, *Heteropticon* continues an interest, shared with many artists, in how we might know ourselves, otherwise.

Note

1 Gene-sequencing of plant DNA has demonstrated that in some cases the similarities between species are more cosmetic than actual, with some species considered distinct to one another found to be closely related and others belonging to new genera (Shmahalo 2018).

References

American Meteorological Society. 2015, Available from: www.ametsoc.org/ams/index.cfm/about-ams/ams-statements/statements-of-the-ams-in-force/weather-analysis-and-forecasting/ [accessed 17 July 2019].

Ansell-Pearson K 2010, "Deleuze on the Overcoming of Memory", in Radstone S and Schwarz B (eds.), *Memory: Histories, Theories, Debates*. New York: Fordham University Press, pp. 161–179.

Babel. 2001, A data browser by Simon Biggs. Available from: http://littlepig.org.uk/babel/index.htm [accessed 23 March 2019].

Biggs S 2018, "Co-Reading as a Generative Ontology", *Materialities of Literature*, vol. 6, no. 3. Electronic Literature: Translations. Portugal: Coimbra University Press.

Biggs S et al. 2009, "The 'H' in HCI: Enhancing Perception of Interaction through the Performative", in Shumaker R (ed.), *Virtual and Mixed Reality*. San Diego, CA: Springer.

Bogue R 2003, *Deleuze on Music, Painting and the Arts*. London: Routledge.

Bourdieu P 1990, *The Logic of Practice*. Cambridge: Polity Press.

Burke E 2015 [1757], *A Philosophical Inquiry into the Origin of our Ideas of the Sublime and Beautiful*. Oxford: Oxford University Press.

Cézanne P 1902–1906, *Mont Sainte-Victoire*. In the collection of the Metropolitan Museum, New York. Available from: www.metmuseum.org/art/collection/search/435878 [accessed 3 October 2019].

Dark Matter. 2017, A data browser by Simon Biggs. Available from: http://littlepig.org.uk/darkmatter/index.htm [accessed 23 March 2019].

Debord G 2006 [1956], "Theory of the Dérive", in Knabb K (ed.), *The Situationist International Anthology*. Berkeley, CA: Bureau of Public Secrets.

Deleuze, G 1994, *What is Philosophy*, trans. Tomlinson H and Burchell G. New York: Columbia University Press.

Deleuze G and Guattari F 1987, *A Thousand Plateaus: Capitalism and Schizophrenia*, trans. Massumi B. London: Continuum.

Foucault M 1977, *Discipline and Punish: The Birth of the Prison*, trans. Sheridan A. New York: Pantheon Books.

Foucault M 1982, "The Subject and Power", *Critical Inquiry*, vol. 8, no. 4, pp. 777–795.

Foucault M 1998, "Different Spaces", in Faubion, JD (ed.), *Aesthetics, Method, and Epistemology: Essential Works of Foucault, 1954–1984, Volume 2*, trans. Hurley R. New York: The New Press, pp. 175–185.

Friedrich CD 1818, *Wanderer above the Sea of Fog*. Hamburg: Hamburger Kunsthalle. Available from: www.hamburger-kunsthalle.de/en/nineteenth-century [accessed 3 October 2019].

Giraldo MA and Stavenga DG 2016, "Brilliant Iridescence of Morpho Butterfly Wing Scales is Due to Both a Thin Film Lower Lamina and a Multilayered Upper Lamina", *Journal of Comparative Physiology: A Neuroethology, Sensory, Neural, and Behavioral Physiology*, May. Berlin, Heidelberg: Springer. Available from: https://doi.org/10.1007/s00359-016-1084-1 [accessed 3 October 2019].

Gursky A 2016, *Amazon*. Los Angeles, CA: The Broad Museum of Art, Los Angeles. Available from: www.thebroad.org/art/andreas-gursky/amazon [accessed 3 October 2019].

Heteropticon. 2019, A data browser by Simon Biggs. Available from: http://littlepig.org.uk/installations/hetero/index.htm [accessed 23 March 2019].

Joly M 2018, *Pour Bourdieu*. Paris: CNRS Editions.

Latour B 1999, *Pandora's Hope: Essays on the Reality of Science Studies*. Cambridge, MA: Harvard University Press.

Lefebvre H 1991 [1947], *The Critique of Everyday Life, Volume 1*, trans. Moore J. London: Verso.

Lozano-Hemmer R 2010, *Pulse Index*. Available from: www.lozano-hemmer.com/artworks/pulse_index.php [accessed 3 October 2019].

McLuhan M 1964. *Understanding Media: The Extensions of Man*. London: Routledge and Kegan Paul.

Moretti F 2013, *Distant Reading*. New York: Verso Books.

Perec G 1974 [1973], *Species of Spaces and Other Pieces*, trans. Sturrock J. Harmondsworth: Penguin.

Shmahalo O 2018, "DNA Analysis Reveals a Genus of Plants Hiding in Plain Sight", *Quanta Magazine*, September 4. Available from: www.quantamagazine.org/dna-analysis-reveals-a-genus-of-plants-hiding-in-plain-sight-20180904/ [accessed 5 January 2020].

Wiener N 1961, *Cybernetics: Or Control and Communication in the Animal and the Machine*. Cambridge, MA: MIT Press.

Žižek S 2005, "The Empty Wheelbarrow", *The Guardian*, February 19, London.

Zuboff S 2019, *The Age of Surveillance Capitalism*. London: Profile Books.

13

EPILOGUE: TELEPATHIC EXAPTATION IN LATE COGNITIVE CAPITALISM

A speculative approach to the effects of digitality

Warren Neidich

Introduction

According to a 2013 study by the Oxford Martin School, 47 per cent of all jobs in the US are susceptible to automation. In the not-too-distant future, information and communication technologies like the Internet, big data and global positioning systems, will be joined by neural-based technologies such as brain–computer interfaces, cortical implants, and artificial intelligence, all of which will drastically alter the labour environment. The AI sector alone, which includes the Internet of Things, cloud computing, and big data analytics, could reach US$118.6 billion by 2025. As Singh, the Chief Operating Officer at Markets and Markets suggests: "the marketing, security, health care, and automotive industries are poised to be the top four end-user industries to experience the most significant impact during the next five years" (Singh 2019, np.). According to a report by Grand View Research, the global brain–computer interface (BCI) market size will increase in value to US$1.72 billion in 2022 as a result of neuroprosthetic applications increasingly used for facilitating communication and movement in paralytic patients, virtual gaming, home control systems, and military equipment operations markets. Musk's venture Neuralink, in which an implantable array of electrode threads will act as an interface between the brain and an assortment of external gadgets potentiating human intelligence, like Facebook's thought-to-text technologies – in which brain-typing will be accomplished with your mind rather than your fingertips through a brain–computer interface – are only some of the examples of new technologies that will accelerate the speed of work (Forrest 2017; Markman 2019). This intersection of brain research and Internet interactivity is also likely to circumvent the need for human labour as we now know it, particularly in the mental realm, as an assemblage of technologies may do such work more efficiently (Knapp 2019). Outsourcing mental modules to external devices in the era of widespread GPS use may have

Epilogue: Telepathic exaptation **207**

profound effects on our posterior hippocampus causing brain areas involved in navigation to shrink (O'Connor 2019). But, equally, could new capacities emerge in the spaces left?

We are at the beginning of a transition from knowledge-based economies to a neural or brain-based economy. Just as in the past the burgeoning industrial economy subsumed craft and agricultural economies, and the information and economies of the late twentieth and early twenty-first centuries subsumed the industrial economy, the brain-based economy will subsume those that preceded it. It will use their infrastructures to leap into the realm of 'superintelligence' delineating the latest manifestation of a dystopian future fuelled by the new realities of cognitive capitalism where the brain is the new factory of the twenty-first century, and a new site of commoditisation. Especially relevant for us here is the focus on the brain's neural plastic potential as a site for a new labour force described by Berardi as the cognitariat or mental labourers (Berardi 2005). The brain consists of plastic intracranial components such as populations of neurons and synapses. Its embodied capacities are connected to our situated sensorium. The extra-cranial component includes the cultural, social, communicative, and technological milieus undergoing constant change. Data and cloud computing are important components of this technological milieu, and constitute, as I will argue below, the new sovereign. My conceptual frame of the evolving brain echoes Ihde and Malafouris's in "*Homo Faber* Revisited: Postphenomenology and Material Engagement Theory", where they approach *homo faber* in a way that both retains the power and value of this notion to signify the primacy of creative material engagement in human life and evolution, and reclaims the notion from any misleading connotations of human exceptionalism (Ihde and Malafouris 2019). Other animals make and use tools, too. The difference that makes the difference is that humans both make things and are made by them. I would like to name this relationship between creative material engagement, the evolving artistic and technological processes through which we make things that populate the real, imaginary and virtual worlds, and their effect upon human becoming, the situated-intracranial-extra-cranial-complex. On the one hand, this complex affords the possibility for tremendous freedom and emancipation; on the other, it affords new opportunities for regulation, normalisation, and control. My wager is that the new technological, social, political, and economic formations that define cognitive capitalism will have dramatic repercussions upon the neurological architecture of the human brain, resulting in the expression of latent mental capacities. In the last ten years, my own research as well as that of others has unveiled a host of 'psychopathologies', such as attention deficit disorder, hyperactivity, obsessive-compulsive disorder, and panic attacks, most of which have emerged as the effect of the highly accelerated technological environment on the plasticity of the brain (Rosen 2012; Neidich 2019). Taking a developmental and phylogenetic approach that reaches back into deep history I want to suggest that the brain's plastic potential and internal variation afford it the capacity to change in accordance with contingent changes in the environment (Neidich 2003, 2006; Malabou 2008). Expansions of dedicated cognitive organs for self-reflection and

208 Warren Neidich

autobiographical memory emerged in our predecessors. With them emerged the necessary neural substrates, such as the visual word form area, the *arcuate gyrus*, and the superior longitudinal fasciculus (Torrey 2019). For example, the accumulation of writing and reading materials in Sumaria five thousand years ago had the profound effect of producing dedicated neural modules for reading and writing (Dehaene 2015). A comparable concretion of new technologies in the realm of telemetry and telepathy might have a similar effect. Many agencies and companies such as the Defense Advanced Research Projects Agency (DARPA), Neuralink, and Facebook are already in a race for the telemetric and telepathic devices market. A plethora of new technological contingencies, some unexpected and profound, will in the not-too-distant future populate our experiential universe, calling out to new latent potentialities locked in the human nervous system. Using a similar logic as that espoused by Dehaene, I hypothesise how an environment saturated with telemetric and telepathic apparatuses will transition to a dedicated organic cortical module for telepathy as a result of the confluences of Darwinian, Baldwinian, and Lamarkian evolutionary forces.

Cognitive capitalism

The brain and mind are the new factories of the twenty-first century. We are no longer proletarians working on assembly lines, but cognitarians generating behavioural data that are bought and sold on behavioural futures markets (Zuboff 2019). The early stages of cognitive capitalism marked the recognition of the importance of immaterial labour and the importation of cybernetic methods – feedback and feed forward design – into the work place. It is described by five conditions: precarity, valorisation, the financialisation of capital, real subsumption, and communication capitalism (Neidich 2017a). Late cognitive capitalism commenced at the end of the last century on the coat-tails of what was often referred to as the "decade of the brain" (Goldstein 1994) and was carried forth by Obama in his famous initiative to map the brain. Understanding the brain became a priority public policy of politically expedient doctrines. But underneath the surface another motivation was brewing. In a world where the predominant forms of labour are intellectual and service-oriented, the machinery of the brain acquires an added importance as a locus of capitalist speculation. As I describe in the first volume of *The Psychopathologies of Cognitive Capitalism* (2013), late cognitive capitalism is defined by three conditions: biopower is supplanted by neuropower in which populations of brains and their neuroplastic potential are the new focus of sovereignty and governmentalisation; the Taylorist management techniques (which optimised assembly line labour during Fordism), have given way to Hebbianism, named after the Canadian neuroscientist who discovered the Hebbs postulate (which describes how neural efficiency arises from the synchronous, repetitive stimulation occurring at synaptic junctions between neurons); and finally, the functions of the frontal lobe have become more vital to labouring in the new economy. The cognitariat must have a supple mind sensitive to contingency to adjust to new provocations

Epilogue: Telepathic exaptation **209**

of the precarious labour market; in an overabundance of stimulation, its ability to cope depends upon a well-tuned attentional capacity. In the brain's plastic potential, neuropower suggests an attempt by sovereignty to normalise the neural diversity and create an easy-to-govern, monolithic neural population. Neural diversity results from the variability of the neurons, dendrites, and synapses that make up the central nervous system at birth as well as from its continued variation produced over a lifetime of interactions with changing technological and cultural environments. According to Fuster's *Neuroscience of Freedom and Creativity*, this variability of the brain's "primary repertoire" constitutes the basis of human freedom and emancipation (Fuster 2013). Embedded in this variability is also the possibility for the brain to change its anatomy in accordance with the new requirements of different and contingent socio-cultural, economic and politically inflected material (and immaterial) ecosystems (Neidich 2017b). Throughout human history, culture and technology have combined to create unique assemblages of tools – biface spear points, fire, reading, and writing – all of which conferred survival advantages on humans capable of evolving. Despite the fact that not all changes were beneficial, the capacity to take advantage of the rapid changes in cultural traits or sudden generational improvements is not the result of a slow march of Darwinian evolution acting on the collective genome, but, rather, of a powerful neural plastic potential (Smail 2007). As part of a general investigation of the means by which the anatomy of the brain can undergo changes in the history of our species, of which telepathy might be a future example, I want to suggest that today the brain's neural plasticity is susceptible to algorithmic power increasingly sculpting our contemporary digital environments. In cognitive capitalism, nature and designed urban space have been replaced by the online data-generated environment where, as mentioned above, the cognitariat is spending more and more of their waking/working hours. Google Bubbles and mediated echo chambers – in which, for instance, specific political beliefs are intensely repeated and reinforced – epigenetically interact with the proclivities of our brain's neuroplasticitic potential, sculpting its neural network connections. According to Changeux and Danchin's theory of selective stabilisation of developing synapses, the environment creates enhanced efficiencies of neural populations through acting upon millions of synaptic junctions synchronously (Changeux and Danchin 1976). Could this theory possibly explain how the power of technology, the intimate relationship formed between the architecture of the net and the brain, might lead to unconscious forms of confirmation bias? Or might the Google effects commonly called 'digital amnesia', in which people preferentially forget information they know they can find online, be an example of another effect? The digital age is the latest stage in an ontogeny of human development that goes back to *homo habilus* and the expansion of the parietal and frontal lobes of the brain resulting from the concretion of new capacities, such as stone tool production, foraging, and hunting. Today, the technologies that inhabit the extra-cranial environment are as different as were the accumulated technologies that populated former times and produced the changes to the parietal and frontal lobes. The process(es) are still ongoing and one can speculate that the concretion of

210 Warren Neidich

new technologies that will define our future worlds will foster unique changes in the neural architecture. I am speculating that a dedicated telepathic module could be one result.

Big data and the big other

In "Big Other: Surveillance Capitalism and the Prospects of an Information Civilization", Zuboff investigates the consequences of data generation and accumulation; 'big data' is above all the "foundational component in a deeply intentional and highly consequential new logic of accumulation" called "surveillance capitalism" (Zuboff 2015, p. 75). Big data concerns the "migration of everydayness as a commercialization strategy" and is essential to Zuboff's interpretation of the Big Other as "a ubiquitous networked institutional regime that records, modifies, and commodifies everyday experience from toasters to bodies, communication to thought, all with a view to establishing new pathways to monetization and profit" (81). Zuboff goes on to state that "[f]alse consciousness is no longer produced by the hidden facts of class and their relation to production, but rather by the hidden facts of commoditized behavior modification" (82). Big Data and Big Other are the forces currently remodelling the cognitariat's brain.

We have transitioned from *homo symbolicus*, in which the human being was subsumed by language, to *homo informaticus* where language is subsumed by data as electronic text and the iCloud. The connectome, or brain connections, have been entangled in a process analogous to what has been called tertiary retention through a process of technical exteriorisation and epiphylogenesis (Stiegler 1998). For *homo informaticus*, big data and its apparatuses have become epigenetically linked to the brain through neural plasticity. The neural plasticity is not only a source of docility and flexibility for subjects at the mercy of institutional or corporate regimes; it is also a resource for emancipation and freedom (Neidich 2006; Malabou 2008). The possibility of a future telepathic capacity may therefore subvert the impending regimes of neural capitalist authoritarianism and reroute mental energies away from the techno-noetic sovereignty. Emerging self-organising processes acting in the techno-socio-cultural milieu as well as in the brain may provide an escape from the future of technological demagoguery. I will use these insights to conjure a speculative theory of a future brain that might develop new organs of perception, specifically, an organ of telepathy. To do this I will follow the logic of evolution beginning 2,000,000 years ago.

Evolutionary prerequisites

Commencing with our early ancestors, *homo habilis*, generally considered the first hominin to diverge significantly from its primate ancestors, *homo erectus*, and *homo sapiens*, the evolution of cognitive skills such as intelligence, self-reflexivity, and the theory of mind – an understanding that the behaviour of others is motivated by internal states such as thoughts, emotions, and beliefs similar to our own (Torrey

Epilogue: Telepathic exaptation **211**

2019) – resulted from the evolution of new cerebral organs that evolved along-side human-designed and environmental pressures. About 700,000 years ago, *homo erectus* started evolving into an early *homo sapiens* or Neanderthals. These new species decorated their bodies and tools with ochre, cared for one another, and buried their dead. Worrying about fellow Kinsmen journey into the afterlife implies that Neanderthals may have had a sense of empathy, which is one of the fundamental components of Torrey's "theory of mind"; it is knowledge of another person's motivational states (Torrey 2019). In the history of humanity, moments of extreme innovation created concretions of multiple and confluent socio-economic-political and technological relations that induced concomitant changes in the interior neurobiological substrate. Both at rest and during the execution of cognitive tasks, the brain continuously creates and reshapes complex patterns of correlated neural dynamics or resonances that are synchronised to analogously link activities in the real–imaginary–virtual world (Papo 2014). These correlated and synchronous activities can alter the neural architectonics in the hippocampus, a part of the brain relevant for memory consolidation. As Axmacher et al. suggest in "Memory Formation by Neural Synchronization":

> [c]ognitive functions not only depend on the localization of neural activity, but also on the precise temporal pattern of activity in neural assemblies. Synchronization [...] provides a link between large-scale EEG recordings and cellular plasticity mechanisms [...] in different frequency ranges, [it] induces specific forms of cellular plasticity during subsequent stages of memory formation.
>
> *(Axmacher et al. 2006, p. 179)*

Over time, repetition of events within specific temporal windows, as in rituals or religious performances, has the capacity to alter the brain's architecture (Torrey 2019). This process is akin to Marxian accumulation as a form of cultural invest-ment and increase in potential for collective learning (Beasley-Murray 2000). In what follows, I link cultural accumulation to Baldwinian evolution in which bio-logical traits can be transmitted upon polymorphous variations in the gene pool favouring predisposed individuals.

Ontogeny, phylogeny, Lamarkian, Darwinian and Baldwinian evolution

Uneven and non-linear accelerations across the socio-cultural-political-technological landscape induce uneven accumulations, which produce selective pressures upon the brain with varying neuroanatomical consequences. Different machinic assemblages induce different neural mixologies, depending on what cognits are necessary for the use of a particular tool or tool assemblage. This mix-ology forms the basis of the emerging neural material phenomena. For instance, in the case of *homo erectus*, a completely terrestrial lifestyle, and a brain averaging about

1,000 cubic centimetres in a relatively small body, allowed this proto-human to reach new horizons of behaviour. *Homo erectus* was the first hominin to control fire and cook food. It extended its territory with a mass migration and spread halfway around the globe. Key to many of its capacities was cooperation, and a symbolic system that could be thought of as a precursor to human language (Torrey 2019). Over time, crude tools became more sophisticated and weapons for hunting animals appeared. Stone-tipped spears, dated to around 460,000 years ago, gave humans a chance to hunt larger animals, requiring cooperation between large numbers of people. Using a similar logic to that of Changeux and Danchin in "Selective Stabilisation of Developing Synapses as a Mechanism for the Specification of Neuronal Networks", one cannot disregard the possibility that the repeated neural correlations acquired during a tool's production and use may have stabilised labile synapses into dedicated cognits (Changeux and Danchin 1976). The large temporal and frontal lobes, the expanded parietal lobe, enlarged cerebellum and the lateralisation of the hemispheres, all characteristic of the *homo erectus* brain, may have resulted from the pressure to use their new tools physically and mentally. For instance, throwing a spear may have created hand and arm dominance, and, eventually, asymmetric cerebral hemispheres. Group hunting for large game may have necessitated future planning and a larger frontal lobe. Similarly, in cognitive capitalism, ADD, ADHD, and even the differences between the cognitive behaviours of 'digital natives', born into wired cultures, and 'digital immigrants' who encountered the Internet later in life, are cases in point. Could using the contemporary digital tools within cognitively ergonomically designed virtual platforms result in different digital capacities that, over time, might drive different neural architectures?

Lamarckian evolution presupposes that humans are capable of profiting from the experience of their predecessors, and that progress in history, unlike evolution in nature, rests on the transmission of acquired characteristics (Smail 2007). Quoting Gould, Smail suggests that

> [w]hat we learn in one generation, we transmit directly through teaching and writing. Acquired characters are inherited in technology and culture. Lamarckian evolution is rapid and cumulative. It explains the cardinal difference between our past, purely biological mode of change, and our current, maddening acceleration toward something new and liberating.
>
> *(Gould quoted in Smail 2007, p. 88)*

With the advent of civilisation, the process of biological evolution dependent on genes gave way to the much faster process of cultural evolution capable of inducing a generational mutation of the neurobiologic architecture through the process of synaptic epigenesis acting through and upon its neural plasticity and changing the function of designated networks (Chagneux and Danchin 1976).

Baldwinian evolution, on the other hand, states that under some conditions, learnt behaviours can affect the rate of evolutionary change by natural selection (Depew 2003). Cultural evolution acts as a bridge between Darwin's genomic-based theory

Epilogue: Telepathic exaptation **213**

of natural selection, and Lamarck's theory of inheritance of acquired characteristics. The broad claim made by Baldwin and his supporters, most recently anthropologist Deacon, is that learning can modify the environment for a species in such a way as to influence its selective potency for that learnt behaviour if there is a consistent genotype-phenotype relationship over generations (Deacon 2010). In other words, inherited factors favourable to adaptive behaviour will move along the channel already cut by culture converting learnt behaviours into genetic adaptations. The so-called 'Baldwin effect' expresses the possibility that traits, which are not strictly biological, could also be transmitted via learning and other cultural practices acting upon a polymorphous assortment of individual variations in the gene pool. Yet unexpressed individual genetic variations not relevant in one sociological context could give selective advantage in another. If that sociological context remains stable over generations, it could act on the conspecific gene pool and skew it in favour of a particular genetic variation, which first becomes fixed as an acquired then inheritable trait. Writing about language in particular, Deacon proposes that once a few members of a population developed the ability to communicate symbolically, the advantage of such an ability would, in itself, create intense selection pressure promoting its further evolution (Deacon 1998).

Neural capitalism, brain–computer interfaces and telepathy

Neural capitalism is an alliance between science, information technology, big data, AI, Big Pharma, neuroeconomics and neural consumerism, such as the Internet of Things. It is the driving force of late-stage neo-liberal cognitive capitalism. Technoceuticals are a unique class of innovations related to big data and to what Zuboff terms the Big Other through advanced technologies like brain–computer interfaces; data collection is here no longer limited to mouse clicks and keyboard directives but is fed by brainwave signals involved in thought itself. In the jargon of cognitive capitalism, real subsumption, in which all of life is work, will expand to include neural subsumption transcribing our thoughts into digital code to be registered, collated, and analysed. I call this new form of governmentalisation the Statisticon. The Statisticon is the third phase in the ontology of surveillance following Foucault's panopticon and Deleuze's society of control. The functions of telepathy can be seen as a counter-intuitive form of resistance to this impending surveillance system. Telepathy is defined as the ability to know what is in someone else's mind, or to communicate with someone mentally, without using words or physical signals. It is related to such notions as precognition, psychokinetics, sixth sense, premonition, augury, precognition, telekinesis, and telesthesia. A bevy of new technoceuticals that has technologically assisted telepathic capacity is already in use: brain–computer interfaces (BCIs); cortical implants; bio-neuro-headsets; neural or 'smart' dust. Musk created Neuralink to overcome what he considers to be the main obstacle to optimum human–machine interaction in communication: bandwidth. Touch screens and keyboards are slow and inefficient means to interact with a computer. A better way is a much faster high-bandwidth type of interaction using "neural lace" and neural dust (Lopatto 2019). Musk hopes to make consensual telepathy possible for everyone by using brain–computer interfaces, currently used to enable disabled individuals to participate more fully in society, to enable able-bodied, developmentally neurotypical individuals to intensify their mental capacities in the work place. Emotiv, another company specialising in neurologically based monetisation, produces software that allows for the visualisation of brain activity in 3D, to control drones, robots, and video games. BCIs have recently entered the realm of ubiquitous computing military operations. As Drinkall suggests, telepathy is "weaponised in video-game use of EEG bio-neuro-headset interaction" to enable gamers to practice virtual telekinesis with the "world as their weapon" (Drinkall 2017, p. 345). Some examples of this are *Son of Nor*, which uses Emotive EPOC headsets, to alter the environment with "terraforming abilities" such as "telekinetic powers to bend the dynamic surroundings" (346).

If this seems aggressive and quasi-militaristic – it is. As early as 2010, Kotchetkov et al. waxed lyrical about the applications of brain–computer interfaces on the battlefield, for example DARPA's programme called "Silent Talk" whose aim is "to develop user-to-user communication" through EEG signals of "'intended speech' thereby eliminating the need for any vocalizations or body gestures", capabilities that are "of particular benefit in reconnaissance and special operation settings" (Kotchetkov 2010, p. 4). Enhancements of soldiers' perception and control of vehicles or heavy machinery with BCIs are within the realm of the possible; a recent DARPA proposal for a "Cognitive Technology Threat Warning System" also includes a requirement for "operator-trained high-resolution BCI binoculars that can quickly respond to a *subconsciously* detected target or a threat" (4). Neural interfaces are on the horizon, too, in the form of smart dust and neural dust, which create environments to send signals back and forth or a techno-cultural-brain loop. Smart dust refers to a collection of tiny micro-electromechanical sensors (MEMS) that are the size of a salt crystal but have the capacity to detect light, vibration, and noise, and communicate that data back to a receiver. Their miniscule size allows them to be spread invisibly on any terrain or environment. Their lightness allows them to be dispersed by the wind. Camera lenses the size of a grain of salt but taking high definition images have been produced by researchers at the University of Stuttgart (Dorrier 2016). Neural dust is part of the emerging field of neurotechnology, which aims to mimic complex neural circuitry in the brain. It refers to very small, wirelessly powered nerve sensors, less than a millimetre in size that can be attached to a wire mesh, or implanted directly into the brain. Neural dust motes consist of a pair of recording electrodes, a custom transistor and a piezo-electric crystal capable of recording brain activity from the extra-cellular space. Recently, a more accurate neural dust, using ultrasound rather than radio signals, has been used for BCI applications with great success; the DARPA Cortical Modem connects the brain directly to the computer for electronic telepathy and telekinesis (Cuthbertson 2015). It is possible that in the future, a tele-signalling environment made of clouds and fields of superimposed populations of smart dust particles will connect to networks of neural lace infested with neural dust bots to produce a

Epilogue: Telepathic exaptation **215**

supplemental nervous system in addition to the one we already have. When neural dust becomes small enough to interact directly with our nervous system, neural sculpting of our own organic tissue will become a distinct possibility. Wirdatmadja et al. have created a model in which an optogenetically linked cerebral cortex is connected to wireless nano-networking devices, optogenetics being a method of artificially manipulating neurons using light at a specific wavelength, a construct obtained by genetically engineering neurons with the opsins from green algae that can be turned on and off by lasers of particular wavelengths (Wirdatmadja et al. 2017). Liu et al. describe the process of creating a fear memory in the hippocampus of a rat with opsins and turning the network on and off by stimulating the neuron network involved in the fear response with a laser light recreating the fear response; they conclude that repeated stimulation of this network can lead to long-term memories in the entire downstream network showing that simulated environments built with smart dust and linked to optogenetically engineered neural dust meshes present a new step in the control and manipulation of the neural mental apparatus (Liu et al. 2014).

Neuronal recycling hypothesis, exaptation and telepathy

So, how might a dedicated telepathic module, cognit, or network develop in the intracranial brain while linked to an accelerating evolving technological counterpart in the extra-cranial brain? In this section, I explore Dehaene's "neuronal recycling hypothesis", in which a dedicated module for reading and writing is believed to have evolved in the 5,000 years since the invention of writing on Sumarian tablets. This theory is a form of what Gould and Verba have called 'exaptation'. In exaptation, a trait like bird feathers, first evolved for the purpose of warmth, progressed to be used in flight (Gould and Verba 1982). Dehaene's theory of neuronal recycling explains how reading and writing colonised what became the visual word-forming area of the left temporal lobe. A similar process might be applied to create a dedicated module for telepathy. We are experiencing a confluence of cultural, technological and sociological relations with neural material consequences; might their intense interrelation combine to form the necessary evolutionary pressures to modify an existing predisposition of the brain to generate new forms of telepathic cognitive behaviours? Neuronal recycling is based on the idea that novel cultural or cognitive processes invade cortical areas initially devoted to different functions (Dehaene 2007). The cortical architecture presents hindrances prior to learning, but, through neuronal recycling, novel functions may be acquired, so long as they find a suitable cortical area to accommodate them, an area referred to as a cognitive function's "neuronal niche" (Dehaene 2015). The novel cultural function must locate a cortical area whose prior function is similar and plastic enough to accommodate it. In the human brain, this area is called the visual word form area and is located in the lateral temporal locus near the fusiform gyrus, dubbed 'the brain's letterbox'. For example, reading rests upon primitive neuronal mechanisms of primate vision for object and facial recognition that have been preserved over the course of evolution. Collectively, these neurons contain a stock of elementary shapes whose combinations can encode any visual object. In some individual macaques, neurons even respond to line junctions resembling our letter shapes (Dehaene 2015). According to the 'neuronal recycling' hypothesis, when we learn to read, part of the neuronal system converts to the new task of recognising letters and words. What does this mean for telepathy? The scientific data on the human telepathic powers is still meagre, although a telepathic module in the area of the parahippocampal gyrus, important for visualising environmental scenes like cityscapes and landscapes, has been reported (Venkatasubramanian 2008). That notwithstanding, recent interest in technologically mediated telepathy via cortical modems, BCIs, and neural dust has translated into a tremendous amount of capital flow being directed toward the investigation of telepathy. The need for increased brainpower in cognitive capitalism is expressed succinctly in the title of Gates' 1999 book *Business @ the Speed of Thought*. In concordance with Moore's Law – that computation power doubles every two years – (Neidich 2019) we can only assume that the technologically supported telepathy will develop exponentially. Following Deacon's example of reading in writing in *The Symbolic Species, The Coevolution of Language and the Brain*, I hypothesise that telepathy will find its way into activities such as driving a car, communicating with another person, playing video games, or shopping online. It will integrate our brains into the Internet of Everything. Here is how Deacon expresses it: "once symbolic communication became even slightly elaborated in early hominid societies, its unique representation functions and open-ended flexibility would have led to its use for innumerable purposes with equally powerful reproductive consequences" (Deacon 1998, p. 349). The culture of telepathy will have profound effects on our life world, which itself will become more immaterial and more like a noosphere. Perhaps likely candidates for the vector by which telepathic functions will be manifested via neurobiology are the dedicated intracranial modules developed in archaic *homo sapiens*. Neuroimaging studies conducted on experimental subjects during theory of mind-related tasks have revealed a number of brain activation patterns emanating from the temporoparietal junction, and parts of the frontal lobe (anterior cingulate, insula, frontal pole, and medial frontal cortex) (Torrey 2019). The diversity of human beings is the result of the inherent variation of the brain's neural populations created during its foetal life and post-natal interaction with diverse and contingent environments that make up the real, imaginary, and virtual world. No two brains are alike, not even between identical twins. As we saw in the above discussion of the Baldwin Effect on human language acquisition, learning and behavioural flexibility might have played a role in amplifying and biasing natural selection because learnt abilities enable individuals, in a varied population of differently abled individuals (with different capacities to learn a new trick, like language), to pass that skill on to the next generation. Assuming the stability of a social environment to support this new socially acquired linguistic ability over many succeeding generations, and understanding that, as Deacon has argued, the flexibility to learn

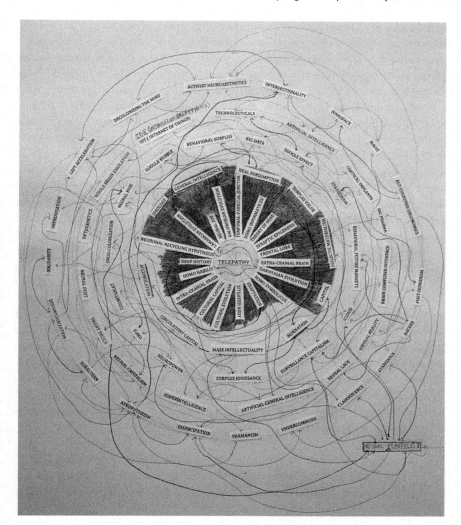

FIGURE 13.1 Warren Neidich, *Telepathy Drawing*, Artist Studio, Los Angeles, California, 2019.

Source: Photo: Warren Neidich. © Warren Neidich

new behavioural responses during a lifetime can produce rapid and radical evolutionary consequences (Deacon 1998), the assimilation of telepathy poses itself as a logical question.

Conclusion

In any population of individuals who are genetically, as well as neuro-biologically, dissimilar there are individuals who have predispositions to telepathy. History is filled with stories of shamans who communicate with other worlds as well as psychics, empaths, mentalists, and mind readers. Could these differences be accentuated as a result of selective pressures operating on predisposed areas like the medial frontal cortex and temporal-parietal junction? We know that, generally speaking, different people have greater or lesser abilities to empathise. I have made an argument for a gradual accumulation of telepathic technocueticals in the socio-political-cultural field. At some moment a critical point might be reached when telepathy could become a necessary skill for successful adaptation in this new environment, similar to the necessity of being able to read in today's society. Gradually, the sexual and selective advantage would enable these predisposed individuals to distribute these innate capacities to more and more members of their species. Conceivably, over time, the entire population could become telepathic but possibly to different degrees. A certain number of individuals would be eliminated because they could not adapt to the new socially constructed situation. As Deacon suggests, in the end, an organism's behavioural tendencies come to represent configurational features of its environment as this correspondence perpetuates the same synergistic processes (Deacon and Cashman 2011). It is hypothetically possible that as the techno-socio-cultural accumulative pressure continues to accelerate, necessitating telepathic communication and data production, it becomes ever more entangled with that neural diversity through epigenesis. Emerging and self-organising processes coming into play could have non-linear effects upon the predisposed and sensitised neural tissues, creating new organs of perception and cognition. We saw this happen in other moments of humanity's collective ascendance from *homo habilis* to *homo sapiens*. Concretions of new technologies produced unsuspected results instantiated as new formations of grey matter–white matter. Of course, there is a limit to change, which both Deacon and Dehaene understand:

> I emphasize that cultural reconversion or "neuronal recycling" of our genetic organization, has created a cerebral architecture that is both constrained and partially plastic, and that delimits a space of learnable cultural objects. New cultural acquisitions are therefore possible only inasmuch as they are able to fit within the pre-existing constraints of our brain architecture.
>
> *(Dehaene 2015, p. 148)*

But within these evolutionary constraints simultaneous pressures on both the intracranial milieu and its material matter or brain, via its neural plasticity, and its extra-cranial counterpart, via cultural plasticity, could partake in a co-evolutionary process in which a new organ of telepathy could emerge.

References

Axmacher N et al. 2006, "Memory Formation by Neuronal Synchronization", *Brain Research Reviews*, vol. 52, no. 1, pp. 170–182.

Beasley-Murray J 2000, "Value and Capital in Bourdieu and Marx", in Brown N and Szeman I (eds.), *Pierre Bourdieu: Fieldwork in Culture*. Lanham, MD: Rowman and Littlefield.

Berardi, F 2005, "What does Cognitariat Mean? Work, Desire, Depression", *Cultural Studies Review*, vol. 11, no. 2, pp. 57–63.

Changeux JP and Danchin A 1976. "Selective Stabilisation of Developing Synapses as a Mechanism for the Specification of Neuronal Networks", *Nature*, vol. 264, pp. 705–712.

Cuthbertson A 2015, "DARPA Cortical Modem Connects Brain Directly to Computer for 'Electronic Telepathy and Telekinesis'", *International Business Times*, February 18. Available from: www.ibtimes.co.uk/darpa-cortical-modem-connects-brain-directly-computer-electronic-telepathy-telekinesis-1488476 [accessed 6 November 2019].

Deacon T 1998, *The Symbolic Species, The Coevolution of Language and the Brain*. New York: W.W. Norton and Company.

Deacon T 2010. "A Role for Relaxed Selection in the Evolution of the Language Capacity", *PNAS*, 11 May, no. 107 (supp. 2) 9000–9006. First published 5 May, 2010.

Deacon T and Cashman T 2011, "Eliminativism, Complexity and Emergence", in Haag J et al. (eds.), *The Routledge Companion to Religion and Science*. London: Routledge. Available from: www.academia.edu/28779686/Eliminativism_Complexity_and_Emergence [accessed 3 December 2019].

Dehaene S 2007, "Cultural Recycling of Cortical Maps", *Neuron* vol. 56, no. 2, 25 October, pp. 384–398.

Dehaene S 2015, "Evolution of Cortical Circuits for Reading and Arithmetic: The Neuronal Recycling Hypothesis", in Dehaene S et al. (eds.), *From Monkey Brain to Human Brain*. Cambridge, MA: MIT Press.

Depew DJ 2003, "Baldwin and His Many Effects", in Depew DJ and Weber BH (eds.), *Evolution and Learning: The Baldwin Effect Reconsidered*. Cambridge, MA: MIT Press, pp. 3–33.

Dorrier J 2016, "Smart Dust is Coming: New Camera is the Size of a Grain of Salt", *Singularity Hub*, 28 June. Available from: https://singularityhub.com/2016/06/28/smart-dust-is-coming-new-camera-is-the-size-of-a-grain-of-salt [accessed 3 December 2019].

Drinkall J 2017, "Neuromodulations of Extro-Scientific Telepathy", in Neidich W (ed.), *The Psychopathologies of Cognitive Capitalism, Volume 3*. Berlin: Archive Books, pp. 319–367.

Forrest C 2017, "Facebook Planning Brain-to-Text Interface so you can Type with your Thoughts", in *Tech Republic*, 20 April. Available from: www.techrepublic.com/article/facebook-planning-brain-to-text-interface-so-you-can-type-with-your-thoughts/ [accessed 3 December 2019].

Fuster J 2013, *The Neuroscience of Freedom and Creativity*. Cambridge: Cambridge University Press.

Gates B 1999, *Business@the Speed of Thought*. New York: Werner Books.

Goldstein M 1994, "Decade of the Brain: An Agenda for the Nineties", *Western Journal of Medicine*, vol. 161, no. 3, pp. 239–241.

Gould SJ and Verba ES 1982, "Exaptation – a Missing Term in the Science of Form", *Paleobiology*, vol. 8, no. 1, pp. 4–15. Available from: doi:10.1017/S0094837300004310 [accessed 4 August 2020].

Ihde D and Malafouris L 2019, "Homo faber Revisited: Postphenomenology and Material Engagement Theory", *Philosophy & Technology*, vol. 32, pp. 195–214.

Knapp A 2019, "Elon Musk Sees His Neuralink Merging Your Brain With AI", *Forbes Online*, 17 July. Available from: www.forbes.com/sites/alexknapp/2019/07/17/elon-musk-sees-his-neuralink-merging-your-brain-with-ai/#1597462c4b07 [accessed 3 December 2019].

Kotchetkov IS et al. 2010, "Brain–Computer Interfaces: Military, Neurosurgical, and Ethical Perspective", *Neurosurg Focus*, vol. 28, no. 5, E25. Available from: https://thejns.org/focus/view/journals/neurosurg-focus/28/5/2010.2.focus1027.xml [accessed 3 December 2019].

Liu X et al. 2014, "Inception of a False Memory by Optogenetic Manipulation of a Hippocampal Memory Engram", *Philosophical Transactions of the Royal Society of London, Series B, Biological Sciences*, 5 January, vol. 369, no. 1633. Available from: https://royalsocietypublishing.org/doi/full/10.1098/rstb.2013.0142 [accessed 4 August 2020].

Lopatto E 2019, "Elon Musk Unveils Neuralink's Plans for Brain-reading 'Threads' and a Robot to Insert Them", *The Verge*, 16 July. Available from: www.theverge.com/2019/7/16/20697123/elon-musk-neuralink-brain-reading-thread-robot [accessed 3 December 2019].

Malabou C 2008, *What Should We Do with Our Brain? (Que faire de notre cerveau?)* New York: Fordham University Press.

Markman J 2019, "Elon Musk's Neuralink Is Sci-Fi Made Real", *Forbes.com*, 30 August. Available from: www.forbes.com/sites/jonmarkman/2019/08/30/elon-musks-neuralink-is-sci-fi-made-real/#4bd157f94e2f [accessed 3 December 2019].

Neidich W 2003, *Blow-up: Photography, Cinema and the Brain*. New York: DAP.

Neidich W 2006, "The Neurobiopolitics of Global Consciousness", in Narula M et al. (eds.), *Sarai Reader: Turbulence*. Delhi: Raqs Media Collective, pp. 222–236.

Neidich, W 2017a, "Introduction", in Neidich W (ed.), *The Psychopathologies of Cognitive Capitalism, Volume Three*. Berlin: Archive, pp. 11–37.

Neidich W 2017b, "The Brain without Organs: Ayahausca and the Theory of Neural Regression", in Neidich W (ed.), *The Psychopathologies of Cognitive Capitalism, Volume Three*. Berlin: Archive, pp. 223–249.

Neidich W 2019, *Glossary of Cognitive Activism*. Berlin: Archive Books.

O'Connor MR 2019, "Ditch the GPS. It's Ruining your Brain", *Washington Post*, 5 June. Available from: www.washingtonpost.com/opinions/ditch-the-gps-its-ruining-your-brain/2019/06/05/29a3170e-87af-11e9-98c1-e945ae5db8fb_story.html [accessed 3 December 2019].

Papo D 2014, "Reconstructing Functional Brain Networks: Have We Got the Basics Right?", *Frontiers in Human Neuroscience*, 27 February. Available from: https://doi.org/10.3389/fnhum.2014.00107 [accessed 4 December 2019].

Rosen LD 2012, *iDisorder: Understanding our Obsession with Technology and Overcoming its Hold of Us*. Basingstoke: Palgrave Macmillan.

Singh S 2019, "The Impact of Artificial Intelligence Over the Next Five Years" *Forbes*, 30 May. Available from: www.forbes.com/sites/forbesbusinessdevelopmentcouncil/2019/05/30/the-impact-of-artificial-intelligence-over-the-next-five-years/#3a55e2764498 [accessed 3 December 2019].

Smail DL 2007, *On Deep History and the Brain*. Berkeley, CA: University of California Press.

Stiegler B 1998, *Technics and Time 1: The Fault of Epimetheus*, trans. Beardsworth R and Collins G. Stanford, CA: Stanford University Press.

Torrey EF 2019, *Evolving Brains Emerging Gods*. New York: Columbia University Press.

Venkatasubramanian G 2008, "Investigating Paranormal Phenomena: Functional Brain Imaging of Telepathy", *International Journal of Yoga*, vol. 1, no. 2, pp. 66–71.

Wirdatmadja SA et al. 2017, "Wireless Optogenetic Nanonetworks: Device Model and Charging Protocols", *rXiv:1706.06495v1* [cs.ET] 20 June. Available from: https://arxiv.org/pdf/1706.06495.pdf [accessed 4 December 2019].

Zuboff S 2015, "Big Other: Surveillance Capitalism and the Prospects of an Information Civilization", *Journal of Information Technology*, vol. 30, pp. 75–89.

Zuboff S 2019, *The Age of Surveillance Capitalism: The Fight For a Human Future at the New Frontier of Power*. New York: Public Affairs.

INDEX

absence 6, 63, 170–1, 173, 197
abstraction 48, 66, 97, 108–9, 111, 122, 149, 170–71, 182, 193
acceleration 18, 26, 28, 36, 92
additivity 145
ADHD 212
aesthetics 10, 111, 115, 129, 163, 165, 171–4, 204
affect 10, 26, 49, 52, 66, 102, 110–1, 141, 170, 173, 176, 178, 183–4, 189, 201
Agamben, Giorgio 65, 70–2, 77
algorithm 1–2, 12, 21–2, 36, 41, 53–5, 65, 81, 83–4, 86, 88–90, 96, 140, 149, 157, 159, 65–6, 173, 182, 184, 190, 193, 198
alienation 33, 80, 92–3
Amazon Mechanical Turk 80, 82
analogue 130, 140, 151, 165, 171–2, 184, 187
analytics 4, 11–13, 17–18, 55, 58, 65, 68, 80, 82, 121, 129, 132, 140, 165, 167, 175, 177–9, 181, 192; analytic tools 166
anarchive 10, 149, 155–8
Andersen, Christian 181, 189
anonymity 189, 195
anthropocene 203
anthropocentrism 28, 47
appendage 81, 83
architecture 4–5, 49, 53–4, 96–7, 99, 101–2, 104–5, 109, 131, 133, 138, 144, 173, 175, 180, 183
archive 10, 50, 53, 128–31, 133–7, 139, 141–3, 148–9, 156, 158–9

artificial intelligence 9, 12, 35–6, 42, 44, 53, 58, 92, 130, 137, 175, 180
assessment 17, 19, 58, 103–4, 122
Assmann, Aleida 131, 141, 156, 158
asylum seekers 67–8, 73, 76
attractor 199
audit culture 17, 30
Aufhebung 32–4
augmented reality 10, 147, 151, 154, 157, 197
authority 2, 39, 67, 72, 133–4, 139, 142; authoritarianism 210
automation 7, 18, 29, 40, 42; automaton 9, 32, 35–8, 40, 44, 83, 87
autonomy 9–10, 40, 86, 89–90, 93, 130–1, 133, 135, 137, 139–41, 143

Baldwin effect 213, 216, 219
basho 155
Baudrillard, Jean 32–6, 41, 43–5
becoming 18, 23, 26–8, 30, 66, 73–4, 87, 133, 150, 154, 169, 177, 185, 201–3
behavioural modification 82, 89
Benjamin, Walter 7–8, 11, 155, 158
Berardi, Franco 80, 83, 86–9, 91, 207
Bergson, Henri 150–1, 158, 180–1
bias 86, 119, 140, 190
bi-conditional articulation 153
biometrics 9, 65–7, 71–5, 77, 79
biopolitics 9, 70, 77–8, 80–1, 83–5, 87–9, 91, 93; bio-political tattooing 65
biosociality 75–6
black box 133, 140

222 Index

blockchain 65, 71, 188
Boden, Margaret 94, 100, 102
body technique 152, 155–6
Bourdieu, Pierre 193
brain 12, 23, 36, 44, 85–7, 95–6, 99, 186;
  brain-computer interface 206, 213–14,
  216; brainpower 163, 173
Bratton, Benjamin 1–2, 48
Burke, Edmund 171, 191

calculation 47–50, 52, 55, 57, 85, 145
capitalism 4, 9–10, 17, 33, 35, 37, 79–80, 87,
  91, 179, 206–10, 213, 216, 219
Carpo, Mario 38, 41–2
cellular 41, 88
Celmins, Vija 169–71, 173
Cezanne, Paul 200–3
chaos 5, 11, 13, 32–3, 37, 44, 201; chaos
  theory 5
Chun, Wendy Hui Kyong 23, 29,
  46–7, 52, 55
Ciccarelli, Roberto 82–4, 88
cinematic apparatus 147, 177–8
circulation 4, 47, 50, 53, 56, 116–25,
  181–2, 184
class 6, 20, 81, 91, 98, 136, 152
clinamen 149, 154–5
cloud 36, 52, 55–6, 122, 165, 174, 180–2
code 9, 35–40, 42, 84–5, 90, 96, 105–6, 151,
  178, 181, 185
co-dependent origination 146
cognitariat 207–10
cognition 1, 47, 52, 111, 159
cognitive capitalism 10, 17, 30, 92, 143
collections 130, 133, 136–8, 140, 151
collectivity 41
colonialism 18, 20
commoditisation 207
communication theory 157
compatibility 4, 131, 183
complexity 2–3, 12, 41, 48, 108, 130,
  133–5, 138, 140–3, 158, 172, 174, 181,
  188, 193
compression 51, 53, 186, 193
computation 20, 23–4, 34–5, 43–4, 104,
  112, 143, 150, 168
computational models 100
condition 4, 6–7, 20, 34, 38, 40, 44, 53,
  57–8, 68–9, 82, 85, 90, 96, 132, 147, 164,
  173, 195, 203
conjunction 34, 37, 39, 41–2, 184, 198
connectivity 41
consciousness 7–8, 32, 35, 44, 85, 150, 159,
  186, 201

Consortium of European Social Science
  Data Archives (CESSDA) 131
constellation 3, 7–8, 120, 138, 149
contagion 150–1, 153
contingency 208; contingent 70, 72, 89,
  149, 192, 207, 209, 216
continuity 22, 120, 150, 155, 157, 171, 173
Continuous Bag of Words (CBOW) 106
control 4, 21–3, 25, 36, 40, 47, 55, 65–8,
  70–7, 80, 83, 85, 93, 99, 102, 110, 118,
  124–6, 140, 168, 170, 175, 178, 185,
  188–9, 197–8; border control 67, 71,
  75–6, 188
cooperation 67, 87
co-presence 10, 149, 151, 153, 157
cortical modem 214, 216
Crary, Jonathan 87–8
creativity 90, 94–7, 100, 102, 110–11,
  129, 146
Cubitt, Sean 46, 53
curriculum 18–19
cybernetics 13, 21, 59
cybertime 89

Damasio, Antonio 150–1
Darwin, Charles 115–16, 208–9, 211–12
data 1–13, 17–40, 42–4, 46–60, 65–70,
  73–84, 86, 88–9, 91–2, 96, 100, 102,
  105–6, 108–9, 111–12, 115–17, 119–49,
  151, 156, 158, 163–89, 191–9, 201–4;
  data-double 179, 181, 183, 185, 187, 189;
  data harvesting 3, 182; data tissue 146;
  semi-structured data 5, 166; structured
  data 141, 165–7; unstructured data 5, 12,
  137, 165–7
database 19, 60, 65–70, 72, 106, 123, 130,
  148, 163, 165–6, 188, 195
data extraction 36–7, 39, 76, 89, 122,
  181, 187–8
dataism 66, 79, 132, 144
dataveillance 66, 76–7, 79, 144
datification 3, 9–10, 33, 36–8, 44
Deacon, Terrence 213, 216, 218
Dean, Jodi 7, 10, 143, 164
Debord, Guy 33, 199, 201
DeepDream 98–100, 102, 110
deep neural network (DNN) 102
Deleuze, Gilles 11, 44, 53, 85, 164, 174–5,
  177–8, 183–5, 187, 191, 201–2, 213
Deliveroo 80, 88, 93
deprivation 88
depth 10, 121, 153, 163–5, 167–9, 171–5
Derrida, Jacques 2, 22–4, 28, 122, 131,
  135

Index 223

determination 33, 39, 42, 153; self-determination 86, 153
determinism 9, 32, 35, 42–3, 131, 146, 203
Dewey Decimal 195–6
diachronic omniscience 50, 58
digital humanities 18–21, 28–31, 120–4, 128–9, 141, 143
digitalisation 19
Digital Research Infrastructure for the Arts and Humanities (DARIAH) 131
discontinuity 22, 155, 157, 170–1, 194
disorder 5, 156–7
disposition 53, 150, 193
distribution 50, 67–8, 104, 117, 120, 131, 201
dividual 10, 177–9, 181–7, 189
dividuation 179, 183, 185, 187, 190
DNA 36, 192, 204
dormancy 141
dynamic Random Access Memory (DRAM) 157
dynamics 34, 56, 85, 134, 166, 168, 180

Eames, Charles and Ray 5, 9, 119–20
Earth 7, 48–50, 58–9, 120
echo chambers 187, 209
economy 9–10, 34–6, 40, 58, 76, 78, 80–2, 87–9, 92–3, 131, 134, 139, 159, 193
efficiency 84, 89, 110
Eigenpraxis 6, 147
ek-stasis 154, 157
embodiment 33, 156, 178, 187, 189
enhancement 99
Enlightenment 18, 26–7, 44
entanglement 18, 21–2, 25, 27–8, 35, 52
enunciation 38–41
environment 4, 6, 9, 13, 18, 21, 34–5, 40, 46–8, 52, 55–7, 60, 90–1, 100, 104, 128, 143, 146, 151, 156, 168, 172, 179, 181, 197
epigenesis 212, 218
epiphylogenesis 210
epistemology 13, 26, 52, 128, 143, 173–4, 204; epistemological 6, 21, 24, 57, 122, 163–4, 167, 170, 173

Facebook 7, 64–5, 81, 90, 132–3, 137, 163, 176, 183
facial recognition 63–5, 77–9, 174, 188, 193
feedback 2, 4, 9, 19, 58, 154
feedforward 154
filter bubble 40, 45
Floridi, Luciano 10, 163–4, 168, 173–4
flow 12, 34, 40, 42, 68, 84–6, 132, 168, 173

folding 174
forecasting 47, 55–7, 59, 191, 203–4
Foucault, Michel 8, 139, 178, 185, 194–5, 203, 213
fragmentation 25, 33, 183
Friedrich, Caspar David 171, 191
frottage 10, 145, 149–51, 153; digital frottage 10, 145, 149–51, 153
Fujihata, Masaki 10, 147, 149–51, 156
future 2, 4–5, 9–10, 13, 19, 21, 24, 29, 32, 35–40, 42–6, 48–50, 52–8, 60, 65, 72, 77, 84, 90–2, 115, 130, 133, 137, 140–1, 144, 154–5, 157, 164, 175–6, 179, 202–3

Galloway, Alexander 173–4
gatekeeping 130–1, 133
gene 204
genealogy 59, 121, 129, 165, 173
Generative Adversarial Networks (GAN) 174, 188
generative programming 95
genetics 163
geography 11, 143
geology 12
gestalt 5, 42
Google 2, 4, 12, 36–7, 39–40, 58, 64, 68, 81–2, 90–1, 107, 137, 139–40, 163, 176
governance 9, 24–5, 30, 33, 38–40, 46–7, 49, 70, 73–4, 79, 87
government 20, 38, 40, 66, 68, 71, 132, 176
Guattari, Felix 7, 44, 85, 177–8, 190, 202
Gursky, Andreas 191, 194–5

habitus 193
Hadoop 151
hallucination 9, 46–7, 49, 51–3, 55, 57, 59
Han, Byung-Chul 8, 29, 132, 148
Hardt, Michael 17, 80, 87, 89
heritage 3, 9, 113, 130–5, 137–42
heterogeneity 166, 185
heteropticon 194–5, 199, 201
heterotopia 194–5
hiddenness 140–1
homo informaticus 210
homo sapiens 210–11, 216, 218
humanitarianism 66, 68–70, 73, 76
hybrid 158, 192, 197

ID2020 66, 71–2
identity 1, 28, 33, 44, 65–73, 75–7, 119, 127–8, 141, 158, 202
image 6, 9–10, 27, 29, 46–60, 85, 94, 96–102, 107–12, 115–16, 119, 129, 133, 135, 138, 141, 146–51, 153–4, 157, 159,

163–5, 169–71, 173–84, 186–7, 189–90, 198–201, 203; image aggregates 151, 175, 180

imagination 27, 33, 35, 52, 57, 89, 110, 141, 158, 167–71, 173, 175, 191, 194, 202

indeterminacy 6, 42

individuation 178, 184–7, 189

infolabour 88

information 2, 5, 10–11, 13, 23–4, 32, 34, 36–7, 46–7, 52, 55–6, 58–60, 66–70, 75, 77, 80, 82–3, 85, 96, 102, 106, 112, 115–17, 120–1, 123, 131–4, 145–6, 156–7, 166, 172–6, 178–9, 181, 183, 186, 191–3, 196–7, 203

innovation 10, 19–20, 23, 28–9, 118, 167

inscription 4, 9, 36–40, 43, 141, 156–7

installation 146–7, 158, 197–8, 200–1

institution 8–10, 17, 19, 28–9, 44, 54, 66, 74–5, 130–4, 136–41

integration 35, 37, 185

interactant 154–6

interactive artwork 199

inter-expression 146, 148–51, 153

interface 38, 41, 46–7, 56, 75, 86, 121, 140, 157, 165, 174–5, 179, 181–2, 185–7, 195–6; metainterface 180–9

Internet 3, 45, 121, 147, 163–4, 168, 181, 195

Internet of Things 3, 181

interpellation 84

interval 54, 168, 171

invisibility 188

iridescence 10, 191, 194, 201, 203–4

iteration 5, 90, 146, 168, 199

Kant, Immanuel 24–5, 171, 175

Kepes, Gyorgy 5

Kitchin, Rob 3–4, 85, 133, 165–8, 170, 172, 174

knowledge 3, 8, 10, 15, 17–31, 37, 46, 50, 74–6, 78, 95, 99, 105, 109, 115, 121–2, 129–43, 145, 149, 154, 164, 166, 172–4, 176, 191, 193

Knowledge Complexity Study 133–5, 141

l'avenir 2

labour 74, 79–84, 87, 90

Lamarck, Jean-Baptiste 212–13

Latour, Bruno 133, 138–9, 193

Lazzarato, Maurizio 83, 85, 89

learning 1–2, 9, 12–13, 18–19, 46–8, 51–3, 55–60, 65, 94–7, 99, 102–4, 106–7, 110–12, 130, 138, 140, 166–7, 174–5, 180, 186, 193; learning architecture 99;

learning networks 180; machine learning 1–2, 9, 13, 46–8, 51–2, 55–8, 65, 95, 130, 138, 140, 166–7, 174, 186, 193

legitimacy 67, 70

Leibniz, Gottfried Wilhelm 33–4, 172–4

Lozano-Hemmer Rafael 191

Lyotard, Jean-Francois 22, 24–5, 28

machinery 27, 72, 81–3, 87, 95, 110

MacKenzie, Adrian 53–5, 85, 155, 164, 175, 180–1, 183, 185

Malabou, Catherine 4, 207, 210

market 4, 11, 17–18, 23–4, 31, 37, 57–8, 73, 78, 80, 82, 84–6, 88, 91–2, 118–19, 178–9, 188

Marx, Karl 9, 22, 81, 83, 87, 89

Massumi, Brian 81, 92, 167, 171

materiality 48, 121, 140, 204

matrix 70, 100, 146, 181–2, 185, 195

mechanism 9, 24, 47, 49, 65, 67–8, 72, 77, 83, 94, 96–7, 100, 102, 108, 110–11, 115, 147, 194

medium 6–8, 66, 87, 112, 130–1, 134, 136, 146–7, 149, 151, 155–7, 164, 171

memory 3–4, 9–11, 29–30, 35, 40, 89, 105, 113, 119, 130–3, 135–6, 138, 140–3, 145–59, 191–2, 200, 202, 204; memory institution 136; prosthetic memory 10, 145, 147–9, 151, 153, 155, 157, 159

message 7, 39, 83, 88, 94, 157, 172, 182

metaphor 57, 105, 111, 115, 119, 138, 165, 168–9, 188

methodology 5, 9–10, 21, 28, 34, 43, 50, 94, 117, 136, 138, 166–7, 194

microphysics 8, 59, 147

micropolitcs 178

microtemporality 48, 50

migrant 67–8, 71, 91

missing visuals 180–3, 185–9

model 2, 10, 12, 19, 23, 32–3, 39, 43, 47–8, 53–60, 75, 80, 97, 100, 103–5, 110, 112, 116, 118, 120–1, 133, 146–9, 166, 173, 175, 186, 193–4, 199–200

modulation 57, 178, 183, 185–7; module 10, 133

molarity 177, 185; molar 177–9, 183, 185–6, 188

molecularity 177, 185; molecular 177–9, 181, 183, 185–6, 188, 201

monad 34

monitoring 9, 36, 46, 48, 50, 55, 57–8, 66–8, 71, 73–4, 76–7

Moretti, Franco 117, 120, 123, 192

Morozov, Evgeny 86

morphogenesis 32, 42
motion capture 54
Moulier-Boutang, Yann 17, 80, 87, 91
multiperspectivalism 194
Munster, Anna 150, 164, 175, 180–1, 183, 185
mutability 178
Myers, Natasha 26–8

Nancy, Jean-Luc 22–3, 149, 154, 157
Negri, Antonio 17, 80, 83, 87, 89, 135
neoliberalism 11, 30, 78, 142, 158
network 2, 9, 18–19, 23, 26, 28, 36, 50, 53–4, 56, 59, 66, 68, 75, 84–7, 89, 95–112, 119, 143–4, 165, 171, 174–5, 178, 180–3, 187–8, 193
Neumann von, John 23
Neuralink 206, 208, 213
neurobiology 216
neuron 97, 112, 138, 151, 193; neural architectures 183; neural dust 214–16; neural network 9, 54, 96–7, 102, 105, 109, 183, 188; neuronal recycling 215–16, 218
neuroscience 23, 163
neurotechnology 214
Nishida, Kitaro 146, 153, 155, 157
node 85–6, 96, 99, 103–4, 110, 133, 165, 171
noise 2–3, 13, 23, 44, 122, 147, 151, 155–7, 168, 171–4, 192
nowcasting 9, 55–60
numerical weather prediction 55–6

obfuscation 140, 186, 193
occlusion 140–1
ontogeny 209, 211
ontology 6, 10, 12, 48, 67, 128, 191, 194, 204; ontological 6, 25, 70, 164, 167–8, 192
oppression 12
optimisation 23, 28, 36
order 2, 4–5, 9–10, 12–13, 17–19, 21–3, 26–7, 29, 32, 34, 37–8, 40–1, 53, 55, 63, 68–9, 71, 74, 82, 85, 98–100, 102, 107, 115, 121, 131, 133, 138, 157, 165, 178, 180, 182–3, 191, 193, 199, 202–3
otherness 153, 194
Ott, Michaela 178, 184–5
Oulipo 193

Paik, Nam June 147, 155
panopticon 83, 188–9, 194–5
paradox 18, 23, 29, 137, 156, 165–6, 180

passability 25, 28
pattern 1–3, 5, 7–8, 11–13, 41, 46, 48, 50–2, 55, 60, 65, 68, 90, 98–100, 104, 106–7, 109–12, 115, 117, 122, 128, 136, 151, 163–4, 167, 179, 183, 192, 195, 202–3; pattern recognition 1–2, 13, 46, 48, 60, 65, 111–12, 115, 192
perception 1, 4–5, 7, 11, 34, 47–9, 95–8, 108, 110–12, 136–7, 140, 148–51, 155–7, 159, 172, 178, 180, 184, 191, 193–5, 199, 202–4
Perec, Georges 10, 191–4
persecution 72, 189
perspective 9–10, 26, 28, 42, 66, 92, 100, 129, 136, 138, 143, 169–72, 195
photogrammetry 147, 151–2
photography 7, 47, 59–60, 142, 149–50
physics 26, 56, 119, 163, 174, 191, 199
plasticity 178, 180
platform 9, 18, 25–6, 30, 58, 68, 75–6, 78, 80–92, 121, 133, 159, 164–5, 174, 176, 178, 180–3, 185, 190; platform economy 81–2, 87–9; platform seeing 159, 176, 180–3, 185, 190
Point of View (POV) 10, 177–89
Pold, Soren 181
postphenomenology 207
potentiality 8, 87–90, 168, 192
prediction 2, 9, 38–9, 43, 47–8, 50–7, 59–60, 68, 76, 102–3, 110, 183, 203; Next Frame Prediction 9, 48, 51–2, 55
prescription 35–6, 38–9
presence 6, 10, 139, 153, 155, 157, 170–1, 192, 194
prosthetic presence 155
ProGres database 69–70, 78
prophecy 9, 32–3, 35, 38–40, 65, 84
prototype 33
psychopathology 207–8

quantified self 73–4, 76–9

randomness 109; random access 157
ranking 17, 19, 22, 25, 136, 182
rating 38, 84, 103, 133, 182, 189–90
reactivation 150–1
reading 2, 9–10, 18, 20, 30, 56, 102, 115, 117, 119–22, 124–5, 128–30, 132–3, 147, 191–2, 195, 198, 202, 204; close reading 9, 18, 30, 117, 120, 124, 128, 133; distant reading 117, 120–2, 128–9, 192
reality 5, 10–11, 27, 33–6, 38, 40–1, 43–4, 47, 57, 76, 80, 85, 87, 115, 122, 143, 145,

147–9, 151, 154, 157, 175, 187, 194, 197, 204
recombination 33–4, 44
reconfiguration 141
Recurrent Neural Network (RNN) 102–4
register 6, 26, 53, 69, 154, 166, 168, 173–4
relationality 6, 146, 149, 151–2, 155, 180
replicant 9, 32–3, 35–7, 39, 41, 43, 45
representation 5, 27, 33, 38–41, 47, 49, 57, 59, 85, 94, 100–7, 110–11, 123, 131–2, 135–6, 138, 142–3, 165, 170, 180, 193, 203
Rosenblat, Alex 82–6, 88, 91

satellite 48–50, 52, 55–6, 58–9
satisfice 137
Schengen Information Systems (SIS) 67, 135
Scholz, Trebor 81–2, 86–91
Schor, Naomi 122
screen 46–7, 52, 85, 87–8, 152, 168, 177–8, 181–2, 184, 187, 191, 196–7, 200–1
securitisation 66, 76
security 37, 50, 57–8, 65–6, 68, 71, 74, 77, 188
sensus communis 25
sentiment 97, 102–4, 110, 112
Shannon, Claude 23
signal 2, 18, 22, 49, 111, 122, 147, 151, 155–7, 174–5, 181, 198
Simondon, Gilbert 89–90, 184–5
simulation 33, 35–6, 39, 41, 43–4, 48, 55, 120, 156, 174
Sloterdijk, Peter 121
The Smart Set 116–17, 124, 127–9
software 11, 18, 21–3, 29, 46, 49, 53, 80, 85, 90, 140, 151, 176, 195, 199–200
sovereignty 11, 13, 159; sovereign 70, 77
Spark 151
Srnicek, Nick 81–2, 88–9
Steyerl, Hito 3, 55, 100
Stiegler, Bernard 4, 6, 23, 131, 135, 187, 210
structure 2, 5, 7, 11, 23, 38, 43, 56, 66, 94, 105–6, 109, 111–12, 121, 133, 138, 145–7, 165–6, 173, 179, 182–4, 193
Spark 151
Srnicek, Nick 81–2, 88–9
Steyerl, Hito 3, 55, 100
Stiegler, Bernard 4, 6, 23, 131, 135, 187, 210
structure 2, 5, 7, 11, 23, 38, 43, 56, 66, 94, 105–6, 109, 111–12, 121, 133, 138, 145–7, 165–6, 173, 179, 182–4, 193, 201–2

subjugation 83, 85–8, 90
sublime 25, 28, 129, 171, 175–6, 191–2, 201, 204
subsumption 83
surface 5, 10, 48–51, 57, 94, 109, 119, 147, 150–1, 163, 165, 167, 169, 171–5, 182, 194; superficial 10, 18, 27, 119, 165–70, 172–3
surveillance 4, 8, 13, 17–18, 22, 25–6, 36–7, 45, 59, 64, 66–8, 71, 73, 77–9, 83–4, 93, 144, 176, 179, 190, 192; surveillance capitalism 4, 13, 36–7, 45, 93, 176, 179, 190
swarm 192
synapse 4, 97; synaptic connections 97, 209
synchronous 155

technicity 30, 74
technics 31
technique 5, 9–10, 13, 17–18, 20, 22, 24–8, 40, 46–58, 60, 65–9, 73–4, 92, 99–101, 106, 112, 121, 141, 149–50, 152, 155–6, 159, 186, 191–2, 194, 196–9
technology 6, 9, 11, 18–19, 21–30, 32, 35–7, 44, 55–6, 58–9, 64–78, 80–2, 84, 86, 89–90, 92–3, 131–2, 137–40, 142, 144, 154, 158, 175, 179, 181, 183–4, 188–9, 192
telemetry 208
telepathy 208, 210, 213–18
temporality 46–7, 50, 56–7, 154–5, 164, 167, 182
Terranova, Tiziana 80, 83
Tinder 182–3, 189–90
totalitarianism 4, 11, 37
Totalizierung 32
tracking 4–5, 73–9, 146, 188, 199; self-tracking 9, 66, 73–7
training 1–2, 53–4, 96, 98–9, 102–6, 108–10, 174, 186
transformation 7–8, 33, 35–8, 41, 47, 50, 67, 79, 108, 159, 171–2, 178, 185, 187
trans-individuation 187
transversal 151, 153, 155
truth 12, 27, 29, 34, 49, 53, 55, 74–5, 132, 188–9, 202
Turing, Alan 94; Turing test 94, 111
Twitter 21, 176

Uber 80–6, 89–90, 92, 170, 181
United Nations (UN) 18, 40, 65, 69–72, 79
United Nations High Commissioner for Refugees (UNHCR) 69–70, 78

university 1–13, 17–21, 24–6, 28–31, 42, 45, 58–60, 65, 77, 79, 91–3, 111–12, 116, 119, 128–9, 141–4, 158–9, 174–6, 189–90, 204
unknown knowns 203
utopia 195

value 3, 7, 10, 21, 31, 34–5, 37–8, 71, 73, 76, 82, 100, 104–5, 118–19, 132, 134–6, 139–41, 148, 157, 163, 177, 189, 196, 203
Varela, Francisco 154
velocity 3–4, 6, 145–6, 166–8, 170, 176, 181
Virilio, Paul 47–9, 55–7
virtuality 148; virtual 34, 44, 53, 64, 67, 84, 137, 146, 148, 154–6, 176, 197, 199–201, 204
Visa Information System (VIS) 22, 66–7, 75

visibility 10, 42, 49, 52, 164, 177, 180–2, 188–90, 194
vision 5, 11, 19, 22–3, 29, 33–5, 42, 47, 49–50, 52, 56–7, 60, 98, 111, 139, 158, 171, 195, 198–9, 201
Vismann, Cornelia 6, 147, 150–1
visualisation 3, 18, 27, 46, 48, 51–2, 57–9, 121–2, 124, 173, 176, 181, 191, 195–7

Weaver, Warren 23, 157
Wiener, Norbert 1, 151, 173, 193
Winkel, Camiel van 180–1, 183
Wittgenstein, Ludwig 169

Zuboff, Shoshana 4, 36–7, 82, 86, 89, 91, 168, 179, 193, 208, 210, 213

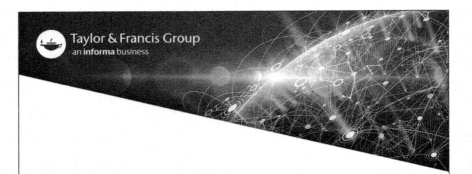